Playing the Market

A volume in the series
CORNELL STUDIES IN POLITICAL ECONOMY
edited by Peter J. Katzenstein

Playing the Market

A Political Strategy for Uniting Europe, 1985–2005

NICOLAS JABKO

CORNELL UNIVERSITY PRESS

Ithaca & London

First published 2006 by Cornell University Press

First printing, Cornell Paperbacks, 2012

Printed in the United States of America

Library of Congress Cataloging-in-Publication Data

Jabko, Nicolas.
    Playing the market : a political strategy for uniting Europe, 1985–2005 / Nicolas Jabko.
        p. cm. — (Cornell studies in political economy)
    Includes bibliographical references and index.
    ISBN-13: 978-0-8014-4463-0 (cloth : alk. paper)
    ISBN-13: 978-0-8014-7791-1 (pbk : alk. paper)
        1. European Union. 2. European Union countries—Politics and government.
3. Europe—Politics and government—1989- . 4. European Union countries—
Economic integration. I. Title. II. Series.
JN30.J32 2006
341.242'2—dc22
                                                            2006008389

Cornell University Press strives to use environmentally responsible
suppliers and materials to the fullest extent possible in the publishing
of its books. Such materials include vegetable-based, low-VOC inks
and acid-free papers that are recycled, totally chlorine-free, or partly
composed of nonwood fibers. For further information, visit our website
at www.cornellpress.cornell.edu.

For Che

The question that was on the table was the re-launching of Europe, but how? . . . I had to fall back on a pragmatic objective that was also in tune with the Zeitgeist [of the mid-1980s], since at the time everybody talked about deregulation and about the elimination of barriers to competition and to the operation of the market.

Jacques Delors, president of the
European Commission, 1984–94

I am seeking to play my part in making the Community deregulatory and in opening it to the outside world. That is my agenda. I make no secret of it.

Sir Leon Brittan,
member and later vice president of the
European Commission, 1989–99

Contents

Preface

This book is the product of many years of ruminations and research on Europe's late-twentieth-century push for the single market and the euro. As a French graduate student embarking on an American PhD in the mid-1990s, I asked myself what I now realize has been an increasingly nagging question for the French: What is the role of liberal economic ideas in the drive for a united Europe? On May 29, 2005, France held a referendum on the Treaty establishing a Constitution for Europe, and 55 percent of French voters rejected it. The tipping factor according to opinion polls was not the fear of European integration as such but a widespread opposition to its perceived "neoliberal" orientation. Many voters, especially on the left, were wary of the European Union's market liberalization and anti-inflationary policies. Clearly, the degree of Europe's market and monetary integration since the 1980s raises troublesome questions of political identity. This is true for all European citizens but particularly so for the French (including me), because of the historically central role of the state in the economy.

My motivation for reflecting on the single market and the euro is the assumption that Europe's past carries interesting lessons for its future and for politics more broadly. At this time, the future of European integration appears highly uncertain. The French *non* may have inadvertently made it more difficult for the European Union to move beyond the economic focus that voters criticized. In any event, significant further advancements of European unification cannot be contemplated as long as the legacy of the European Union's past is not properly understood and digested. When I started working on this project ten years ago, it seemed clear to me that liberal economic ideas played *some* part in Europe's market and monetary integration. But I wanted to understand how this worked in practice. Many fellow Europeans have often asked me with a touch of irony why I had gone all the way to the University of California at Berkeley in order to study European politics. In my view, Berkeley's ivory-tower environment was ideal for this scholarly investigation. I was immersed in a world-class intellectual community where I learned to use and address political science methods. And as a young French citizen researching the role of liberal economic ideas, I was also better able to establish a necessary critical distance from a highly polarized debate in my own country.

An established custom now dictates that I open a long list of acknowledgments; and I will gladly comply. I express my gratitude first to Steve Weber and to my other advisers: Chris Ansell, Jonah Levy, Neil Fligstein, and John Zysman. All helped me specify what I was doing and saying, and they often rescued me from scientific dead ends. I owe a special intellectual debt to Ernie Haas, who was my adviser at the start and who taught me a lot. I also learned an incredible amount in long and still ongoing conversations with my peers, especially Keith Darden and Craig Parsons. After Berkeley, I joined the research faculty at Sciences Po in Paris. I thank especially Patrick Le Galès, Bernard Manin, and Michael Storper for their collegial encouragements and precious feedback on my work. I was also fortunate to spend time as a postdoctoral fellow at Princeton University's Center for International Studies, which enabled me to work on this book in a stimulating intellectual environment. Thanks especially to Kate McNamara, Sophie Meunier, and Ezra Suleiman.

Many other people helped me at various points along the way. For their enthusiastic support as editors, I thank Roger Haydon and Peter Katzenstein, as well as two anonymous referees for Cornell University Press. I am grateful for the useful comments on draft chapters that I received from seminar participants at Syracuse University, Johns Hopkins University, Harvard University, the University of Pennsylvania, New York University, Northwestern University, and the University of Washington. Thanks especially to Mark Blyth, Jim Caporaso, Frank Dobbin, Dan Kelemen, Andrew Martin, Jon Mercer, Andy Moravcsik, Paul Pierson, Claudio Radaelli, Rudra Sil, David Stasavage, and Amy Verdun. I thank Jeremy Richardson and two anonymous referees for the *Journal of European Public Policy*, who gave comments to me on a previously published version of my chapter on economic and monetary union ("In the Name of the Market," *JEPP* [September 1999], published by the Taylor & Francis Group/Routledge). I also thank David Michel and Todd Shepard for reading through the entire manuscript and helping me fix some glaring problems. Last but not least, I thank the many EU and member-state officials as well as industry executives who granted me interviews on an anonymous basis.

Finally, I acknowledge the main funding sources and institutional support for my research. For generous financial support, I thank the MacArthur Foundation, the Institute of Global Conflict and Cooperation, the Center for German and European Studies, and the Department of Political Science at UC Berkeley. I also acknowledge Princeton University's precious postdoctoral fellowship. I thank Sciences Po's Center for European Studies for its support of a political economy seminar that has provided me with a stimulating intellectual environment. Although grateful for all the assistance and support I have had, I take all responsibility for any shortcomings in the book.

NICOLAS JABKO

Paris

Playing the Market

ONE

A Quiet Revolution

The move toward greater European unity in the 1980s and 1990s is widely seen as the acceleration of an arcane process that began in the 1950s. Conventional wisdom holds that the global quest for trade liberalization and market reforms "relaunched" Europe around the single market and the euro. Market globalization and European integration thus come into view as relentless and mutually reinforcing processes. The problems facing Europe at the turn of the twenty-first century, then, stem from a political backlash against the logic of past integration. "Citizens are calling for a clear, open, effective, democratically controlled Community approach," as European leaders put it at the beginning of their protracted constitution-drafting exercise in December 2001.[1] In other words, many Europeans regard the process of regional integration as opaque, elitist, ineffective, and technocratic. This public perception that Europe has a democratic deficit is relatively new. With the fading of World War II memories, the founding fathers' high-minded purpose of establishing peace on a war-prone continent began to sound somewhat abstract. Europe's original promise has been so successfully fulfilled that what the European Union stands for has become hazy.

Without denying the importance of this new predicament, in this book I dispute the underlying assessment of the latest big push for European unity. Contrary to conventional wisdom, the revival of Europe in the 1980s and 1990s cannot be easily explained by the combined logic of market globalization and regional integration. Global economic interdependence was, in fact, perhaps more likely to lead to fragmentation than to further integration.[2] Instead, the integration process was relaunched and Europe underwent a quiet revolution. The launching of the single market and the euro signaled a fundamental reinstitutionalization of the European economy. Market reforms reached deep into economic and social structures, while the European

1. Laeken Declaration on the Future of the European Union, adopted by the European Council in Laeken, December 15, 2001.
2. See especially Ernst B. Haas, "Turbulent Fields and the Theory of Regional Integration," *International Organization* 29, no. 3 (Spring 1976): 173–212.

Union's decision-making process moved decisively toward the center of the European political stage. The contrast between the late twentieth-century period of revolutionary change and the incremental diplomacy of early European integration in the 1950s and 1960s is striking. The push for European unity quickly went far beyond international trade liberalization and functional institution building. In less than two decades, economic governance in Europe went through its deepest transformation since the end of World War II, leading to the emergence of a distinctive European model of political economy.

If we want to understand the European Union's quiet revolution, we need to think harder about what was original about it. Market liberalization in Europe mirrored in many respects what was happening in the rest of the industrialized world. But only in Europe did this process go hand in hand with a process of deep institutional integration. Globalization certainly played a role, but it is not a sufficient explanation for what happened in Europe. Nor can the European Union's quiet revolution be explained simply as a victory of European ideals. European federalism had its die-hard advocates, but they remained a minority. The quiet revolution was supported not only by federalists but by a broad coalition of actors with extremely diverse motivations. Actors who previously had little interest in European integration increasingly saw it as a way to pursue their various agendas. New converts to the European cause included free-marketeers and critics of the free market, politicians of the left and the right, bureaucrats and business leaders, as well as high-level government officials in all the member states. For all these strange bedfellows, the European Union unexpectedly became an important terrain of political action and policymaking.

The birth of such a heterogeneous coalition was not a fortuitous development. A carefully balanced political strategy that catered to a variety of constituencies made the European Union's quiet revolution a success. The promoters of Europe, especially within the European Commission, understood the need to rally a broad-based political clientele as the precondition for integrating Europe. They chose "the market" as a convenient banner for this coalition-building exercise, but they did not commit to a single-minded pursuit of market liberalization. They realized that the coalition in support of the quiet revolution did not share common interests or ideas. In order to sustain such a broad coalition, the promoters of Europe defined the objective of building a market in a very open-ended fashion. This purposefully inclusive vision of the market served to bring together many actors behind the European cause.

THE CONUNDRUM OF MARKET REFORMS

This argument goes against the conventional view of late twentieth-century European integration as being the straightforward adoption of a global market reform agenda within the European policy-making framework. In the academic literature, three widespread interpretations echo this line. A first group of scholars adopt a utilitarian perspective on the integration of Europe.[3] They primarily stress the shifting interests and power relations induced by market globalization. In the European context, they point out that multinational corporations and financial actors acquired the political clout to advance market-friendly policies. A second strand of scholarship subscribes to an institutionalist view of European integration.[4] Unlike their utilitarian counterparts, institutionalist scholars believe that material interests are embedded in and filtered through complex webs of institutions. They view European integration as an incremental and path-dependent development, where consequences are often unintended and periods of acceleration and stagnation alternate. Finally, a third group of scholars embrace a constructivist view of European integration.[5] These scholars belong to the institutionalist tradition, but they emphasize the importance of ideas, especially in times of uncertainty. They note that the perceived failure of Keynesian policies in the 1970s and the rising hegemony of the free market in the 1980s provided a favorable ideological ground for the relaunching of Europe around the single market and the euro.

Each of these three influential interpretations sheds light on particular aspects of the broad structural and ideational context of late twentieth-century Europe. Roughly speaking, the old continent's market and monetary integration can be plausibly envisioned as the quaint European way of adjusting to material and ideological shifts in the global economy. There is a strange mismatch, however, between the aloofness of scholarly interpretations and the pathbreaking nature of change in European economic governance in the 1980s and 1990s. To cite only the most obvious example, the creation of a supranational currency run by an independent European Central Bank (ECB) with an anti-inflationary mandate was a major breakthrough after decades of nationally focused monetary management that had produced resilient policy divergence and creeping inflation. There is little reason to believe that globalization and Europe's developmental dynamic would seamlessly work together and prompt Europe to undergo such a revolution. Unlike their predecessors

---

3. Studies of European integration in the 1980s and 1990s have often adopted this perspective since the launching of the single market program. See Jeffry Frieden, "Invested Interests," *International Organization* 45 (Autumn 1991); Geoffrey Garrett, "International Cooperation and Institutional Choice: The European Community's Internal Market," *International Organization* 46, no. 2 (Spring 1992); Andrew Moravcsik, *The Choice for Europe* (Ithaca: Cornell University Press, 1998).

4. Scholars who focus on the development of European law or specific policy areas generally take this long-term institutionalist view. See esp. Joseph Weiler, "The Transformation of Europe," *Yale Law Journal* 100 (June 1991); Paul Pierson, "The Path to European Integration: A Historical Institutionalist Analysis," *Comparative Political Studies* 29, no. 2 (April 1996).

5. The scholarship on the EMU is often informed by this ideational perspective. See esp. Kathleen R. McNamara, *The Currency of Ideas: Monetary Politics in the European Union* (Ithaca: Cornell University Press, 1998); Amy Verdun, "The Role of the Delors Committee in the Creation of EMU: An Epistemic Community?" *Journal of European Public Policy* 6, no. 2 (June 1999); Kenneth Dyson and Kevin Featherstone, *The Road to Maastricht: Negotiating Economic and Monetary Union* (Oxford: Oxford University Press, 1999).

in the 1970s, most scholars of the EU today fail to interrogate the link between market globalization and European integration. Although the changes of the 1980s and 1990s in European economic governance took place without a change of political regime, they were genuinely revolutionary—they could not have resulted simply from self-propelled global and regional integration.

The problem with established interpretations of the single market and European Economic and Monetary Union (EMU) is that they miss the *politics* of the European Union's quiet revolution. Actors who had a stake in the institutional status quo were not going to give in without a fight—however powerful the logic of interests, institutions, or ideas. Thus, the quiet revolution could not have taken place without some creative crafting of new institutional settlements that were broadly acceptable to a majority of actors. To gloss over this political process is not a minor oversight, since it affects the way we understand the new EU model of economic governance and institutional change more generally. In a nutshell, we are not talking merely about the tidy victory of economic interests, supranational institutions, or neoliberal ideology. We are talking about a revolutionary yet variegated phenomenon, which calls for a more disaggregated and a more political interpretation of Europe's version of market reforms.

The characteristics of the European Union's quiet revolution of the 1980s and 1990s are actually quite diverse and puzzling, especially in two respects. First, the shift toward market-based economic governance does not neatly correlate with the presence of market pressures. This is exactly the opposite of what we would expect in a market-driven modernization scenario. In fast-changing sectors like finance or telecommunications, Europe's drive toward a single market only accelerated existing processes of regulatory reform at the domestic level. By contrast, the effects of the single market were much more profound on the provision of collective services such as energy or public transportation, despite the weakness of market pressures. Second, the shift in the locus of policymaking toward Brussels enabled a considerable reassertion of public powers. This makes it difficult to speak of a true neoliberal revolution. For example, the promotion of growth through competitiveness policies had an active developmental character. Likewise, Europe's Economic and Monetary Union transferred monetary policy powers not to the market but to the European Central Bank, a public body. Insofar as the euro sheltered Europe's economic policies from the threat of currency fluctuations, EMU also dampened the free operation of the market.

In sum, the convenient label "market reform" conceals a conundrum. The European Union's quiet revolution went much further and deeper than one could have expected. Yet the shift toward market-based governance was far from homogenous, and it was not most evident in the areas where market forces were the most present. In addition, market-oriented reforms often went hand in hand with a market-mitigating concentration of powers at the EU level.[6] Altogether, neither Europe's internal developmental dynamic nor external market pressure nor the rise of neoliberal ideology is the primary determinant of the quiet revolution.

MARKET IDEAS AS STRATEGIC RESOURCES

The solution to this conundrum, I believe, is to envision the market not as a driving factor or ideology of change but as a strategic repertoire of ideas. The European Union's quiet revolution was the product of an innovative political strategy by an actor that used market ideas as a way to compensate for a lack of power resources. Simple constructivist explanations do not work very well, yet ideational dynamics should not be dismissed entirely. The very notion of "market reform" had a peculiar appeal within the context of the 1980s and 1990s. In the course of the European Union's quiet revolution, market ideas had an impact not so much because of a general conversion to neoliberal ideology but because they were incorporated into a well-crafted political strategy. In the 1980s and 1990s, "the market" served as a rallying banner for pro-European actors to advance their integrationist goals.

This political strategy was invented within the European Commission, the central administrative body of the European Union. These early promoters of Europe found in market ideas a way to compensate for their relative weakness and to overcome institutional inertia.[7] Compared with the leaders of the member states, Commission officials were in a relatively weak position. By playing "the market" as part of a broad integrationist political strategy, they essentially found a way out of their quandary. Depending on the venue, they sold Europe either as a straightforward process of economic adjustment to new market conditions or as a more political and managerial approach to market globalization.[8] They were thus able to build Europe without choosing clearly between these two very different rationales for the push toward greater European integration. At a time of rapid economic change, "Europe" provided a

---

6. This counterintuitive phenomenon has very well-known historical precedents at the *national* level. See esp. Karl Polanyi, *The Great Transformation* (Boston: Beacon Press, 1957 [1944]), and, more recently, Michael Moran, *The Politics of the Financial Services Revolution* (Basingstoke: Macmillan, 1991); Steven K. Vogel, *Freer Markets, More Rules* (Ithaca: Cornell University Press, 1996).

7. Organization sociologists often stress the importance of "doctrines" and other cultural artifacts as a way for the weak to "co-opt" the powerful. See Philip Selznick, *TVA and the Grass Roots* (Berkeley: University of California Press, 1949), and, more recently, Husayin Leblebici, Gerald D. Salancik, Anne Copay, and Tom King, "Institutional Change and the Transformation of Interorganizational Fields," *Administrative Science Quarterly* 36, no. 3 (September 1991); John F. Padgett and Christopher K. Ansell, "Robust Action and the Rise of the Medici, 1400–1434," *American Journal of Sociology* 98, no. 6 (May 1993).

8. I am suggesting an important strategic component in the different "images of governance" that Liesbet Hooghe, Gary Marks, and their students have found in their studies of ideological preferences among EU officials. See esp. Hooghe, *The European Commission and European Integration* (Cambridge: Cambridge University Press, 2001).

formula to overcome the continuing political struggle between supporters and critics of the free market. This fundamental ambiguity was never clarified because it was the necessary glue for putting together a winning coalition in favor of European reforms. Generally speaking, the strategy was designed to draw support from the most powerful political clienteles—the German, the French, and the British governments, but also the Left, the Right, and the business community. All these actors were given a stake in the European Union's quiet revolution and thus encouraged to reframe their interests around the achievement of Europe's market and monetary integration agenda.

In essence, the market served as a conveniently broad repertoire of justifications.[9] The Commission's goal and guiding motivation was to reform the economy but it was also to build political power at the European level—although not necessarily in its own hands. This explains, in turn, the contrast between the rather loose programmatic coherence of EU reforms and the consistent reinforcement of EU powers. In the minds of many Commission officials who drafted key legislation, market ideas were subordinated to the higher goal of building Europe. Other actors who joined the pro-European coalition had different motivations, but the common focus on intermediate goals served to defuse conflicts on long-term goals. The unprecedented pervasiveness of market rationality among European elites could be used as a basis for broad institutional transformation. Acting as a pivotal actor within the pro-European coalition, the European Commission developed a political strategy that consisted in promoting "Europe" as a generic solution to the tensions arising from market globalization. Across the board, the promoters of Europe consistently exploited the fact that "the market" meant rather different things in different contexts and for different actors.

First and perhaps most obvious, the market operated as a constraint that undermined existing institutional forms. This corresponds to familiar images of the market as a set of forces that allocate resources. Market forces obviously do not exist in a vacuum. But once a sufficiently large number of people conform to these forces in their daily interactions, it becomes pointless and costly to resist the mechanical reality of the market. In certain competition-driven parts of the economy, such as the financial sector, the removal of trade barriers and the full establishment of a single market seemed to make sense simply as a matter of pragmatism.

Second, the market worked as a norm of economic organization. The principle of market competition is by no means the only principle according to which economic activity is organized. But it is arguably the most legitimate in our day and age. It constitutes a normative model that extends well beyond the strict sphere of the market economy. Accordingly, various liberalization en-

---

9. This concept of repertoire is adapted from the sociological literature on social movements and culture. See esp. Charles Tilly, *From Mobilization to Revolution* (Reading, Mass.: Addison-Wesley, 1978), and Ann Swidler, "Culture in Action: Symbols and Strategies," *American Sociological Review* 51, no. 2 (April 1986).

deavors were launched in Europe as part of a general drive toward greater economic efficiency, even in areas such as energy provision that were previously exempt from market competition.

Third, "the market" evoked a space for the pursuit of economic prosperity and development. Gains from trade can be fully realized only if market participants make certain adjustments to exploit their comparative advantages. Since market integration per se does not ensure a fair distribution across space or a continuous progress of economic development over time, the transformation of the EU into a developmental actor was sold as the natural complement to market integration. The folding of Europe's regional and social policies into a market-compatible "structural" policy thus enabled a considerable increase of the community budget.

Fourth, the market functioned as a talisman of political discourse that brought together otherwise divergent views of the world. By the late twentieth century, the market had become the most legitimate principle of economic organization in Europe. The limits of this apparent consensus remained extremely clear, however. While some actors embraced the market wholeheartedly as a salutary source of discipline, others accepted it merely as a pragmatic prerequisite to the pursuit of normatively superior goals. Accordingly, EMU was peddled either as a further extension of the market logic or as a way to reassert some measure of political sovereignty over the economy.

Altogether, the polyvalence of market ideas served to cement an otherwise heterogeneous coalition to a far-reaching reform agenda. For the purpose of political mobilization, the advocates of Europe found it useful to appeal to the market as a central mode of justification for reform. Beneath the surface, the specific rationales that they advanced in favor of market reform were actually quite different across various policy areas. All actors always tried to push for outcomes that would bring them closer to their respective and often sharply different political visions. In all cases, however, "the market" remained a very convenient and effective spin for the advocates of EU-level reforms. Through a flexible use of market ideas, the promoters of Europe achieved a set of reforms that went far beyond what was to be expected from the sheer evolution of economic interests, ultimately resulting in a considerable boost for European unity.

FROM POLITICAL STRATEGY TO INSTITUTIONAL CHANGE

When envisioned as a phenomenon of large-scale institutional change, the European Union's quiet revolution carries broad theoretical lessons. To explain why institutions change, scholars who adopt a utilitarian approach generally focus on changes in material interests, whereas institutionalist and constructivist scholars search for unintended consequences and ideational shifts. In this book, working from a constructivist perspective, I underscore the power of certain ideas—in this instance, how market ideas served to re-ignite European integration.[10] Yet I also take a slightly unusual cut on the explanatory role of ideas, which can be characterized as *strategic constructivism*. I identify the politics of ideas, rather than ideas themselves, as the primary engine of institutional change. From this standpoint, ideas are important not so much as pure beliefs but because, in any given policy area, the parties involved must resort to ideas to articulate and advance their interests. Therefore, ideas can be crucial resources in the hands of strategic actors who understand their usefulness as rallying grounds for those in pursuit of diverse or even incompatible goals.

Obviously, the success of a political strategy based on a less-than-coherent set of ideas and invented by weak pro-European actors was neither preordained nor uniform. The inertia of existing institutions was strong and difficult to overcome. Yet institutions are plentiful, and people are constantly challenged to deal with the tensions between the various institutions that govern their existence. Institutionalist and constructivist scholars see institutions and ideas as strong causal determinants and often downplay the importance of tensions and inconsistencies.[11] By contrast, I start from the assumption that that these tensions are very important for understanding institutional change, because they represent opportunities for reform-seeking actors. The existence of tensions creates room for the emergence of political strategies and, ultimately, for institutional change. In the late twentieth-century drive for a united Europe, the changing relative status of the market and the state was a potent source of institutional dynamism. The growing aura of the market highlighted considerable tensions within economic governance institutions. In turn, this prompted an increasing number of actors to support European solutions to these tensions.

What this process bodes for the future of European integration is not altogether clear, in that the peculiar dynamic power of that political strategy of playing the market grew out of a highly specific historical situation. The integrationist momentum was so powerful in the 1980s and the 1990s that it is difficult today to imagine the European Union without the single market and the euro. Yet the European Union in its current form may have gone as far as it can go in playing the market for the purpose of uniting Europe. In the absence of a unified EU government elected by a united European people, there is still no fully legitimate selection procedure among competing actors and their visions at the EU level. The EU is therefore especially prone to conflict resolution by deferment, because EU actors know that they can only pursue

10. Scholarship on the impact of ideas in political economy and in European integration more specifically includes McNamara, *Currency of Ideas*; Sheri Berman, *The Social Democratic Moment* (Cambridge: Harvard University Press, 1998); Mark Blyth, *Great Transformations* (Cambridge: Cambridge University Press, 2002); Craig Parsons, *A Certain Idea of Europe* (Ithaca: Cornell University Press, 2003); Juan Diez Medrano, *Framing Europe* (Princeton: Princeton University Press, 2003).

11. Only recently have institutionalist scholars begun to question the assumption of institutional coherence and inertia. See Kathleen Thelen, "How Institutions Evolve: Insights from Comparative-Historical Analysis," in *Comparative-Historical Analysis in the Social Sciences*, ed. James Mahoney and Dietrich Rueschemeyer (New York: Cambridge University Press, 2003).

their partisan agendas in roundabout ways. Past a certain threshold, however, it becomes difficult to carry on like this because the risks of popular backlash against such insulation of the decision-making process increase.

At the same time, the widespread tendency to underestimate the importance of political strategy and leadership in past European integration certainly contributes to Europe's difficulties at the beginning of the twenty-first century. Even in the most democratic settings, elections do not take place every day. Insofar as the European Union's quiet revolution can be analyzed as a normal instance of modern institutional change, the argument's underlying analytical model can thus be applied more broadly. Institutional tensions are always present and they generate strategic opportunities for institutional change. Institutions are therefore the source not only of inertia but also of dynamism. From this standpoint, all ambitious reform-minded actors encounter the same sort of challenge. Reformist actors must constantly find ways to exploit institutional tensions and the polyvalence of timely ideas in pursuit of complex goals. Such political strategies represent adventurous gambles, and not all of them encounter good fortune. But the paradox is that political strategies that emerge from an institution-rich context can sometimes provoke a major change of institutional context.

TWO

The Conundrum of Market Reforms

In the 1980s and 1990s the wind of market reforms blew over the entire world. In Europe, this global trend coincided with a visible renewal of the region's political unification—with the launching of the single market in 1986, the official creation of the European Union in 1992, and the advent of the euro in 1999. What happened at the "institutional level" in the EU was only the tip of the iceberg. This is not to deny the importance of the changing patterns of interactions between the member states, the Commission, the European Court of Justice, the European Parliament, and other European institutions. But what made these interactions so important in the first place is that they were taking place within a much broader process of institutional change in the political economy of European nations. In less than two decades, Brussels became the epicenter of successive waves of reforms that deeply affected structures of economic governance throughout Western Europe.

This chapter presents the case for analyzing recent European integration through the lens of economic governance. Market globalization was clearly a factor in the late twentieth-century renewal of European integration. Yet contrary to conventional wisdom, the relationship between market globalization and European integration is highly problematic. The European Union's quiet revolution, considered as a dependent variable, represents a surprising shift in the character and locus of economic policymaking over two decades. When institutions change profoundly and quickly without any outbreak of physical violence, it appears to contradict a defining characteristic of institutions—namely, their inertia. On closer examination, the European Union's quiet revolution was especially puzzling in two respects. First, the shift toward market-based economic governance is not neatly correlated with the presence of market pressures. Secondly, "market reforms" often meant a considerable reassertion of public powers in the economy at the EU level, so that the label "neoliberal" becomes highly questionable. In sum, the momentum of that process can be adequately explained neither by an imperative need to adapt to global economic trends nor by a wholesale shift to a neoliberal paradigm. Market reforms at the European level are a genuine conundrum.

Three views prevail in the scholarly literature on the relationship between events that occurred at the level of the European Union and the broader process of institutional change in the world's political economy. According to the *utilitarian* view, European integration is fundamentally driven by changing actors' economic interests in the context of market globalization. The *institutionalist* view stresses the long-term momentum of the European Union and the dynamics of unintended consequences, over and beyond the short-term logic of economic interests. Finally, the *constructivist* view highlights the integrative power of ideas and policy paradigms, including neoliberal economic ideology. Going back to the writings of an earlier generation of scholars, I argue that these three bodies of scholarship tend to miss the problematic relationship between market globalization and late twentieth-century European integration.

Three Conventional Views

With its single market, its currency, and its constitution, the European Union now exhibits many traits that set it completely apart from any international bargaining forum. It remains to be seen whether the EU will one day turn into a "normal" federal polity. For now, the important point is that the Single Act of 1986 marked the beginning of a quiet but long-lasting revolution in Europe's political and economic landscape. In the early 1980s, Europe's political economy was organized as a rather loose grouping of national economies that traded with each other within the Common Market and whose currencies were further linked by a semifixed exchange rate agreement called the European Monetary System (EMS). Although these national economies were already characterized by very significant trade openness, they could each be envisioned as self-contained models in relative isolation from one another and from Community institutions. Two decades later, the nature of economic governance in Europe has been so radically altered that this is no longer possible. What began as a frenzy of "negative" integration, with the removal of trade barriers across Europe, soon turned into a powerful movement of "positive integration," that is, the creation of new institutional governance mechanisms and policies at the European level. In particular, Europe's Economic and Monetary Union, built around the European Central Bank and the euro, is a critical parameter for any analysis of economic policies in Europe. Seen in this light, the constitutional process of 2002–04 was both a way to acknowledge the depth of this integration and to address unprecedented concerns about its "democratic deficit."

The centrality of an economic agenda in the mid-1980s renewal of European integration was reflected in the increased academic focus on the political economy of European integration. Scholars who wanted to understand the politics of Europe's economy had to come to terms with the growing importance of the European Union as a sphere of policymaking and interest organization. A variety of policy concerns such as the preservation of market competition or the definition of common European objectives on trade, the environment, or regional development became much more salient. The tide of institutional change profoundly affected such diverse matters as the allocation of financial resources in the economy, the supply of collective services such as telecommunications and energy, the economic development of subregional territories, and the management of currencies within Europe. In assessing the renewal of European integration and the accelerating modernization of the European economy, scholars have paid particular attention to the context of market globalization.

The utilitarian standpoint envisions the material momentum of the market as the primary raison d'être of European integration.[1] In the tradition of "endogenous policy theory," this perspective points out the importance of economic interests in politics and the force of broad economic trends as factors of institutional change.[2] According to Andrew Moravcsik, "European integration resulted from a series of rational choices made by national leaders who consistently pursued economic interests . . . that evolved slowly in response to structural incentives in the global economy."[3] Some scholars recognize nonetheless that institutions—and specifically EU institutions—can be important when they define the rules of the game and provide focal points for actors to pursue their preferences.[4] With some variation among scholars, the wave of regional integration in Europe is interpreted as the ultimate result of changes in actors' rationally motivated behavior. The drive toward a united Europe is seen as a logical albeit peculiarly European response to economic globalization.

The institutionalist strand of scholarship stresses that Europe's institutional integration has its own logic, autonomous from global economic trends. Largely in reaction to the utilitarian view, institutionalist scholars stress the European Union's complex political, legal, administrative, and societal dimen-

---

1. Seminal works in this literature include Andrew Moravcsik, "Negotiating the Single European Act," in *The New European Community*, ed. Robert Keohane and Stanley Hoffmann (Boulder: Westview Press, 1991); Garrett, "International Cooperation and Institutional Choice"; Geoffrey Garrett and Barry Weingast, "Ideas, Interests, and Institutions: Constructing the European Community's Internal Market," in *Ideas and Foreign Policy*, ed. Judith Goldstein and Robert Keohane (Ithaca: Cornell University Press, 1993); Moravcsik, *Choice for Europe*.

2. I use the label "utilitarian" in reference to a particular analytical model of human behavior that belongs to the tradition of nineteenth-century classical political economy. Most scholars would use the label "rationalist" instead, but this label is misleadingly broad. Scholars who work within this perspective adopt a *utilitarian* definition of rationality. Of course, "utilitarian" is not without problems either, but it is more appropriate to qualify the scholarship that I have in mind in this book.

3. Moravcsik, *Choice for Europe*, 3.

4. Garrett and Weingast, "Ideas, Interests, and Institutions"; Geoffrey Garrett and George Tsebelis, "An Institutionalist Critique of Intergovernmentalism," *International Organization* 50 (Summer 1996); George Tsebelis and Geoffrey Garrett, "The Institutional Determinants of Supranationalism in the European Union," *International Organization* (forthcoming); Walter Mattli, *The Logic of Regional Integration* (Cambridge: Cambridge University Press, 1999); Simon Hix, "The Study of the European Union II: The 'New Governance' Agenda and Its Rival," *Journal of European Public Policy* 5, no. 1 (March 1998); Mark A. Pollack, *The Engines of Integration* (Oxford: Oxford University Press, 2003).

sions.[5] They do not believe that market forces are so powerful as to completely overwhelm existing institutional dynamics. The impact of the global economy on actors' interests is seen as less determinative for the integration process than the institutional environment within which these interests are formed. Paul Pierson thus describes European integration as a process that follows "a consistent direction over time": "As the density of EC policymaking increases, such interaction effects become more prevalent, unintended consequences multiply, and the prospects of gaps in member states controls multiply."[6] Likewise, scholars of comparative politics and public policy generally analyze the dynamics of Europe as the progressive development of a federal or "multilevel" or "Europeanized" political system, while legal scholars grant primary importance to the progress of European law.[7] In sum, European integration is understood as a self-sustaining path-dependent and incremental process, rife with unintended consequences.

A constructivist view underscores the role of ideas in fueling European integration, including neoliberal ideas in the context of market globalization. Scholars who subscribe to this interpretation often advance it to remedy shortcomings in the institutionalist perspective. Although the spirit of institutionalism is to search for elements of continuity, many scholars in the institutionalist tradition also recognize that major contingencies can arise and reshape the institutional landscape.[8] They are also willing to recognize the importance of ideas in certain processes of institutional change. As Peter Hall put it, "Although complexly determined, [the single market initiative] was inspired by the general enthusiasm for market mechanisms surging through Europe at the time."[9] Working from the assumption that ideas matter, constructivist

5. For clarity of classification, I refer here only to the "thick" version of institutionalism, as opposed to the relatively "thinner" rational-choice institutionalism that overlaps a great deal with the utilitarian tradition. Seminal articles in this literature include Weiler, "Transformation of Europe," and Pierson, "Path to European Integration."

6. Pierson, "Path to European Integration," 139.

7. Fritz Scharpf and Vivien Schmidt, *Welfare and Work in the Open Economy* (Oxford: Oxford University Press, 2000); Liesbet Hooghe and Gary Marks, *Multi-level Governance and European Integration* (Lanham, Md.: Rowman and Littlefield, 2001); Maria Green Cowles, James A. Caporaso, Thomas Risse, eds., *Transforming Europe: Europeanization and Domestic Change* (Ithaca: Cornell University Press, 2001); Joseph Weiler, *The Constitution of Europe* (Cambridge: Cambridge University Press, 1999); Karen J. Alter, *Establishing the Supremacy of European Law* (Oxford: Oxford University Press, 2001).

8. An elaboration of this reasoning in terms of "punctuated equilibrium" can be found in Stephen Krasner, "Approaches to the State: Alternative Conceptions and Historical Dynamics," *Comparative Politics* 16 (January 1984): 223–46. For an application to the 1992 initiative, see Wayne Sandholtz and John Zysman, "1992: Recasting the European Bargain," *World Politics* 42, no. 1 (October 1989).

9. Peter A. Hall, "The Political Economy of Europe in an Era of Interdependence," in *Continuity and Change*, ed. Herbert Kitschelt et al. (Cambridge: Cambridge University Press, 1997), 154. Although Hall does not elaborate this point, one potential explanation for this "enthusiasm" would be the emergence of a new paradigm similar to that outlined for the case of Britain in a seminal article: Peter Hall, "Policy Paradigms, Social Learning, and the State: The Case of Economic Policymaking in Britain," *Comparative Politics* 25, no. 3 (April 1993). See also Ben Rosamond, "Discourses of Globalization and the Social Construction of Identities," *Journal of European Public Policy* 6, no. 4 (1999): 652–68, and Colin Hay and Ben Rosamond, "Globalization, European Integration, and the Discursive Construction of Economic Imperatives," *Journal of European Public Policy* 9, no. 2 (April 2002): 147–67.

scholars highlight the complex construction of actors' interests around ideas, frames, and paradigms, especially in times of uncertainty.[10] They have repeatedly drawn attention to the importance of neoliberal economic ideology in the run-up to the single market and EMU.[11] Altogether, constructivist scholars put more emphasis than do most institutionalists on the power of ideas, yet they concur with the institutionalist view of European integration as being relatively autonomous of global economic trends.

Although these three prevailing scholarly positions say very different things, they all fail to really problematize the link between European integration and market globalization. To understand why, let us reflect on what scholars wrote in the 1970s about the prospects of future integration before "Europe" was "relaunched" in the 1980s. Most observers predicted an increasing *fragmentation* of European interests and policies in an age of increasing global interdependence. Echoing a widespread perception, a leading theorist of economic interdependence offered a particularly ill-fated prediction: "The European Economic Community as a center of economic decision-making is rapidly becoming obsolete in the face of growing economic interdependence."[12] Leading neofunctionalist theorist Ernst Haas saw the global trend toward "interdependence" as a central cause of the "obsolescence of regional integration theory."[13] As Haas pointed out, the emergence of "global" issues meant that the advocates of European integration now had to contend with the temptations of "fragmented" approaches to common problems.[14] And in fact, during the 1970s, European cohesion was routinely sacrificed on the altar of national economic strategies. By the late 1970s, political

10. Neil Fligstein and I. Maradrita, "How to Make a Market," *European Journal of Sociology* 102, no. 1 (July 1996); McNamara, *Currency of Ideas*; Markus Jachtenfuchs et al., "Which Europe? Conflicting Models of a Legitimate European Political Order," *European Journal of International Relations* 4, no. 4 (December 1998); Thomas Christiansen et al., eds., "The Social Construction of Europe," special issue of *Journal of European Public Policy* 6, no. 4 (1999); Neil Fligstein and Alec Stone Sweet, "Constructing Polities and Markets: An Institutionalist Account of European Integration," *American Journal of Sociology* 107, no. 5 (March 2002): 1206–45; Parsons, *Certain Idea of Europe*; Diez Medrano, *Framing Europe*. Claudio Radaelli and Vivien A. Schmidt, "Policy Change and Discourse in Europe," *West European Politics* 27, no. 2 (March 2004): 183–379.

11. McNamara, *Currency of Ideas*; Verdun, "Role of the Delors Committee"; Dyson and Featherstone, *Road to Maastricht*.

12. Richard N. Cooper, "Economic Interdependence and Foreign Policy in the Seventies," *World Politics* 24, no. 2 (January 1972): 181.

13. See Ernst B. Haas, *The Obsolescence of Regional Integration Theory* (Berkeley: University of California, Institute of International Studies, 1975); Haas, "Turbulent Fields and the Theory of Regional Integration." Haas's reassessment of the theory he fathered responded to certain criticisms of regional integration by Stanley Hoffmann. In particular, the 1974 version of Hoffman's famous article "Obstinate or Obsolete" described the European Community as a "halfway house" between the nation and the wider Western international community. See Stanley Hoffmann, *The European Sisyphus* (Boulder: Westview Press, 1995), 101.

14. In apparent contrast to many present-day political scientists, earlier theorists of regional integration acknowledged that political backlashes against European integration and the emergence of centrifugal forces could compromise the very prospect of continuous institutional integration. On the possibility of backlash, see Ernst Haas's preface to the 1968 edition of *The Uniting of Europe* and the preface to Leon Lindberg and Stuart Scheingold, *Europe's Would-Be Polity* (Englewood Cliffs, N.J.: Prentice-Hall, 1970); on centrifugal forces, see Haas, *Obsolescence of Regional Integration Theory*.

scientists who examined European responses to the 1970s oil shocks in a comparative framework concluded that the differences between national models of political economy were more visible than they had been since the end of World War II.[15] If anything, global interdependence in the 1970s seemed to carry the seeds of a renationalization of economic policymaking and reforms.

In contrast with their predecessors, today's scholars typically theorize about European integration as if market globalization was unproblematic. Scholars who adopt the utilitarian perspective often take the reality of market reforms for granted, whereas institutionalist and constructivist scholars believe that the effects of market globalization on the EU are indeterminate. It is important to remember that neofunctionalist scholars—whose intellectual legacy is often claimed simultaneously by all sides of the current scholarly debates—came to focus on "global interdependence" as a cause for the "obsolescence" of their theory. They still believed in the power of the "Community method," associated with father of the European Community Jean Monnet and based on the idea of "upgrading common interests" through the daily work of common institutions. But they came to think, like most scholars in the 1970s, that the accelerating pace of globalization considerably impeded the progress of Europe. With the advance of global interdependence, the circle of common interests broadened beyond Europe's borders. Thus, the centripetal appeal of regional integration competed with the centrifugal forces of global market integration. For mysterious reasons, market globalization apparently did not have the same fragmenting effect in the 1980s and 1990s. A few scholars have pointed out the European Union's complex identity within a global economy—where it has acted either as a facilitator of or as a protector against global market integration.[16] Yet there has been no systematic scholarly attempt to reassess the problematic link between globalization and European integration.

The Problematic Status of Globalization

The benefit of hindsight has allowed scholars to dismiss the potentially detrimental effects of globalization on European integration. Once again, the heroic tale of "ever closer union" seems to explain the history of European integration in the 1980s and 1990s. According to common lore, the relaunching of Europe dates back to the Fontainebleau summit of European heads of state in 1984. After years of foot-dragging and "Euro-sclerosis"—that is, stagnant growth, rampant inflation, and rising unemployment—Europe's political leaders resolved a long-standing financial dispute about the British contribution to the European budget and issued a call for further European integration, thus opening the path for subsequent initiatives. In 1985, the European

15. Peter J. Katzenstein, ed., *Between Power and Plenty* (Madison: University of Wisconsin Press, 1978).
16. Vivien Schmidt, *The Futures of European Capitalism* (Oxford: Oxford University Press, 2002), and Sophie Meunier, *Trading Voices* (Princeton: Princeton University Press, 2005).

Commission, the administrative body of the European Community, led by its newly appointed and charismatic president Jacques Delors, produced a white paper called *Completing the Internal Market*. Building on European Community case law, the white paper established a detailed policy agenda of about three hundred measures aimed at eliminating all remaining nontariff barriers within the Community. It was soon endorsed by the member states and followed in 1987 by their signing the first major European treaty since the 1957 Treaty of Rome. The main achievement of this new treaty, the Single Act, was to forcefully rule out the use of national vetoes in matters relating to "the establishment and functioning of the internal market" (Article 100a, now Article 95 in the consolidated text of the EC Treaty).

From then on, presumably, it was just a matter of implementing the single market and going on to the "logical" next step of monetary integration. The European Commission drafted European legislation ("directives") in order to meet the official 1992 deadline for the implementation of the white paper on the internal market. In February 1988, the member states finally agreed on a six-year budgetary plan, including doubling the amount of the Community's budgetary resources. In June 1988, a landmark directive on the liberalization of all capital movements was adopted. The first major piece of legislation, it not only consecrated the white paper but went far beyond the letter of the document that the member states had originally endorsed. The late 1980s and early 1990s ushered in a series of European legislative acts. The Second Banking Directive (SBD), adopted in 1989, mandated the creation of a European financial market for credit institutions. That same year, the Merger Control Regulation drastically reinforced European Community powers in the area of competition policy, and the Public Procurement Directive mandated equal treatment of national and other EC bids for public works contracts. Discussions also began in Brussels about liberalizing major industrial and service sectors including finance, telecommunications, energy, postal services, trucking, railroads, and airlines. By the time the Treaty on European Union (Maastricht treaty) formalized the creation of the European Union in 1991, "Europe" had become synonymous with far-reaching changes in the governance of domestic economies. Thus, the high-mindedness of Europe's political leaders at Fontainebleau had brought Europe significantly nearer to the Community founding fathers' goal of an "ever-closer union among the peoples of Europe."

This may be good material for a larger-than-life epic, but it entirely overlooks the politics of the regional integration process of the 1980s and 1990s. When the *Economist* called the Single Act a "smiling mouse," it was merely voicing a widespread sentiment. Longtime observers of European politics received the Single European Act with reserve or even skepticism. After all, the idea of a Single European market sounded a lot like the Rome treaty's objective of a common market. Since the Common Market remained a somewhat distant ideal almost thirty years after its inception, many believed the January 31, 1992 deadline for completing the white paper's single market proposals was exuberantly optimistic.[17] There were many reasons to believe, when the Single Act was adopted in 1987, that European integration would again be quickly caught in a political mire. The Single Act's requirement of qualified-majority voting clearly had the potential to upend the status quo, but it was primarily a reassertion of an already existing principle. There was no substantive guarantee that the formal principle would be respected, especially if the reform agenda became too bold. Although a certain rapprochement had occurred between member states whose national economic policies diverged dramatically in the early 1980s, the persistence of fundamental disagreements over the future political shape of "Europe" did not seem to bode well for deep political integration and institutional change.

This point can be illustrated by a survey of elite and mass political opinions. Elite opinion can be sketched from a few representative examples from the published memoirs of high-level government officials in Britain, France, and Germany—three leading parties to the Single Act. However self-serving these memoirs may be, they clearly suggest that nobody fully anticipated nor perhaps wished the market-building process to go as far as it did. Although British prime minister Margaret Thatcher originally supported the EC 1992 agenda wholeheartedly for the sake of the free market, she only later realized that market building was not happening in a political vacuum. She came to recognize that Jacques Delors, the moderate French socialist at the head of the European Commission, was committed to building a "political" Europe—not just a free market.[18] Symmetrically, there is compelling evidence that François Mitterrand and his French socialist government decided to champion "Europe" for reasons that had little to do with the single market per se. The French saw this endeavor primarily as a promise of future progress toward common social and industrial policies.[19] Thus, the French government was surprised that European integration after the Single Act gave continued momentum to economic liberalization.[20] Finally, although German officials at first seemed generally sat-

17. Commissioner Arthur Cockfield, whose team within the European Commission drafted most of the white paper in 1985, summarized a then-prevailing sentiment: "At the time few people thought that we would complete the program, or complete it on time." See Cockfield, "The Real Significance of 1992," in *The Politics of 1992*, ed. Colin Crouch and David Marquand (Oxford: Basil Blackwell, 1990).

18. In her memoirs, Thatcher expresses considerable bitterness about "gestures which seem to be of minor significance at the time but adopt a far greater one in light of events." See Margaret Thatcher, *The Downing Street Years* (London: Harper and Collins, 1993), 549. See also Nigel Lawson, *The View from No. 11* (London: Bantam, 1992).

19. This is especially clear in Jacques Attali, *Verbatim I* (Paris: Fayard, 1993), esp. 31 and 789. See also Hubert Védrine, *Les mondes de François Mitterrand* (Paris: Fayard, 1996), and Pierre Favier and Michel Martin-Rolland, *La décennie Mitterrand*, 2 (Paris: Seuil, 1993).

20. Longtime Mitterrand diplomatic adviser Hubert Védrine acknowledges that "nobody, except perhaps Jacques Delors" realized the full meaning of what it would take and how politically controversial it would be to implement the agenda set forth in the Commission's white paper. See Védrine, *Les mondes de François Mitterrand*, 398. Even French industry minister Roger Fauroux, a former industrialist and leading member of the European Roundtable of Industrialists, confided in an interview: "I thought the single European market of 1992 was just a symbol, but this symbol has now become a reality." See "Wheel Comes Full Circle for France's Industrial Pragmatist," *Financial Times*, July 1, 1988.

isfied with the concurrent progression toward a more liberal Europe and stronger EC institutions in Brussels, neither of these two developments was central to German support of the Single Act. German support for European integration continued a long-standing foreign policy orientation, according to which almost any step toward the integration of Europe was seen as the best avenue for the consolidation of Germany's status and integrity in a Europe divided by the cold war.[21] And they certainly did not anticipate such a rapid expansion of the European policy domain, nor the concurrent need for increased budgetary resources in Brussels.[22] Thus, the uncanny success of the EC 1992 operation and the depth of subsequent institutional change in the 1980s and 1990s at the EU level apparently took the very policymakers who initiated that process by surprise.

On the level of mass politics, the dilemmas of European integration and globalization were not so visible at the beginning but became starker as the single market and monetary union became a reality. Many social groups in Western Europe were bound to feel increasingly threatened by the prospect of market-oriented institutional change. Beneath the superficial consensus to "build Europe" under the auspices of the single market and monetary union, regional integration was bound to become much more controversial and conflict ridden. The traditionally favorable attitude of European citizens toward European integration—what scholars in the 1970s called a "permissive consensus"—disappeared somewhere down the road toward market liberalization.[23] The cross-national data gathered as part of the Eurobarometer public opinion survey project details this trend.[24] Although in 1990 a record proportion—over 70 percent—of the European population considered their country's membership in the European Community as a "good thing," that proportion almost continuously decreased in subsequent years, dropping to less than 50 percent in 1996. For Britain, support dropped from 72 percent to 46 percent; for France, from 70 percent to 46 percent; and for Germany, from 73 percent to 37 percent. In each case, the percentage drop in popularity had never been so sudden and the 1996 figures were the lowest since cross-national population surveys were first conducted on this issue in 1962. Europe's general public woke up to the reality of institutional change later than European political leaders, but public opinion surveys suggest that they had similar misgivings about its direction.

21. The views expressed by long-serving German foreign minister Hans-Dietrich Genscher are quite representative: "The European Community must not be allowed to lag behind [the East-West detente process] if balance in Europe was to be maintained." See Genscher, *Rebuilding a House Divided* (New York: Broadway Books, 1997), 136.

22. On these questions, see the views expressed by longtime German finance minister Gerhard Stoltenberg, *Wendepunkte* (Berlin: Siedler Verlag, 1997), 320–25.

23. See esp. Matthew J. Gabel, *Interests and Integration: Market Liberalization, Public Opinion, and European Union* (Ann Arbor: University of Michigan Press, 1998).

24. See the "Standard Barometer" data sections in European Commission, *Eurobarometer* (May 1994), esp. 71–90; European Commission, *Eurobarometer* (Autumn 1998), 31–41.

In light of these diverse motivations among both elite and mass publics, what is most surprising about recent European integration is not the signing of what looked like a fairly minimalist Single Act but that the single market became a reality. Once again, hindsight is highly misleading. It is tempting to analyze the 1980s and 1990s era of market reforms as a favorable context for European unification, yet very few actors who bought into the idea of relaunching Europe in the 1980s acted on the premise that market reform would carry the day. The Single Act, generally identified as the moment that sealed Europe's renewal, has aptly been called a "triumph of self-delusion."[25] Retrospectively, there is something deeply counterintuitive about the political appeal of the single market. Although Delors had secured the approval of European capitals on the principle of building a genuine single market as early as 1984, it was only later that this mandate was clarified, in the course of its practical implementation and in the evolving context of political battles. Initially, the common ground consisted of a fairly minimal consensus on the diagnosis of Eurosclerosis and on the general sense that "more Europe" could help remedy this situation, rather than on a detailed set of prescriptions. The task of building a single market was not particularly well defined in specific policies. Until about 1988, it was far from clear that the 1992 agenda set forth by the European Commission would amount to anything other than another one of the many failed attempts to revive the European Community.

To some extent, a similar dynamic was at play with EMU. On the one hand, it was obvious at the time of the Maastricht treaty that the idea of European unity had become more powerful than at any time since the early steps of the European Coal and Steel Community in the 1950s. Whereas the Single Act had been an object of widespread skepticism in 1986, the Maastricht treaty and the prospect of EMU were taken very seriously when new treaty was agreed on in December 1991. The context of German reunification and the end of the cold war division of Europe certainly gave the treaty historical panache. On the other hand, the treaty itself was the outcome of a long and difficult political process, and it was only the beginning of the painful and politically perilous march toward the euro. Denmark's referendum on the new treaty yielded a negative outcome, while it barely passed in the French referendum. With a widely derided "petit oui" of 50.7 percent, a majority of the French did vaguely support "Europe," but they had not really thought through the changes it would require.[26] In retrospect, therefore, the wave of Euro-optimism peaked with the signing of the Maastricht treaty. With the advent of a deep economic recession and the emergence of numerous political hurdles, the EU suffered a severe crisis of confidence, from which it arguably never fully recovered. A few

25. Nicholas Colchester and David Buchan, *Europe Relaunched* (London: Hutchinson Business Books, 1990), 14.
26. See George Ross and Sophie Meunier, "Democratic Deficit or Democratic Surplus? Comments on the French Referendum," *French Politics and Society* 11, no. 1 (Winter 1993): 57–69.

important steps were taken in the 1990s, including the decision to extend membership to eastern European countries, but for the most part the EU seemed to have lost its original momentum. Even the definitive introduction of the euro on January 1, 2002, was an anticlimax after such a prolonged pregnancy. From this perspective, the failed referenda of May 2005 on the EU constitution in France and the Netherlands, with respectively 55 percent and 62 percent of voters rejecting the new treaty, are only the latest episode in a growing trend of public dissatisfaction with the European Union.

In sum, the relatively peaceful nature of institutional change in the 1980s and 1990s should not be taken to mean that the European Union's quiet revolution was somehow inscribed in a broader logic of interests, institutions, or ideas. The fortunes of the market and monetary integration agenda constantly fluctuated. Battles were fought, and the forging of new settlements created winners and losers. Scholars who speak of a succession of "bargains" or "deals" imply that the terms of the exchange were known. Yet the Single Act and ensuing European initiatives more often took the form of what Delors called a "dynamic compromise." Treaties were only the beginning of the integration process and were not guarantees of success. Member governments still held very different conceptions of what "Europe" should be about, and that alone could easily have perpetuated the institutional status quo. To make sense of the European Union's quiet revolution, we must disaggregate the various elements of that process and evaluate theoretically derived hypotheses at a more concrete level.

DISAGGREGATING THE QUIET REVOLUTION

How can we make sense of the European Union's quiet revolution—the series of profound economic governance reforms that came with the single market and economic and monetary union—in relation to market globalization? Market globalization is often understood as an inescapable economic requirement or as the hegemonic diffusion of neoliberal ideology. But if we want to explain the particular character and locus of European reforms, we must go beyond the superficial similarity between market integration movements on a global level and those on the European level. We must first look at the reform process and ask whether we would expect various reforms to take place in a "pure" market globalization scenario; we can then construct a selection of cases that seem interesting to study. Once we have identified these cases, it will become possible to highlight the most important puzzles that deserve to be resolved.

Characteristics of the Reforms—Four Select Cases

When we examine the many facets of the European Union's quiet revolution, we observe a certain variation in the pace, scope, focus, and profile of EU reforms. The most ambitious, and presumably the most revealing, reforms are those that are characterized by a fast pace, wide scope, divergent focus, or high profile in relation to market globalization. These characteristics can serve as a basis for selecting corresponding cases: the single financial area; the internal energy market; structural policy; economic and monetary union.

Fast Pace

In some fast-moving sectors like finance and telecommunications, market reforms occurred quickly and combined deregulation with reregulation. The single financial area, as the objective came to be called, is an interesting case. A centerpiece of the European 1992 agenda was to bring regulation down to "essential minimum requirements," scrapping counterproductive rules. In finance, this led to landmark pieces of European legislation such as the 1988 directive mandating full liberalization of capital movements. This deregulatory enterprise typically targeted overly bureaucratized licensing procedures and red tape. A wave of financial reforms swept through Europe with staggering speed. The 1980s and 1990s saw a rapid and far-reaching succession of market-oriented reforms in banking, securities, and insurance. New regulatory frameworks granted more room to market-based governance mechanisms.

Although market pressures had become very pressing and certainly pushed the financial sector in the direction of change, the sudden acceleration of reforms is nonetheless remarkable. Bankers, stockbrokers, bond dealers, and, later, financial market regulators became paragons of popular culture across the world. Socialists and conservatives alike started to heap praise on the virtues of the stock market. Changes in financial institutions are generally difficult to carry out because financial establishments are nationally entrenched and prone to waging political resistance against reforms. Of course, European finance was already changing dramatically at the domestic level. In the mid- to late 1980s, virtually all the EU member states with significant financial markets undertook some liberalization measures, albeit very unevenly. What is striking, however, is the speed of this phenomenon, to which the momentum of EU-level reforms certainly contributed. All over Western Europe, states eliminated financial regulations and administrative controls they had slowly built since the end of World War II.

Wide Scope

The European market reform movement spread to sectors where market forces for change were not pressing. The provision of collective services was generally controlled by public utilities subject to low market and technological pressures—with a few important exceptions such as telecommunication services. European Union countries nevertheless initiated the gradual liberalization of many collective services. In the energy sector, they adopted the objective of an internal energy market as early as 1988. In 1996, they adopted an electricity reform regulation after almost a decade of debate. That first reform was not a big bang—it was phased in slowly, and it allowed member states to establish entry conditions for new firms. Market access initially concerned only

big industrial consumers, and it was extended very slowly to individual consumers. Yet it was a step toward the full liberalization of energy services scheduled to take effect in 2007. One outcome of this gradual process was the reorganization of energy supply around a small number of corporate giants. In
some cases, it involved not only a liberalization of markets but also a privatization of public sector corporations.

Analysis of market reforms in slow-moving sectors controls for the impact of
technological and economic evolution. Despite superficial analogies to other
sectors, utilities and governance mechanisms were not under massive competitive threat from the emergence of alternative providers or substitute services.
The occurrence of reform is especially interesting because public utilities,
often in a monopolistic position, were important domestic political actors and
therefore able to wage a political fight against reform. Although existing structures of energy supply had their problems, many state officials and industry
representatives thought marketization was not the most rational way to address them. In most member states, energy liberalization initially did not figure on the domestic reform agenda before the late 1990s, or even after 2000 in
a few cases. Yet the EU reforms were carried through, and the scope of market
reforms was thus considerably widened.

Divergent Focus

Institutional change at the EU level centered not only on market integration but also extended into areas that were highly tangential to—if not contradictory with—that agenda. Policies designed to promote competitiveness
often combined an unprecedented degree of centralized control with decentralized implementation. Perhaps the most novel and certainly the best funded
of EU competitiveness efforts was the establishment of "structural policy." The
objective of this new policy was to foster regional development and help European regions to compete in the single market. With roughly one-third of the
EU budget, structural policy became the second largest EU expenditure (after
the common agricultural policy or CAP) and the fastest growing expenditure.
The EU budget increased considerably, mostly to cover an increase in the
Structural Funds. Through two successive reforms in 1988 and 1993, the member states agreed to set up a redistributive budgetary mechanism between EU
regions.

Although the EU budget remained capped at a modest 1.24 percent of the
European Union's GDP even after this increase, the likelihood of reform in
this area was not self-evident. On the one hand, structural policy redistributes
only 0.4 percent of EU GDP, strictly on the basis of eligibility rather than entitlement criteria. From this standpoint, it seems to be compatible with a
market-based paradigm of policymaking. On the other hand, the newly conceived structural policy explicitly aims to correct market outcomes. Not only
did the wealthiest and biggest member states stand to lose from EU-wide inter-

regional transfers but the reform also seemed to go against the free-market principle of competitive allocation of resources. By the turn of the century, diminished economic growth and the concentration of poor regions in the ten new member states clouded the political future of EU structural policy. Yet the rationale for preserving a geographically based developmental policy remained comparatively much stronger than many other EU expenditures such as the common agricultural policy. Once again, this seems to contradict the common perception of the single market as an artifact of market globalization.

High Profile

In some cases, the EU adopted very high-profile reforms in relation to the broad, yet less visible, process of market globalization. This was most clear for economic and monetary union, with the creation of a single currency, the euro, managed by an independent European Central Bank. The stakes of EMU were high, the ultimate distribution of costs and benefits largely elusive, and the long-term consequences potentially enormous. In this case, the surprise stems from the fact that a core group of EU member states prepared for and carried through what was in many respects a leap of faith. Twelve member states abandoned their respective national currencies and adopted the euro in a three-step process from the late 1990s through January 1, 2002. The ECB was freed from any political tutelage and assigned the primary task of fighting inflation. With the so-called Maastricht convergence criteria in 1992 and with the Stability and Growth Pact in 1997, the member states also adopted a fairly extensive framework of budget deficit ceilings and fiscal policy rules and guidelines.

Economic and monetary union represents a shift to market-friendly policies, but it also enabled a concentration of powers at the EU level. On the one hand, the birth of the euro went along with a reorganization of macroeconomic policies under more market-friendly terms. European Union governments set up an independent central bank and important safeguards against profligate fiscal policy. This would seem to confirm the common perception of EMU as the apotheosis of neoliberal economics. On the other hand, EMU can also be described a form of public empowerment against the vagaries of the free market. Under EMU, member states transferred monetary powers to a single central bank that de facto sheltered them from the previously enormous pressure of currency fluctuations. While they recognized the need to fight inflation, member governments also regained maneuvering room vis-à-vis market actors in the exercise of economic policies. Their fiscal priorities are now subject to a process of peer evaluation, which enables them to avoid the harsher verdicts of financial actors. The Maastricht treaty also provides an embryonic framework for central bank accountability and fiscal policy coordination, which opens the possibility for political leaders to assert collective priorities other than low inflation.

TABLE 1.
Case Selection and Outcomes

Select cases	Characteristics	Outcomes
Single financial area	High pace	Deregulation and re-regulation; started at domestic level
Internal energy market	Expanded scope	Progressive liberalization; deep sectoral changes over time
Structural policy	Divergent focus	Upgrade of non-market resource allocation; procedural and budgetary centralization
Economic and Monetary Union	High profile	New macroeconomic policy framework; partial transfer of sovereignty

Two Puzzles

This is not yet the place to delve into the details of each case and to explain their characteristics, but two puzzles already stand out. First, the correlation between the occurrence of market reforms and the presence of market pressures is anything but straightforward. Scholars who adopt a utilitarian perspective identify market forces as a prominent pushing factor in internationally exposed sectors such as finance. But to push through liberalization, the reformers also had to fight difficult political battles. The political dimension of market reforms is especially obvious if we compare the internal energy market to the single financial area. How "market reform" became a mantra that even extended to sectors relatively sheltered from market forces is not so easy to understand in conventional scholarly terms. Contrary to a common utilitarian assumption, the occurrence of market reforms in the context of market globalization cannot be taken for granted. Conversely, institutionalist scholars, who stress the incremental character of institutional change, can be criticized for discounting the novelty of European market reforms. Finally, the market reform process can hardly be described in constructivist terms as a wholesale ideological conversion or learning exercise, even though constructivist scholars are right to detect a greater acceptance of the liberalization logic. In sum, the challenge is to explain not only why liberalization occurred but also why it did not entail a triumph of the market, that is, why the glass is both half full and half empty.

A second puzzle is that market reforms often went hand in hand with a considerable buildup of policy capacity at the EU level. Various explanations have been offered for the upgrading of structural policy and EMU. Utilitarian explanations usually focus on big member states pursuing their national economic interests and extending "side payments" to less developed member states for going along with them. Institutionalist scholars often present these policy innovations as incremental steps toward "ever closer union," in line with longstanding Community commitments. Constructivist scholars point out the cross-national prominence of policy paradigms such as "regulated capitalism" or "sound money" ideas. There is a gap, however, between these interpretations and the complexity and magnitude of the power concentrations they are supposed to explain. In structural policy, two seemingly opposite rationales—economic and social—coexisted to justify a significant budgetary and procedural centralization. Even more conspicuously in the case of EMU, a clear desire to establish "market-friendly" monetary and fiscal policies somehow went along with the creation of enormous new EU powers.

What made the prospect of a united Europe seem obsolete in the 1970s, and suddenly very timely in the 1980s and the 1990s? In the literature, conventional views of Europe's late twentieth-century renewal have developed without any systematic attempt to answer this question. Perhaps because the European Commission's 1985 white paper seemed so boringly technical, the concrete meaning of Europe's "market reforms" has not attracted much attention. The recent acceleration of market globalization certainly spurred, but did not determine, the transition to new political settlements. Behind the particular problem of spelling out the logic of the European Union's quiet revolution, the larger question is how peaceful institutional change can be hammered out in a global economy. We know from the works of Karl Polanyi and other institutionalist scholars that it takes political power to build a market. But this does not really tell us why key policy areas ceased to be the exclusive preserve of nation-states. From this standpoint, it is important to pay closer attention to the political strategies that actors develop in the context of market globalization.

THREE

The Politics of Market Ideas

T he European Union's quiet revolution was the result of a political strategy. In a specific historical context, the advocates of Europe chose the market as a central rationale for building power at the European level. They appealed to market ideas across a variety of policy areas, but on close examination these ideas were not particularly coherent. They pursued a variety of integrationist goals and used different market ideas for these different purposes. My argument, then, is primarily about political strategy as a causal factor of institutional change and only secondarily about the power of ideas. The politics of market ideas, not these ideas themselves, fueled the European Union's quiet revolution. On the one hand, the many variants of institutional change cannot be traced back to a sharply delineated and consensual idea or doctrine of ideas, say, neoclassical economics. In this sense, the quiet revolution was not a neoliberal revolution. On the other hand, market rationality functioned as a very effective repertoire of loosely articulated ideas. Actors were able to pick and choose from this repertoire to advance their integrationist agenda. Different market ideas thus served to justify different integrationist actions. This was possible precisely because the market was anything but a systematic and rigid ideology.

This argument essentially rests on a theoretical stance that can be characterized as *strategic constructivism*. It highlights the complex motivations of the political strategy that led to the European Union's quiet revolution. A political strategy, as I define it, is a socially constructed method of collective action that brings together actors with diverse motivations. In politics, actors do not just maximize and trade utilities in explicit bargains, nor do they consistently follow clear-cut ideas. They constantly have to make choices in the present while knowing that these choices will have unpredictable and contentious consequences beyond the short term. Actors formulate and pursue broad visions of what they want to achieve. These visions provide them with a sense of direction, but they rarely spell out rigid ideological or material goals. By necessity, actors often have to embark on a course of action without being sure where it will lead them. In late twentieth-century Europe, various actors were pursuing various long-term goals—a united Europe, a free market economy, or a socially oriented market economy. Although these visions were partly or wholly incompatible, the key actors who held them were willing to gamble on the future. The breadth and remoteness of their long-term goals enabled them to agree on an intermediate objective of "building a market," even though they disagreed on a fundamental level. The market-building agenda thus became the receptacle of divergent long-term motivations. The promoters of Europe not only gambled on the future, they knowingly entered into an essentially ambiguous agreement on market integration. In practice, the actors who implemented the common goal of a Europe-wide market resorted to a variety of market ideas in pursuit of their different long-term visions. As a result, the quiet revolution was carried out under the auspices of the market, but it did not follow a predominantly economic logic.

GOAL COMPLEXITY IN POLITICS

There is no doubt that the European Union's quiet revolution is somehow linked to market globalization. As Europe's national models of economic governance faced difficulties, combined with the looming collapse of the Soviet bloc, a majority of elite actors in Europe increasingly began to view the market as a powerful reality on a global scale. Although the fortunes of the market as a body of discourse have widely fluctuated, market ideas experienced a new golden age in the late twentieth century.[1] Of course, the market was already a central institution of European liberal democracy even before the 1980s. But the aura of the free market had lost much of its glow in the wake of the Great Depression and World War II. During the cold war, market forces in Western Europe were held in check by nonmarket institutions designed to dampen the destabilizing effects of economic cycles.[2] That is why the 1980s redemption of the market after a long period of purgatory marked a certain watershed and has often been described as the beginning of a neoliberal age.

What Peter Hall calls the "general enthusiasm for market mechanisms" is not so straightforward, however. Western Europeans did not all suddenly fall in love with the free market—or with Europe. Mainstream European political actors perceived market globalization as an important fact, but they often de-

---

1. The historical origins of the market as a canonical way of thinking about economic organization can be dated approximately to the beginning of the industrial revolution. See Karl Polanyi, *Great Transformation*, esp. chaps. 4–6; Polanyi, "The Economy as an Instituted Process," in *Trade and Market in the Early Empires*, ed. Polanyi, Conrad M. Arensberger, and Harry W. Pearson (Glencoe, Ill.: Gateway, 1957); Albert O. Hirschman, *The Passions and the Interests* (Princeton: Princeton University Press, 1977).

2. For seminal works on the domestic and international foundations of postwar political economy, see Andrew Shonfield, *Modern Capitalism: The Changing Balance of Public and Private Power* (London: Oxford University Press, 1969); John G. Ruggie, "International Regimes, Transactions, and Change: Embedded Liberalism in the Postwar Economic Order," *International Organization* 36 (Spring 1982).

rived opposite conclusions from it. The market's return to favor was greeted with mixed feelings because various actors remained committed to starkly different long-term visions of the ideal polity. The conflict of visions between the advocates and critics of the free market remained central. Free-market liberals were convinced of the value of free markets with minimal government intervention. This liberal economic orientation became more widespread, but its proponents were never a majority. Many actors remained critical of the free market and concerned about the social consequences of market globalization. Although these critics increasingly acknowledged the absence of full-fledged alternatives to the market economy, they did not regard the free market as a categorically superior mechanism for allocating resources and values. Finally, aside from advocates and critics of the free market, there was also an active federalist minority that considered Europe's political integration a desirable end in itself. Thus, beneath the superficial European "enthusiasm" for the market, differences of political vision among key actors ran particularly deep.

Political Strategy as a Social Construct

Although various political actors held a variety of long-term purposes, they were nonetheless able to agree on a common political strategy of market and monetary unification. The key political actors who became the promoters of Europe in the 1980s and 1990s were extremely strange bedfellows. They shared a desire to change the status quo, but for very different reasons. Many on the right saw Europe as a way to promote the free market; they often did not care for European unity as such. Conversely, many on the left considered the free market potentially harmful; they saw the European Union as a countervailing force against the free market. There was no way they could reconcile their fundamentally different visions. Yet they were able to agree on an immediate goal that also suited the federalists, namely the completion of an internal market with a single currency at the European level.

At first glance, it might seem surprising that the promoters of Europe were able to agree on a strategy of action even though they did not pursue the same goals. We generally assume that people who act together must share at least *some* common interests or values. However commonsensical it may sound, this is not a safe assumption for political analysis. In politics it is not at all unusual to see actors form alliances despite fundamental disagreements. This routinely occurs in electoral periods for the simple purpose of gaining power; but unholy alliances can also persist over longer periods of time. Actors do not need to agree on everything to accomplish things together. In fact, it is perfectly possible to agree on a strategy without sharing the same long-term goals—just as it is possible to agree on goals and disagree on strategy. In such cases, all actors take the risk of deviating from their respective long-term goals in carrying out their common strategy, but they each also work hard to retain the initiative and to make progress toward their long-term goals.

Seen in this light, the drive for a united Europe via market and monetary unification embodied above all a complex collective gamble on the future of the European Union in the context of market globalization. The promoters of Europe did not trade off preferences any more than they converted to a coherent set of neoliberal ideas. There was no explicit bargain between the Left and the Right or between member states such as Germany and France. On the contrary, the main actors who chose to put their weight behind European integration each retained the hope that their respective long-term vision would ultimately prevail. Yet the visions that the various actors pursued were sufficiently broad and remote that they were able to find common ground for immediate action. Rather than risk an open conflict and a continued stalemate in European integration, they muted their disagreements, struck a tactical truce, and adopted a common strategy. "The market" provided a good ground for this truce because it had captured the imagination of European elites at the time. Actors continued to disagree over their different long-term purposes, but they pursued a common political strategy that led to various integrationist reforms.

Goal Complexity as a Core Element of Political Strategy

The goal complexity inherent in this political strategy is difficult to square with conventional conceptions of strategy in political science. When they speak about strategy, most political scientists who work from constructivist, institutionalist, or utilitarian perspectives rarely pay sufficient attention to the complexity of actors' goals. In constructivist and institutionalist scholarship, actors' strategies are often seen as by-products of the ideational and institutional environments in which they find themselves. For example, the market is typically conceived as the core figure of a neoliberal policy paradigm that can, under certain institutional conditions, frame the action of governments. Actors' strategies are seen, in turn, as generally subordinate to these broad cognitive and institutional frameworks. Of course, it would be difficult to deny the impact of cognitive and institutional variables. After a long period of Keynesian-style policymaking, neoliberal ideas gained ground in the 1970s and 1980s, while existing institutions continued to shape and constrain actors' behavior.[3] But it would also be a mistake to reduce actors' strategy to the institutionally constrained implementation of a neoliberal paradigm. Although the European Union's quiet revolution can certainly be approached from a constructivist perspective, it is impossible to demonstrate that the strategy of mar-

3. On the institutionally constrained impact of Keynesianism and neoliberalism, see Peter A. Hall, ed., *The Political Power of Economic Ideas* (Princeton: Princeton University Press, 1989), and Hall, "The Movement from Keynesianism to Monetarism," in *Structuring Politics: Historical Institutionalism in Comparative Analysis*, by Sven Steinmo, Kathleen Thelen, and Frank Longstreth (Cambridge: Cambridge University Press, 1992).

ket integration directly stemmed from a single coherent and widely shared body of ideas.

The political strategy that led to the quiet revolution embodied complex long-term motivations and expectations. Standard constructivist and institutionalist conceptions of strategy are often unsatisfactory because ideas and institutions do not completely preempt actors' goals.[4] In opting for a broad market-building strategy, those critical of neoliberalism and those who wanted to build nothing more than a free market at the European level engaged together in a risky and complex gamble. In the unfolding of the European Union's quiet revolution, however, actors' visions of the ideal polity were never far below the surface. The fact that different actors' pursued different long-term goals mattered a lot, not only because these actors had their goals clearly in mind when they chose their common political strategy but also because these different goals continued to shape actors' behavior throughout the reform process. Although the market was the dominant trope of the quiet revolution, it was invoked to legitimize a surprisingly wide range of policies. Just as Keynesian economics had been used to buttress a large panoply of choices, political declarations about the "end of Keynesianism" went well beyond the subtle evolution of scientific debates within economics. As a consequence, rarely spoken but nonetheless pressing political goals overshadowed the economic reasoning and ideas that the promoters of Europe held out to justify their reforms.

To say that actors' goals mattered is not to revert to a purely utilitarian view of strategy, however. Goal complexity and gambling are practically absent from the standard utilitarian conception of strategy as a tool. From a utilitarian perspective, strategy is simply the art of choosing the best course of action in a given setting.[5] Utility-maximizing actors pursue clear, rank-ordered preferences, and they trade them off whenever it is rational to do so. Not very surprisingly, economic interests often play a central part in utilitarian assumptions about actors' preferences.[6] This tends to result in a rather thin utilitarian conception of strategy, which can be criticized for missing the broad political dimension of actors' strategies. Political strategies are unwieldy tools at best, in that the actors who adopt them often do not share the same goals. In the run-

4. In part because of the challenge of rational-choice institutionalism, old-style institutionalist scholars have come to recognize that more attention should be paid to actors' goals and strategies. See Peter Hall and Rosemary C. R. Taylor, "Political Science and the Three Institutionalisms," *Political Studies* 44, no. 5 (December 1996), and Kathleen Thelen, "How Institutions Evolve: Insights from Comparative Institutional Analysis," in *Comparative Historical Analysis in the Social Sciences*, ed. James Mahoney and Dietrich Rueschemeyer (Cambridge: Cambridge University Press, 2003).

5. According to Jeffry Frieden, for example, "given [a] strategic setting, strategies are tools the agent uses to get as close to its preferences as possible." Frieden, "Actors and Preferences in International Relations," in *Strategic Choice and International Relations*, ed. David A. Lake and Robert Powell (Princeton: Princeton University Press, 1999), 45.

6. For an elaboration of this point, see ibid.; for an empirical analysis of actors' strategies in terms of their economic interests, see Moravcsik, *Choice of Europe*.

up to the quiet revolution, the collective choice of a political strategy of market integration cannot be described as a straightforward least-common-denominator bargain among utility-maximizing actors, since the promoters of Europe were pursuing largely incompatible long-term visions.[7] Only the passing of time would decide whose vision was the most foresighted, but it was clear from the outset that the process would necessarily entail winners and losers.

What the utilitarian perspective fails to recognize is the social construction of political strategy. In politics, even the most rational and foresighted actors must accept the fact that the distant future is shrouded in a veil of fog. And since any bold political initiative must be supported by a sufficiently broad coalition, actors thus face strong incentives to take risks and to work with allies who have different motivations and long-term goals than their own. A strategy becomes political only when it spurs a collective mobilization beyond the small circle of its individual initiators. The resulting social construction of strategy undercuts the very definition of strategy as a utility-maximizing tool in the hands of individual actors. Factors other than standard utility maximization and actors' calculations of economic interests often play a crucial role in shaping strategies. In late twentieth-century Europe, the promoters of Europe agreed on market and monetary integration knowing that this strategy was risky. They chose to temporarily set aside their disagreements over long-term goals in order to push through a more immediate agenda. The collective character of their political strategy meant that none of the promoters of Europe could be sure they were choosing a winning strategy in the long run. The market-building strategy simply embodied a tactical truce that effectively launched the quiet revolution, even though the various promoters of Europe each knew that their respective visions might ultimately not prevail.

Although goal complexity and gambling on the future are seldom fully acknowledged by political actors or analysts, they are widespread facts of political life. When trade-offs are too stark and visions too polarized, there is a risk of deadlock. To avoid paralysis and to forge ahead as a group, actors must sometimes agree to defer controversial choices. It sometimes pays to remain elusive over the ultimate direction of change.[8] Truces between opposing factions are routine within political parties and coalitions, or in any setting where there is no clear-cut selection procedure among competing actors and their visions. The absence of a unified government at the EU level precluded any clear resolution of fundamental goal conflicts. It was not easy to maintain this elusiveness and to keep everyone on board, with different actors wanting to go

---

7. Even with short-time horizons, scholars have found it is empirically problematic to envision strategies as utility-maximizing tools. In recent years, an entire subfield of economics and psychology has developed to overcome the limits of the utility-maximization assumption. For a useful survey applied to international relations, see Jonathan Mercer, "Rationality and Psychology in International Politics," *International Organization* 59 (Winter 2005): 77–106.

8. On the political value of saying as little as possible in situations of intense political conflict, see Padgett and Ansell, "Robust Action and the Rise of the Medici."

in different directions. At first glance, the choice of a market and monetary integration strategy would seem to give the advantage to free-market liberals in achieving their long-term agenda. But since actors who remained critical of the free market also bought into it, they must have had good reasons to believe that this strategy left the future sufficiently open. To understand these reasons, we must ask what market integration actually meant.

The Market as a Repertoire of Ideas

Once we recognize the complexity of actors' goals, we are naturally led to question the conventional view of the Europe Union's market reforms as the embodiment of a global neoliberal agenda. Beneath the surface, there are many different meanings of the market and, hence, many different ways to integrate a market. From an anthropological perspective, the market is a highly abstract representation of the world. As a set of ideas that people have in their heads and rarely question, the market constitutes what sociologists and anthropologists call an institution.[9] On the one hand, the market has become a deeply ingrained way of making sense of the world. Whether we like it or not, the market today comes close to being perceived as a natural phenomenon, like "planets fixed in the sky."[10] On the other hand, the institution of the market is so broad that it is very loosely constraining. In sociological parlance, the market can be depicted as a broad "repertoire" or "tool kit" for action.[11] Thus, actors agreed to build a Europe-wide market not simply because they recognized the power or the normative superiority of market mechanisms but because the repertoire of market ideas legitimized their actions while leaving them significant maneuvering room. Precisely because the market is anything but a rigid and sharply delineated reality, the promoters of Europe were able to undertake market and monetary integration without losing sight of their respective long-term goals.

9. Some anthropologists would call it an "ideology," but what they have in mind is much broader than the popular (Marxist) meaning of ideology as a "cloak" for material interests. See Clifford Geertz, *The Interpretation of Cultures* (New York: Basic Books, 1973), esp. chap. 8, "Ideology as a Cultural System"; Louis Dumont, *From Mandeville to Marx: The Genesis and Triumph of Economic Ideology* (Chicago: University of Chicago Press, 1977). Although political scientists usually reserve the word *institution* for formal artifacts of law and government, they sometimes describe the market much as anthropologists do as a "meta-institution." See Kathleen Thelen and Sven Steinmo, "Historical Institutionalism in Comparative Politics," in Steinmo, Thelen, and Longstreth, *Structuring Politics*, 31.

10. According to anthropologist Mary Douglas, "A convention is institutionalized when, in reply to the question, 'Why do you do it like this?' although the first answer may be framed in terms of mutual convenience, in response to further questioning the final answer refers to the way the planets are fixed in the sky or the way that plants or humans or animals naturally behave." Douglas, *How Institutions Think* (Syracuse: Syracuse University Press, 1986), 46–47.

11. On these concepts, see Charles Tilly, *From Mobilization to Revolution* (Reading, Mass.: Addison-Wesley, 1978); Swidler, "Culture in Action"; Elizabeth S. Clemens, "Organizational Repertoires and Institutional Change: Women's Groups and the Transformation of U.S. Politics, 1890–1920," *American Journal of Sociology* 98, no. 4 (January 1993).

The Multiplicity of Market Ideas

The market is often envisioned as a strong material or ideological determinant of actors' strategies, somewhat apart from day-to-day politics. For example, conventional utilitarian and constructivist interpretations of Europe's market and monetary integration generally highlight the coercive power of rising capital mobility or the neoliberal movement in reaction to the perceived failure of Keynesian countercyclical policies. These standard conceptions of the market—as a constraint or as a norm—are obviously important, but they are not the only possible meanings of the market. To appreciate the breadth of the market repertoire, we must build on and also reach beyond conventional notions of the market in political science.

The market is most commonly understood as a constraint, a notion that comes from the political economy of Adam Smith and his followers. In this classical sense, the power of market forces stems from the aggregation of people's "propensity to truck, barter, and exchange." This mechanistic, quasi-natural vision of the market remains influential, having become an object of exploration by modern economics as a discipline. In an age of instant communication and global economic flows, the image of overwhelming market forces acting as strong determinants of public policies makes considerable intuitive sense. The constraining power of the market can be felt directly, when it forces certain policy changes. It can also have indirect effects, when it empowers certain social groups at the expense of others. In varying proportions, both these effects figure prominently in utilitarian explanations of the European Union's quiet revolution as a market-induced modernization process.

The second meaning of the market, as a norm, is also very widespread in the political economy literature. It is related to yet distinct from the first meaning. In many cases, market forces often remain objectively circumscribed or counterbalanced by other factors. From a normative standpoint, however, the market has a certain attraction because it holds the promise of superior (Pareto) efficiency. According to market believers, the free exercise of choice by individuals creates welfare gains for society as a whole; therefore, it makes sense to generalize the market model, even in areas of economic and social life where the market is absent. A critical scholarship has pointed out that the market is not a neutral norm but a political and social construct. For Marx, the market is an ideology that reflects the elite's material interests. For Weber, it is the product of ideal interests that are independent of material interests. In this vein, recent constructivist scholarship on the European Union's quiet revolution often highlights the importance of neoliberal ideas.

The views of the market as a material constraint or a normative ideal do not cover the full range of market ideas, however. Such tidy notions of the market should be taken with a grain of salt, even though they are prominent in the political economy literature as well as in conventional wisdom. When we delve a little further into the meanings of the market, we find other important market ideas. In particular, we commonly think of the market as a space for economic development. We then refer to a geographical or even to a socially embedded conception of the market. This third meaning is not primarily mechanistic, in that the development of the market as a space must often be assisted by active policies. Building a market is not only a question of removing trade barriers but also of ensuring the harmonious development of a certain territory within which economic exchange takes place. Implicitly, then, the free market ceases to appear as a normative panacea. This meaning of the market is complementary to but also partly in contradiction with the second meaning of the market as a norm.

Finally, we can also think of the market as a commonplace yet largely unexamined rationale for action—again, like "planets fixed in the sky." Even when market forces are objectively limited and when actors do not believe in the absolute superiority of the free market, the market can become quite pervasive as a way to rationalize reality and actions. The market then functions as a talisman that concentrates several different and partly contradictory meanings. Precisely because the existence of the market is unquestioned, what it means for political actors to do something because of "the market" is often left implicit. It can range from a wholehearted embrace of the free market as a salutary source of discipline all the way to a reluctant acceptance of the market as a troublesome reality that must be held in check. Such diverse policy justifications framed in terms of the market are thus increasingly widespread, but they should not be taken at face value. The social scientist's task is to make explicit the diverse motivations that give the market its talisman-like quality and to show how actors mobilize contradictory notions of the market in the political arena.

In sum, the market is a pervasive yet malleable institution that encapsulates many ideas. While it may sometimes appear as an exogenous reality "out there," the market is actually available as a repertoire that various actors can appropriate for differing purposes. Although this anthropological perspective is not the only valid way to envision the market, it is especially useful because it prompts us to delve further into what *really* motivates actors when they say that they are doing something because of "the market." It takes us beyond the two conventional understandings of the market as a constraint or as a norm. Although they may be relevant explanatory factors in some cases, these two notions of the market do not reflect the full spectrum of market-centered motivations for action. In an anthropological light, the political power of market ideas does not derive merely from the inner force or logic of the market. Rather, it stems from the relative open-endedness of the market as a diffuse cluster of rationales.

Inconsistencies and Tensions as Opportunities for Change

The anthropological conception of the market as a diffuse cluster of ideas is theoretically challenging. As social scientists, we tend to project our own standards of logical consistency onto the world. We think that ideas, like institutions, are more likely to shape actors' beliefs and behavior when they are crystal clear and sharply delineated. When this is not the case, we are all too ready to discount them. Powerful ideas often do take the form of legitimate models of action upon which institutions are built; and, since institutions usually evolve incrementally, the ideas that support them usually seem remarkably coherent.[12] Even when existing institutions and beliefs are under stress, actors search for coherent paradigms and cognitive roadmaps to make sense of a changing world and to guide their actions.[13] In the bulk of institutionalist and constructivist scholarship in political economy, therefore, ideas and institutions are depicted as orderly. There is usually little room for the tensions and inconsistencies that anthropologists depict in their work.

Yet the political economists' all-or-nothing approach to the role of ideas and institutions is somewhat unrealistic. However uncomfortable it may seem for theory building, reality is closer to the intricate world that anthropologists describe. Like material interests, institutions and ideas most often have murky effects. Situations where institutions constitute a faultlessly coherent order are nowhere to be found.[14] In the real world, the power of institutions is not so overwhelming because institutions are not so neat and tidy. As for true paradigm shifts, they are inherently rare and difficult to make out, except with full historical hindsight.[15] Ideas are seldom sufficiently coherent and glaring to genuinely determine policy outcomes. In the European Union's quiet revolution, for example, the market was above all a Zeitgeist on which actors relied so as to promote a wide range of reforms. The promoters of Europe mobilized market ideas, yet they did not act on a deep ideational consensus any more than on widely shared material interests. In the rough and tumble of politics, few actors have qualms about deviating somewhat from the disciplinary purity

12. According to institutionalist scholars in organizational sociology and comparative politics, institutions change incrementally when new legitimate models of action are diffused. See, for example, Peter Hall's interpretation of the evolution of British and French economic policies as a result of changing sources of legitimacy: Hall, *Governing the Economy* (Cambridge: Polity Press, 1986). See also the discussion of "institutional isomorphism" in Paul J. Dimaggio and Walter W. Powell's introduction to *The New Institutionalism in Organizational Analysis*, ed. Powell and Dimaggio (Chicago: University of Chicago Press, 1991), and, in the same volume, John W. Meyer and Brian Rowan, "Institutionalized Organizations: Formal Structures as Myth and Ceremony."

13. McNamara, *Currency of Ideas*, and Mark Blyth, *Great Transformations* (Cambridge: Cambridge University Press, 2002).

14. Some institutionalist scholars have begun to question the standard assumption of systemic coherence and inertia, usefully pointing out that tensions within the social world create strategic opportunities. See esp. Karen Orren and Stephen Skowronek, "Beyond the Iconography of Order: Notes for a 'New' Institutionalism," in *The Dynamics of American Politics*, ed. Lawrence C. Dodd and Calvin Jillson (Boulder: Westview Press, 1994); Robert C. Lieberman, "Ideas, Institutions, and Political Order: Explaining Political Change," *American Political Science Review* 96, no. 4 (December 2002): 697–712; Thelen, "How Institutions Evolve."

15. In reference to scientific revolutions, Thomas Kuhn pointed out that the scientific community is often able to recognize a paradigm shift only very slowly and many years after the fact. Kuhn, *The Structure of Scientific Revolutions* (Chicago: University of Chicago Press, 1970), 84–85.

of economic theory. This does not mean that actors do not try to act consistently. Yet economic theories and principles, once they have been taken out of economics textbooks and recycled into policy practice, are often reduced to a simpler and blurred body of economic discourse. In late twentieth-century Europe, the market merely provided a common banner behind which actors rallied in order to push through the various reforms that they undertook at the European level.

Thus, instead of considering institutions and ideas like "the market" as orderly matrices of action, we should focus on their tensions and inconsistencies. A key effect of new ideas is to generate tensions in actors' worldviews and thus to create opportunities for institutional change. As market ideas became more prominent in late twentieth-century Europe, ideational contradictions and institutional tensions arose, which created opportunities for reformist actors to alter the status quo. Past a certain threshold, "the market" became the receptacle of diverse aspirations. Institutional constraints and incentives operated, but actors could also exploit the tensions that exist within any institutional framework. Market ideas were crucial not as shared beliefs but as justificatory tools within a political strategy of reform. The strength of these ideas therefore stemmed not from their conceptual coherence but from their relative malleability. The actors who adopted and developed that political strategy appealed to a timely and conveniently abstract metainstitution, namely the market, in pursuit of their diverse goals. Such a broad repertoire was loosely articulated and thus weakly constraining. The fact that the market was only an intermediate goal and that its repertoire was relatively malleable served to defuse the most glaring conflicts. In the end, the invocation of "the market" as a rationale for reform ultimately was an extremely successful recipe for overcoming political resistance and for achieving institutional change.

A POLITICAL STRATEGY AT WORK

The European Union's quiet revolution had a groping, trial-and-error quality. Actors not only had to adjust their actions to the circumstances they faced but they were not all pursing the same long-term purposes. The trend of marketization was neither uniform nor particularly coherent. The market functioned as a repertoire of ideas from which the promoters of Europe could pick and choose, rather than as a coherent factor driving outcomes. As a result of actors' pushing and pulling in different directions, the process of market and monetary integration was much more contentious and choppy than the outward victory of the market would suggest. Of course, the market orientation of the European political economy significantly increased over the 1980s and 1990s. Yet the quiet revolution went very far as well in areas where market forces were not present. In addition, the advocates of Europe were able to build considerable power at the EU level. If economic interests were doing the work, the character of change would be directly correlated to the penetration of market forces. If ideas and cognitive routines were doing the work, institutional change would be consistently guided by the ideology of the free market.

The promoters of Europe exploited the fact that "the market" meant different things in different issue areas and for different groups. They all became increasingly "skillful" in their interpretation of this repertoire of market ideas.[16] They quickly found out that, contrary to what standard utilitarian or constructivist arguments would suggest, there were many different ways to build "a market." Because the different actors who had embarked on that common political strategy did not share a common political vision, they continued to struggle among themselves behind the scenes. Different subgroups had different long-term priorities—less regulated markets, or more European political unity, or more effective public powers over the economy. Though constantly trying to steer reforms toward their favored ends with varying degrees of success, they were able to continue to move forward. As a result, the European Union's quiet revolution marked not just a process of outright marketization but also a new and important phase in the political integration of Europe and in the reform of state action.

A Solution to the Conundrum of Market Reforms

This political strategy had two characteristic effects that together outline a solution to the conundrum of market reforms in the European Union. First, it helps explain the apparent inconsistency of reforms and the paradox that market reforms often went furthest in the areas where market forces were least present. If we envision the market not as a driving factor of change but as a strategic repertoire, then it becomes conceivable that the agility of reform advocates prevailed over the intrinsic logic of the market. Second, it helps explain the market-mitigating tendency of a concentration of power at the EU level. In the reform process, it became increasingly clear that the establishment of effective market-oriented governance required the exertion of considerable political power.[17] The supporters of the free market realized that the market would not naturally impose itself. Their opponents wanted to make sure that the new market structures were properly regulated and managed. Once the decision to implement market reforms was taken, therefore, many actors went along with a buildup of political authority at the European level—albeit often for very different reasons.

Taken together, the first two case studies of this book—finance and electricity—illustrate the paradox of market reforms, that is, that reform went the furthest in areas where the market was least present. In the financial sector, most

16. On the sociological concept of skill, see Eric Leifer, *Actors as Observers: A Theory of Skill in Social Relationships* (New York: Garland, 1991), and Neil Fligstein, "Social Skill and the Theory of Fields," *Sociological Theory* 19, no. 2 (July 2001): 105–25.

17. This is consistent with Polanyi's insight in *The Great Transformation* that it takes considerable power to build and regulate a market. The difference here is that the power buildup occurred at the EU level instead of at the national level.

actors accepted the constraining power of market forces even before the advent of EU reforms. Even though market forces were contained within an elaborate institutional framework, the need for change could be more readily accepted in the financial sector. The promoters of Europe therefore successfully invoked the market as a constraint that made reform necessary and urgent. Yet—and this is the main source of the paradox—the rationale for major EU-level institutional revamping was less compelling, since the market was already operating at the domestic level. European Union reform was fast, but its reach was limited because national actors could block it. Many domestic actors who gave lip service to European market reforms found that they could best defend or extend their prerogatives through marginal reforms that did not go much further than a coordination of national regulators.

The case of electricity liberalization contrasts with financial reform and illustrates the other side of the paradox. At the outset, market forces were much less present in electricity than in finance. Yet the political strategy that the promoters of Europe deployed had a greater relative impact since it led to the creation of a previously nonexistent internal energy market under EU oversight. Pro-European actors drew from the market repertoire once again, but they played up the normative appeal of the market. They understood that in particular historical circumstances the norm of the market could be invoked even to reform sectors where market competition was previously deemed undesirable. At the same time, the promoters of market reforms recognized that the introduction of market rationality involved a radical departure from previous equilibria. To facilitate the transition in the absence of strong market forces, they were careful to introduce liberalization in a progressive fashion. They also successfully pushed for an EU oversight capacity, since many domestic actors were concerned about the fairness of a liberalization process that was inherently difficult to carry out and that could easily backfire.

The cases of structural policy and economic and monetary union are especially interesting because they illustrate the concentration of powers at the EU level. The upgrading of structural policy seemed to mitigate the mechanisms of the free market, since the main effect of the reforms of the 1980s and 1990s was a considerable increase in EU expenditures. Yet the market was also present as a central justification. This time, pro-European actors presented the market as a space for development rather than as a constraint or as a norm. They framed new policy schemes in areas such as regional development or R&D as primarily developmental rather than redistributive mechanisms, even though the main short-term effect was redistributive. This idea of the market as a space for development combined—some would say confused—the economic and social justification of these policies, which were intended to increase both the wealth and the cohesion of the European Union. And because money is always a potential target for abuse, the European Commission and other European-level actors were able to expand the EU sphere of regulatory and financial control to policy areas where it previously had virtually no jurisdiction.

TABLE 2.
Summary of the Argument

Select cases	Use of market repertoire	Resolution of core puzzle
Single financial area	Market as constraint	The market is held as an inescapable reality; actors implement high-paced EU reform after domestic reforms
Internal energy market	Market as norm	The market is held as a normatively desirable mode of organization; actors manage to expand the scope of reform
Structural policy	Market as space	The market is held as a territorial and social as well as economic reality; actors sell a developmental policy
Economic and Monetary Union	Market as talisman	The market is held as a new context, or as source of discipline; actors sell a market-friendly concentration of powers at the EU level

Economic and monetary union is the case that perhaps best exemplifies the strange shift both toward market-friendly policies and increased powers at the EU level. Here, the market rationale functioned, in effect, as a talisman that brought together a heterogeneous coalition of actors. The promoters of Europe presented the market by turns as a new context for the exercise of public powers or as a salutary source of discipline. The apparent contradiction between these two rationales can only be understood as a result of a political, rather than an economic, logic. The advocates of monetary union faced two very different constituencies. The first group believed that market actors had become too powerful under the European Monetary System and rising capital mobility. This group thought that, in the new context of a global market, EMU should serve to reassert political power and policy autonomy against the market. Meanwhile, a second group thought that the foremost priority was to further entrench price stability and fiscal discipline. For them, the raison d'être of EMU was to solidify member states' commitment to these two objectives. The promoters of Europe used the market as a common rationale without choosing explicitly between these two options. The talisman-like quality of the market enabled them to defuse the conflict between radically different conceptions of the desirable balance between public and private power. They skillfully navigated around fundamentally diverging views and interests in order to create new powers at the EU level.

THE ADDED VALUE OF STRATEGIC CONSTRUCTIVISM

The promoters of Europe used the market as an overarching rationale for the quiet revolution, but above all they exploited the multiple meanings of the market. At a time when the market was in vogue, they found it politically expedient to frame their advocacy of reform around market ideas. The reformers not only defended market ideas but also discovered ingenious ways of formulating them in response to objections raised by defenders of the status quo. They appealed to the market as a constraining set of forces, as a norm of resource allocation, as a space for economic development, and as a talisman of political discourse. Each of these figures of the market helps explain the particular variants of the European Union's quiet revolution. Actors struck compromises whenever necessary, and they ultimately utilized market ideas very eclectically to achieve their goals. As a result, the European Union's quiet revolution entailed a relative shift toward more market-oriented forms of economic governance along with a substantial concentration of power at the EU level.

Recognizing the market as a broad and relatively loose mode of rationality leads to a more moderate but also a more strategic version of constructivism. Constructivist explanations often tend to overestimate the power of ideas—which is reminiscent of the utilitarian tendency to overestimate the impact of material factors. It is tempting to assume that people act on coherent ideas—just like it is tempting to assume that they act on their material interests or within orderly institutions. But overly seamless theorizing glosses over the politics of institutional change and often does not lead to a satisfactory resolution of its most puzzling aspects. The most effective way to counter the utilitarian understanding of the market is not to deny it validity but to recognize its power and at the same time to subsume it under a broader conception of market rationality. In the European Union's quiet revolution, there was no big economic push to implement market reform and no mass conversion to the virtues of the free market. In and of itself, the corrosive power of market-related interests and perceptions would not have been sufficient to trigger the profound re-institutionalization of the economy that Europe experienced in the 1980s and 1990s. Some measure of marketization was probably inevitable, but in very limited sectors, and the re-launching of Europe was not at all inevitable. The generalized perplexity in the face of failing policy recipes and the ascendance of market ideas did make it possible, however, for actors to shake up the status quo and engage in radical institutional innovation.

In order to go beyond the misleading depiction of the European Union's quiet revolution as a triumph of the market, we must therefore attend to the fine grain of actors' political strategy. When we observe actors who appeal to similar ideas in multiple contexts, we should question this similarity and examine the concrete meanings of these ideas. The broad repertoires from which actors draw their ideas are crucial to explain the occurrence of change, yet they are rarely as uniform and coherent as it may seem at first glance. We should expect actors to creatively exploit the polyvalence of ideas and the institutional tensions that these ideas create in pursuit of complex and multiple goals. In the European Union's quiet revolution, the fact that the market was only an intermediate goal and that the repertoire of market ideas was sufficiently fluid and malleable served to defuse paralyzing conflicts. It kept a heterogeneous pro-European coalition together and it enabled the promoters of Europe to fight over the modalities rather than the desirability of market and monetary integration.

FOUR

Strange Bedfellows

E ven though national models of economic governance were subject to similar global pressures in the 1980s, the choice of "Europe" as a locus of response to market globalization was not self-evident. Behind the technical tasks of lowering trade barriers and overcoming obstacles to the free movement of capital, labor, goods, and services, the continuing progress of European unification posed the intensely political problem of changing well-entrenched national institutional structures across Europe. The promoters of Europe—a strange coalition of national and European officials, left- and right-of-center politicians, bureaucrats and business leaders—recognized that problem. They sought ways to overcome it despite the European Community's political weakness.

There is no single hero in this complicated story, and my intent in this book is not to create one artificially. Yet the Brussels-based European Commission can be identified in hindsight as the pivotal actor in the pro-European coalition. The Commission was relatively weak in terms of raw decision-making powers, but it played a critical role in launching the European Union's quiet revolution. Faced with a particular ideological and material configuration, the leadership of the Commission invented the political strategy of using market ideas as a rallying ground for reform at the European level. Commission officials were able to compensate for their relative weakness by co-opting a core constituency of reformist actors who favored market and monetary integration. That reformist coalition was heterogeneous and the actors that became the promoters of Europe held very different motivations. But the Commission's recourse to a loose repertoire of market ideas served to sublimate the familiar political cleavage between partisans and critics of the free market. After that political recipe was discovered in the mid-1980s, it acquired a life of its own and sustained a strong pro-European coalition through the end of the century.

THE EUROPEAN COMMISSION AS PIVOTAL ACTOR

The Commission's behavior during the quiet revolution must be understood against the background of its peculiar position in the European Union political system. The European Commission was a relatively weak actor, but Commission officials were able to assert themselves as pivotal actors during the European Union's quiet revolution.[1] Precisely because it was rarely seen as a threat by major national powers, the European Commission was able to broker major reforms.

Relative Weakness

Because it was in many ways a weak actor, the European Commission's pivotal role in the relaunching of Europe is somewhat paradoxical. Jacques Delors, its newly appointed president in 1984, was at the forefront of Europe's single market project from the outset. Whether Delors was acting as a "supranational entrepreneur" or merely as an "agent" of the member states of the European Community has been widely debated in the scholarly literature.[2] Intergovernmentalist scholars—perhaps wrongly—have portrayed Commission officials as narrow bureaucratic agents, but they are nevertheless right in pointing out the Commission's relative weakness within the Community system. The European Commission was born out of international treaties signed in the 1950s by the six founding member states of today's European Union.[3] From the beginning, the European Union was intended as something more than a classic international organization, but it would be incorrect to describe it as a supranational state. Although the Commission is often described as the "executive body" of the European Union, the analogy with an executive branch of government at the national level should not be taken literally. The limitations on the European Commission's powers were always very clear.

1. This is consistent with organization theory findings that institutional change often originates from the "deviant" action of weak or marginal actors. See especially Husayin Leblebici, Gerald D. Salancik, Anne Copay, and Tom King, "Institutional Change and the Transformation of Interorganizational Fields," *Administrative Science Quarterly* 36, no. 3 (September 1991); John F. Padgett and Christopher K. Ansell, "Robust Action and the Rise of the Medici, 1400–1434," *American Journal of Sociology* 98, no. 6 (May 1993).

2. For the "supranational entrepreneurship" view, see Sandholtz and Zysman, "1992: Recasting the European Bargain"; George Ross, *Jacques Delors and European Integration* (New York: Oxford University Press, 1995); Michele Cini, *The European Commission: Leadership, Organisation, and Culture in the EU Administration* (Manchester: Manchester University Press, 1996); Ken Endo, *The Presidency of the European Commission under Jacques Delors: The Politics of Shared Leadership* (New York: St. Martin's, 1999); Helen Drake, *Jacques Delors: Perspectives on a European Leader* (London: Routledge, 2000). For the "intergovernmentalist" view, see esp. Moravcsik, "Negotiating the Single European Act"; Garrett, "International Cooperation and Institutional Choice"; Moravcsik, *Choice for Europe*; Anand Menon, "Member States and International Institutions: Institutionalizing Intergovernmentalism in the European Union," *Comparative European Politics* 1, no. 2 (July 2003): 171–201.

3. In 1951, the treaty establishing the European Coal and Steel Community (ECSC) was the first European treaty; it was followed in 1957 by the treaty establishing the European Economic Community (EEC Treaty) and the treaty establishing the European Atomic Energy Community (Euratom). The EEC treaty quickly became the treaty of reference (*alias* Treaty of Rome), especially after the institutions of the three original European Communities were fully merged in 1968, giving birth to what became known simply as "the European Community" (EC). The treaties signed toward the end of the twentieth century—the Single Act (1986), the Treaty of Maastricht (1992), the Treaty of Amsterdam (1997), and the Treaty of Nice (2001)—consisted primarily of successive revisions of the original treaties.

Delors and other Commission officials were conscious of their lack of power relative to the European Union's member governments. Strictly speaking, the European Commission was a small collegial body of commissioners (fewer than twenty in the 1980s and the 1990s). In one sense, the Commission is a "supranational" body, in that the commissioners may not "seek or accept instructions from any Government or any other body." However, they are not elected officials but international public servants who are appointed by the member governments. The college of commissioners is backed by a relatively small bureaucracy (about twenty thousand European public servants in the 1980s and 1990s).[4] The Commission disposes of "a power of decision of its own" but only in certain limited areas such as competition policy. Its main role is to act as "guardian" of the treaties and to "initiate" legislation at the European level. It does not have the power to draft treaties, since that task is reserved to the member governments within the framework of intergovernmental conferences (IGCs).

The Commission's weakness stemmed both from its organizational limitations and from its insertion in a system of divided powers. Delors and his commissioners could not carry out anything significant without the at least tacit support of the member states, the European Court, and increasingly the European Parliament. The member states remained the most important centers of power within the European Union.[5] The European Council, which brings together the heads of member governments, set broad policies. The Council of Ministers, a body composed of cabinet ministers from the member states, met periodically to examine proposals submitted by the Commission. The Court of Justice also acted as a check on the Commission's powers, since its role is to ensure that the Commission respects its treaty-defined obligations. Still today, when the member states deem that the Commission is stepping beyond its role, they can drag their feet and fight the Commission's actions before the Court. Finally, successive treaties in the 1980s and 1990s considerably upgraded the European Parliament's powers as a "co-legislator" with the Council of Ministers. Even though these powers remained relatively limited compared with parliamentary powers in most modern democratic states, the European Parliament was aggressive in asserting its prerogatives, especially vis-à-vis the Commission.

The Advantage of Surprise and Position

I do not want to imply that the Commission engineered everything, but it did have a pivotal role in launching the European Union's quiet revolution. The

---

4. By extension, the term "European Commission" commonly refers to the collectivity of both the politically appointed commissioners and the bureaucracy of *fonctionnaires*.

5. Milward and Moravcsik have argued that the Community has reinforced the power of the nation-state. Although this thesis is very contested, there nonetheless exist solid reasons for saying that the member states remain formally "in control" of Community-level developments. See Andrew Moravcsik, "Why European Integration Strengthens the Nation-State," CFIA Working Paper, Harvard University, 1993; Alan S. Milward, *The European Rescue of the Nation-State* (Berkeley: University of California Press, 1992); Moravcsik, *Choice for Europe*.

first ingredient in the Commission's success was the factor of surprise. In 1984–85, after two decades of low-level activity in the European political arena, the European Commission was perceived as a weak actor and certainly not as a serious contender in the power games of European politics. When Delors embarked in late 1984 on his tour of the capitals of Europe, he was in search of a "big idea" that would elicit a high-level commitment from member governments.[6] He did not seek to impose his pet project—monetary union—and settled for the apparently less controversial task of creating a "single market without borders." He kept to his role as honest broker between member governments, making sure that the governments would get credit for their support of the European initiative.[7] Although the Commission was in charge of initiating any formal Europe-wide decisions, it was unthinkable for Commission officials to launch a major new initiative without the support of the member governments.

Throughout their campaign for the single market as a relaunching platform for Europe, Commission officials were especially careful to make no unjustified demands for a reinforcement of the Commission's competencies, hence increasing their powers. They trod cautiously behind the front of a broadly acceptable market-building agenda.[8] A program of market integration as proposed in the white paper of 1985, *Completing the Internal Market*, was seen as rather innocuous, since the Commission was apparently keeping to its technical role of promoting regional trade—much like other international organizations such as the GATT (General Agreement on Tariffs and Trade) and the OECD (Organization for Economic Cooperation and Development) were doing at the global level. The Commission acted when an objectively weak actor could wield disproportionate influence in defining the policy agenda, as long as its intentions were perceived as modest and legitimate. Across Europe, the wind was blowing in the direction of market reforms. The movement gathered momentum once the Commission took up "the market" as its banner and secured the member governments' endorsement of its single market agenda.

In many ways, the European Commission was in the right place at the right time. It derived a positional advantage from its permanent presence in Brus-

6. Jacques Delors, *L'unité d'un homme* (Paris: Odile Jacob, 1994). See also Grant, *The House That Jacques Built*, 66–67.

7. Delors alludes to this aspect of his role and method as president of the European Commission: "To make proposals, as opposed to seeking control. To act in such a way that the heads of government could claim credit for the progress that was achieved. . . . To circumvent personal touchiness and to slowly build bridges between different viewpoints." Delors, *L'unité d'un homme*, 222, 224–25. See also Delors, *Mémoires* (Paris: Plon, 2004), 171–228.

8. An interesting example of this dynamic is provided by Delors' gradualist approach to the problem of establishing the rule of qualified-majority voting and the reinforcement of the Commission's budgetary capacities. According to Charles Grant, that approach was conceived as a "triptych," that is, Delors first obtained the member government's approval of his 1992 objective; he then presented the Single Act's main provision on voting and the first "Delors package" on the EC budget simply as the inescapable "means" to achieve the EC 1992 objective. See Grant, *Delors: Inside the House That Jacques Built* (London: Nicholas Brealey, 1994), 76.

sels, at the nexus of a sphere of intense political interaction. Once they had decided on a common initiative, members speaking from their respective national capitals did not have the credibility to make proposals that would be perceived as neutral. Governmental proposals were likely to be criticized and dismissed as selfish expressions of national interests. By contrast, the Commission could play on the Community ethos of compromise.[9] Sitting in Brussels at the crossroads of national political ambitions and interests, the Commission was generally able to maintain an aura of relative impartiality as guardian of the treaties. Most important, the Commission was in charge of setting the formal European policy-making agenda. It had the prerogative of initiating and formulating policies that it deemed appropriate under the treaties. Commission officials were also free to propose and defend novel reforms. Not only did they have little to lose and much to gain from initiating a broad process of institutional change, but they also were not directly subject to the same level of domestic political constraints that often paralyze government initiatives and perpetuate the status quo.

Furthermore, the Commission could count on the support of institutional partners and external constituents, starting with other supranational bodies, namely the European Court of Justice and the European Parliament. Even though the European Court was independent and did not have a specific stake in the success of the Commission's policy initiatives, its judges were favorably predisposed toward the Commission's generic effort to deepen the process of European integration.[10] The Court was entrenched within the framework of European judicial systems and able to strongly back the Commission's apparently modest formal agenda-setting prerogative. As for the European Parliament, it was virtually powerless until the Single Act. Although its relationship with the Commission was sometimes extremely confrontational, since its members wanted to assert their power and sometimes saw their relationship with the Commission as a zero-sum game, that perception was the exception rather than the rule. Much like European Court judges, most members of the European Parliament were broadly supportive of the Commission's integrationist initiatives. Through most of the 1980s and 1990s, the

9. On the ethos of compromise within the European Community, see esp. Weiler, "Transformation of Europe." This ethos, which can also be understood as a social-psychological dynamic of "engagement," goes back to the origins of the Community; see Haas, *Uniting of Europe*, esp. 522–27.

10. The legal literature makes it clear that judicial activism and the "constitutionalization" of the treaties were important factors in Europe's recent renewal, although more questionable is the sweeping claim that they were the root causes of that new political dynamic. See esp. Weiler, "Transformation of Europe"; Anne-Marie Slaughter Burley and Walter Mattli, "Europe before the Court: A Political Theory of Legal Integration," *International Organization* 47, no. 1 (Winter 1993); Martin Shapiro and Alec Stone, "The New Constitutional Politics of Europe," *Comparative Political Studies* 26, no. 4 (January 1994); Joseph Weiler, "The Reformation of European Constitutionalism," *Journal of Common Market Studies* 35, no. 1 (March 1997); Alter, *Establishing the Supremacy of European Law*. For a critical perspective on the powers of the ECJ, see Lisa Conant, *Justice Contained: Law and Politics in the European Union* (Ithaca: Cornell University Press, 2002).

Commission was thus able to increasingly count on the European Parliament as a natural ally.

Delors and other Commission officials recognized their relative political weakness and fully exploited the few advantages at their disposal. But their proposals were not obviously ones that would receive support. The EC 1992 project would never have flown if they had not gained the support of the main centers of power in the EU, namely the member states. To understand how the proreform coalition was built, we must examine the motivations of Commission officials and other actors who participated in the reform movement.

The Commission as a Reformist Actor

The political strategy that led to the European Union's quiet revolution originated within the strange and often stormy tandems formed by President Delors, a French Socialist, and successive internal market commissioners, first Commissioner Arthur Cockfield and then Leon Brittan, the two Conservatives chosen by Margaret Thatcher. These men, along with their colleagues in the European Commission, elaborated and implemented a major integrationist program in the guise of a legal-technical project of market reform. That program was presented as consistent with both the spirit of the European Community's foundational Treaty of Rome and with a historically prominent set of assumptions about how the economy should be organized, that is, as "a market."

Even though the Commission is neither an individual nor a monolithic actor, it is nonetheless meaningful to speak of "its" strategy. Put very simply, the Commission has many of the same features of organizational integrity that we attribute to other corporate actors such as governments or firms. It is a relatively classic bureaucratic agency, with well-defined decision-making procedures, a hierarchical structure albeit with a collegial leadership at the top, and internal channels of communication. Altogether, this enables the Commission to conduct fairly coherent policies that correspond in broad terms to the preferences of its executive leadership. In the cases under consideration, the commissioners' integrationist strategy was effectively communicated down the hierarchical lines of the European Commission and implemented in a variety of domains. To the extent that the college of commissioners managed to agree on a common political strategy, it is therefore reasonable to speak of that strategy, in shorthand, as the Commission's strategy.

The Commission's strategy did not emerge all at once and in a fully worked-out form in 1985. The white paper on the internal market built on numerous proposals that had been under discussion in Brussels since the 1960s. Yet the odds that these proposals would ever be implemented did not seem particularly great at the time. Since the early 1980s, market ideas were increasingly in vogue, but the European Commission was not historically predisposed toward free-market liberalism.[11] The Commission's taste for public intervention in the economy was shared with many member governments at the time, except that Commission officials would have preferred to centralize public intervention at the European rather than at the national level. For this very reason, their aspirations were naturally frustrated by the member states. The initial process of collecting proposals for what was going to become the 1985 white paper, *Completing the Internal Market*, apparently revealed that many departments of the Commission were inclined to establish a big government at the European level.[12] Only under the clear impulse of new guidelines coming from the college of commissioners did the Commission's agenda crystallize around certain proposals that seemed more promising in the ideational environment of the 1980s. From then on, Commission officials worked at constructing a particular integrationist agenda, known as EC 1992, premised on the renewed popularity of market ideas among European elite at that time.

On the face of it, the Commission's ability to transform itself and its style of action is remarkable. It probably had to do with the fact that many Commission officials had learned the hard way, through two decades of stalemate in political integration, some important lessons in modesty. Commission officials, at all levels, were keenly aware of the political difficulties they faced in renewing European integration, even in the apparently innocuous task of market integration. After all, they had been trying, with little success, to achieve a full-fledged common market ever since the European Economic Community was founded in 1957. Beneath the "common" interest in building a Europe-wide market, contradictory interests were present everywhere. Complex cleavages ran not only between member states but also within them, between various institutional actors at the European level—and even within the Commission itself, between officials attached to divergent policy objectives, both for ideological and bureaucratic-political reasons.[13] Throughout its existence, the Commission had lacked the necessary clout to erase Europe's internal economic borders and thus give birth to a genuine common market.

The Commission's slowly emerging political strategy was thus a product of circumstances and of a choice to set aside the divergent motivations held by different Commission officials. The advantage of uniting Europe via market integration was to overcome paralysis and to assuage conflict. The chosen strategy not only established a separation between the short term and the long term but it also defused the clash of motivations. Altogether, the political strat-

---

11. See, for example, Haas, *Uniting of Europe*, 19–29, and David Coombes, *Politics and Bureaucracy in the European Community* (London: George Allen and Unwin, 1970).

12. See Colchester and Buchan, *Europe Relaunched*, 31.

13. On differences of attitude and conflicts within the Commission, see Thomas Christiansen, "Tensions of European Governance," *Journal of European Public Policy* 4, no. 1 (March 1997); Liesbet Hooghe, "Images of Europe," *British Journal of Political Science* 29, no. 2 (April 1999); Liesbet Hooghe, "Supranational Activists or Intergovernmental Agents?" *Comparative Political Studies* 32, no. 4 (June 1999).

TABLE 3.
Motivations of Commission Officials

Motivations	The market as an end in itself	The market as a means to get more Europe
Long-term political vision	Free-market liberalism	Europeanism and/or effective public powers in the economy
Short-term motivation	Integrationist pragmatism	Bureaucratic politics

egy offered a way to accommodate the various short-term and long-term motivations of Commission officials. From this perspective, four ideal-typical motivations can be charted (see table 3).

The main divide ran between those who accepted the market wholeheartedly and those who took it primarily as a means to a higher goal. While some Commission officials believed in the immanent virtues of a single market and a monetary union, others espoused these objectives mainly as a vehicle for deeper political integration. This was the key polarity within the Commission, especially at the top political level.[14] The first group was made up of those officials who self-identified as free-market liberals, including Leon Brittan. There were also a large number of officials who did not necessarily identify as economic liberals yet adopted the goal of market integration as a primarily pragmatic action framework consistent with the Commission's role as "guardian of the treaties." Either by conviction or pragmatism (or both), these officials generally welcomed any step toward a more integrated market and a monetary union that would secure such progress. For this group, market integration was a priority in itself that went hand in hand with the process of building power at the European level. They generally considered the buildup of political power as a necessary step to ensure continued market integration.

A second group saw political integration as the Commission's historical mission, reflecting its distinctive character as a "Europeanist" institution.[15] This group was very large and included many of the Commission's permanent staff of *fonctionnaires*. Obviously, Commission officials' aspiration for deeper political integration could be understood as straightforward bureaucratic politics, since any progress toward European unity held the prospect of a higher dose

14. The protagonists of European renewal in the European Commission have abundantly expressed their views on the single market and European integration. See Jacques Delors and Clisthène, *La France par l'Europe* (Paris: Grasset, 1988); Delors, *L'unité d'un homme*, esp. 219–308; Arthur Cockfield, "The Real Significance of 1992," in *The Politics of 1992*, ed. Colin Crouch and David Marquand (Oxford: Basil Blackwell, 1990); Cockfield, *The European Union*; Leon Brittan, *Globalization vs. Sovereignty?* (Cambridge: Cambridge University Press, 1998); Brittan, *A Diet of Brussels* (London: Little, Brown, 2000).

15. The concepts of "mission" and "distinctive character" are borrowed from organization theory, specifically the works of Philip Selznick. See Selznick, *Leadership in Public Administration* (Berkeley: University of California Press, 1984 [1957]).

of European bureaucracy in the governance of the economy. But this group's commitment to European unity did not only result from a short-term calculus of bureaucratic interest. Many Commission officials were committed to European unity by vocation, as European public servants. During the period under consideration, this group found its best spokesman in the person of President Delors. These individuals accepted the liberal logic of market and monetary integration, because they saw it as an expedient formula to deepen European integration in the ideational context of Europe in the 1980s and 1990s. For Delors as for many Commission officials since the mid-1980s, a market reform agenda was not an end in itself, but a means to a higher yet more remote goal. That goal, in turn, was defined sometimes in opposition to nationalism, as was the case with true "Europeanists" or "federalists," and sometimes in a reaction against excessive economic liberalism, as was the case with Commission officials who saw in Europe the promise of more effective public powers in a global economy.

Altogether, the Commission's political strategy was anything but a full-fledged blueprint for action based on a clear set of consistent preferences collectively held by Commission officials. Rather, it was a general method of action that identified the particular intermediate goal of "the market" as a means to achieve broader and more contentious but also more distant goals—either a united Europe or a free market. Neither Europeanism nor economic liberalism had encountered much success in the past—the former because it appeared to lack programmatic substance or to threaten national prerogatives, the latter because it imperiled the social bases of Europe's postwar political order. But the recipe of the "new" Europe of the mid-1980s was to selectively conjugate these partly contradictory goals in a seemingly nonideological, technical form. This approach took advantage of a particular political context marked by the general discrediting of alternative models of economic governance.

The Commission's official adoption of specific reformist goals framed around market ideas also served an internal coherence imperative. Progressively, the college of commissioners headed by Delors came to focus on a market-building strategy. This strategy was born out of necessity and not completely worked out at the beginning, but it became more self-conscious as the single market program reached the implementation stage. Delors made it increasingly clear that his efforts were directed toward building Europe into an "organized space" around the single market.[16] Although free-market liberals were not wedded to this approach, and more often saw the single market as an end in itself, they nonetheless recognized the value of building a European-level policy-making capacity, if only to provide a minimal regulatory framework for that market. Because their ultimate purposes remained distant, free-

16. On this notion, see especially the study by Ross of the Delors Commission, *Jacques Delors and European Integration*, chap. 4.

market liberals and social democrats within the European Commission could get along and pursue the same intermediate objective, ambiguously defined as "building a market."

That political strategy was effectively communicated down the hierarchical lines of the Commission and became the political strategy of the Commission as a whole. Each department (or "directorate general") of the Commission was assigned particular tasks within the framework of the single market. For example, the Directorate General for Competition was in charge of antitrust policy and the regulation of state aid to industry, an increasingly important area in the context of major corporate and public sector restructuring in the late 1980s. Significantly, this department became one of the most desirable assignments for career-oriented Commission bureaucrats in the late 1980s and early 1990s. Other directorates were in charge of specific sectoral policies, such as financial services, energy, and regional policy. Meanwhile, the Directorate General for Economic Affairs was in charge of monitoring the process of macroeconomic adjustment and the increasingly important task of surveying the convergence of national economic policies in the context of monetary union. In all cases, the Commission's agenda of market building was translated into more specific policy objectives. The goal was to build power at the European level, but only as an integral part of and in the name of the drive toward "the market."

The Commission's strategy informed the official discourse of the Commission on a variety of issues, eventually inducing a remarkable—arguably unprecedented—level of programmatic coherence. The Commission consistently formulated, and, in some cases dramatically reformulated, its area-specific policy goals in terms of a market-building agenda that had been preapproved at the highest national governmental levels. This had the advantage not only of reinforcing internal esprit de corps and morale within the Commission but of making it more difficult for potential opponents to question specific policy items. The enduring legitimacy of the Commission's overall market agenda was useful whenever its officials encountered outside challenges. Commission officials held the higher political ground and their opponents were portrayed as obstructing the march toward European unity. The Commission was long able to invoke the member states' programmatic approval and treaty confirmation of the white paper's market-building agenda as a way to counter potential opposition.

Reformists of All Member States, Unite!

Although a desire to move away from the status quo makes intuitive sense on the part of a relatively weak actor like the European Commission, the fact that a number of powerful actors in the member states also jumped on the bandwagon of European reforms is more problematic. Of course, one reason the EC 1992 agenda worked so well for the member states is that it self-consciously fulfilled a market integration agenda with strong relays among increasingly powerful domestic economic interest groups and national governments. Yet it would be naive to assume that all national European policymakers directly felt the pressures of globalization or somehow changed their minds about how "best" to conduct economic policy and at which level. Various actors, especially at the state level, did try to justify their Europeanist actions from an economic perspective, yet they also faced domestic political concerns and pressures from domestic constituencies.

Put very simply, the single market could not be built by tearing down the existing institutions of advanced market societies. In any political system, reforms are difficult to carry out, given that the groups with a stake in institutional structures generally want to preserve the main elements of the status quo. When difficulties arise, political caution often takes precedence over broad and often elusive economic objectives such as the pursuit of growth and prosperity. The ideal of a free market may have been a palatable project in nineteenth-century England, but it was less likely to become a focus of unlimited faith and expectations in other nations of late twentieth-century Europe. Although some degree of economic liberalization may have become economically "necessary," it is equally clear that these reforms were subject to many obstacles and uncertainties by the mid-1980s. In contemporary Europe's "mixed" structures of economic governance, where public-sector based, corporatist, or centralized resource allocation and policy-making mechanisms existed everywhere alongside market competition and often served the purpose of upholding social and political unity, the prospect of a genuinely unified market and a single currency was bound to antagonize large and powerful constituencies.

Given these strong impediments to radical reform, why did the Commission's market reform agenda elicit so much external political support? The generic answer has to do with the changing basis of Europe's economic governance structures and the fact that the "powers that be" never formed a perfect unitary bloc behind the status quo. Any institutional equilibrium results from a compromise between various corporate actors; by the same token, no single actor is perfectly satisfied with it. Some actors, when given the opportunity or if they have reason to believe that some degree of change is inevitable, may be tempted to defect from the status quo. In such a complex environment, it remains possible to bring about institutional change without colliding with raw power dynamics.

Lacking the sheer power to force its integrationist agenda on other actors, the Commission's main tactic for breaking the status quo was to co-opt a core vanguard of powerful national actors.[17] Its officials undertook the task of translating widespread but diffuse perceptions about economic evolution into a coherent reform agenda that was framed in terms of the market. Building on the increasingly visible tensions in Europe's national models of economic governance, that agenda provided a common ideational baseline for particular sub-

17. On the concept of co-optation, see Selznick, *TVA and the Grass Roots.*

TABLE 4.
Motivations of National Elites

Motivations	The market as an end in itself	The market as a means for more Europe
Long-term political vision	Free-market liberalism	Effective public powers in the economy and/or Europeanism
Short-term motivation	Business interest in expanded markets; "new governance" agenda	Turf expansion of domestic EU-centered networks

sections of the elite that sought reform in various areas. Proreform political actors were persuaded to support "Europe" as a way to advance their own interests or policy preferences. They embraced Europe because they realized that the sole logic of internal contradiction and reform in the face of external economic pressures was inherently a slow process with an uncertain outcome. As a result, the coalition of actors that came out in favor of the European agenda of the 1980s and 1990s were particularly heterogeneous. The spectrum of motivations among those that rallied behind the objective of a united Europe can be understood as a slightly modified mirror image of the motivations among Commission officials (see table 4).

The underlying cleavage of political visions was the same as among Commission officials, with a few differences of emphasis. Europeanism played a less important part and often remained rather diffuse. Federalism as such—that is, the open advocacy of a federal Europe with a radically new division of power between the European level and the member state level—was less frequently advocated in national circles. Europeanism was rarely expressed as a desire to transfer powers to the supranational level, since many national officials remained ambivalent about an intergovernmental versus a supranational Europe. The yearning for more effective public powers in the economy was a more important source of motivation among national officials. Many, especially on the left, saw Europe as a way to reassert public powers and values over the free market. Of course, the paradox is that other national officials saw Europe as precisely the opposite, that is, as a way to better legitimize the victory of the free market. The point is that the European agenda of the 1980s softened the struggle between advocates and critics of the free market because it eluded any clear choice between the two visions. The heads of states' approval of the single market agenda at the European Council in June 1985 encouraged domestic political actors to declare themselves both "pro-Europe" and "in favor of the single market." In most mainstream European political parties of the right or the left, overt support for Europe became a central tenet of discourse in the 1980s. Although this pro-Europe rhetoric sometimes barely concealed fundamental differences in long-term political outlooks, it also made obstructionism more difficult to sustain.

If we now look at short-term political motivations, the first actors to join the movement were the growing number of multinational businesses that considered themselves overly constrained by national regulatory structures and that increasingly looked to Europe as their natural sphere of activity and customer base. These actors lobbied hard in favor of the single market program and their preferred policies in Brussels.[18] From their perspective, a more unified European market served their business-related interests and needs. At the same time, however, a number of bureaucratic actors developed early on a keen interest in the European agenda. The new political imperative did not take very long to trickle down in the public sector. Many domestic actors that belonged to EU-centered networks of policymakers saw the European agenda as an avenue to extend their jurisdiction and reinforce their prerogatives. This applied, most clearly perhaps, to national competition authorities, whose power and autonomy were almost negligible in many member states before the mid-1980s.[19] Another powerful source of motivation was the growing popularity of "new public management" and the "new governance" agenda. Many actors that supported Europe saw it as the way to generalize the use of market-efficiency criteria to evaluate public policies. In particular, the finance ministries and the central banks of the member states were in the forefront of support for that new agenda. They saw liberalization and orthodox monetary policies within the single market as a palatable bulwark against the postwar inflationary trend of devoting growing shares of the national budgets to the funding of social entitlement programs.

For all these actors, then, the newfound legitimacy of European agenda items was an important resource. It enabled them, in turn, to advocate their preferred policy reforms, which sometimes were opposed to the domestic institutional traditions and structures within which they operated. In fact, these actors often had to fight against standard perceptions of "the national interest" in their respective countries. If they had been isolated in their domestic crusade to obtain market reforms, they would have had a much harder time prevailing. For these actors, the market-based arguments that justified reforms were not always deep underlying beliefs or tenets. Although some were true crusaders, pure faith in the free market was rarely the most important motivation. A comparatively much more important source of motivation was the po-

---

18. See Maria Green Cowles, "Setting the Agenda for a New Europe: The ERT and EC 1992," *Journal of Common Market Studies* 33, no. 4 (December 1995), and Sonia Mazey and Jeremy J. Richardson, *Lobbying in the European Community* (Oxford: Oxford University Press, 1993).

19. Although considerations of policy efficiency were the primary justification for the emergence of the so-called European regulatory state, another important factor was the objective interests of national regulators in the reinforcement of their own regulatory powers. On the EC as a "regulatory state," see Giandomenico Majone, "The Rise of the Regulatory State in Europe," *West European Politics* 17 (July 1994); Majone, *Regulating Europe* (London: Routledge, 1996); R. Daniel Kelemen, *The Rules of Federalism* (Cambridge: Harvard University Press, 2004).

litical capital to be gained from positioning themselves on the winning side of a reform process. The benefits varied and included personal reputation and credibility as well as career or electoral success.

In the end, the promoters of Europe were able to temporarily sublimate the long-standing political struggle between free-marketeers and critics of the free market. Those who felt reluctant about European reform initiatives were often faced with a rather stark dilemma—either they agreed to live with it and then might be able to gain some political capital from this move and influence the direction of reform, or they did not and then were forced to wage a rearguard battle against change. It quickly became very difficult even for powerful national actors to resist the logic of the single market. Domestic actors were forced to engage in a series of apparently technical debates about what Europe's single market should look like in their respective field of interests, which they were not always prepared to confront. They understandably did not appreciate being portrayed as petty turf defenders or as bigoted followers of archaic ideas. Although it is relatively easy in principle for powerful actors to resist change, it is not so easy to resist what is perceived as the movement of history. For many well-entrenched domestic actors in the boardrooms of Europe's financial establishments, public utilities, local development agencies, and central banks, an all-out war on European initiatives was simply out of the question.

Member governments were keenly aware that obstruction was inherently a perilous choice under the shadow of qualified-majority voting and that they could waste a lot of political capital and credibility, both in Brussels and at home, by fighting for a lost cause. After the Single Act there was always a clear possibility that individual member states that did not play the game would be outvoted at the Council of Ministers. Yet the main motivation for the member governments to remain within a logic of compromise was that to renege overtly on prior commitments would have been interpreted as a violation of the Community ethos.[20] Barring exceptional circumstances, it is only by building a countercoalition within the Council that a member state could hope to change the general substance of the European reform agenda. To adopt a confrontational or delaying tactic carried the risk of being pilloried for "obstructing the construction of Europe." Commission officials were especially quick to invoke treaty obligations or programmatic commitments and, if necessary, to trigger a crisis in cases of egregious "bad will." By contrast, a member government that consistently displayed a "constructive good will" toward the European agenda was able to reinforce its reputation as a "good European" and thus to build political capital, which was very useful when it came to negotiating the practical modalities of European legislation.

---

20. On the importance of this ethos as a check on go-it-alone temptations among the member states, see Peter J. Katzenstein, "The Smaller States, Germany, and Europe," in *Tamed Power*, ed. Katzenstein (Ithaca: Cornell University Press, 1997); Craig A. Parsons, "Domestic Interests, Ideas and Integration: The French Case," *Journal of Common Market Studies* 38, no. 1 (March 2000).

Thus, when they reiterated their commitment to the single market and then to qualified-majority voting through the Single Act, the member states not only tied one another's hands but perhaps even more important they gave the Commission an implicit mandate to work out many of the details of the single market agenda. The existence of such maneuvering room, however limited, was a necessary condition for the Commission to initiate the quiet revolution. State actors were led to trade off some of their national agenda-setting prerogatives for Community-level political capital. That capital was necessary vis-à-vis their negotiating partners in order to participate in shaping what had become a winning set of reforms under the auspices of the single market. In the end, most actors faced very strong incentives to accept the logic of reform. They placed their hopes on being able to define the concrete contours of European reforms while waiting for a brighter European future.

In sum, the actors that became the promoters of Europe adopted a common strategy for a variety of reasons. At a time when the existing balance between public and private power in Europe was rife with tensions, the Commission presented elite national actors with a new avenue of political action and the chance to reframe their goals around the intermediate rationale of "the market." This political strategy served as the cement for a growing pro-Europe coalition. That coalition was anything but the homogenous product of a changing configuration of economic interest groups, or of some easily identifiable collective learning experience. Although changing global economic circumstances were certainly a factor in the quiet revolution, shifts in elite interests and beliefs are inherently subject to considerable institutional inertia.

The heterogeneous nature of the pro-Europe coalition helps to explain why the quiet revolution was neither seamless nor easily accomplished. It was always difficult to maintain the momentum of reform, in that conflicting motivations often surfaced when it came to making policy choices. As the subsequent chapters illustrate, there was considerable variation both in the character of reform and in the forms of power that were built at the EU level. The willingness of domestic actors to go along with the quiet revolution did not depend merely on the persuasive powers of pro-Europe actors. In a variety of ways, the promoters of Europe leaned on a timely and legitimate rationale of action: "the market." Because they often used market ideas in a deft way and because they adjusted this discourse to the circumstances, their idiosyncratic agenda of reforms often carried the day and overcame the powerful forces of institutional inertia.

FIVE

The Market as a Constraint

In the 1980s and 1990s, a series of financial reforms were adopted all across Western Europe. These reforms opened the gates of national finance to a host of new competitors, in two steps. In the early to mid-1980s, financial reforms were launched first at the national level in the member states that had the biggest financial marketplaces—Britain, then France, Italy, and Germany. In the mid- to late 1980s, and with gathering momentum, EU-level financial reforms pursued the reforms initiated at the national level. Lord Cockfield's 1985 white paper *Completing the Internal Market* contained only a few paragraphs on the need to liberalize European capital markets so as to "create a single market in financial services."[1] Behind this innocuous formula lurked the specter of three decades of almost no action in this area. As it turned out, however, the white paper ushered in an impressive body of European legislation on issues ranging from capital mobility to banking, insurance, investment services, and pension funds regulation. Many observers were later disappointed by the uneven progress of European financial reforms, especially after the advent of the euro, but the movement toward a single financial space was certainly one of the most original early achievements of the 1992 project.

The political strategy pioneered by the European Commission explains the timing, the momentum, and to some extent the nature of EU-level financial reforms. Crucial to the process of EU-level financial reforms was the step-by-step formulation of a legislative agenda that rested on a widespread perception of the market as a constraint. The market is commonly understood as a set of material "forces." Everybody understands that these forces are one step removed from the formal institutions of a market economy. In most cases, this distance between "market realities" and market institutions is small, since the two tend to move in lockstep. Yet there are times in which market realities change so much and so suddenly that they becomes increasingly antagonistic to formal in-

---

1. See paragraphs 101–7 (pp. 28–30) in Commission of the European Communities, *Completing the Internal Market*.

stitutions. The market can then appear as an inescapable constraint that forces drastic reform. In the case of European finance in the 1980s and 1990s, dominant perceptions of economic evolution powerfully contributed to the relatively easy victory of EU reforms. The promoters of Europe therefore seized on this perception of the market as a constraint to buttress their own agenda of institutional change.

Of course, the Commission's political strategy was not the only factor at play. There were many causes which, taken altogether, pushed European finance in the direction of reform. The reforms responded to the widely perceived need for a more market-based governance of the financial sector. Yet this case offers particular insight into the opportunistic and sequential nature of the political strategy behind the European Union's quiet revolution. Commission officials used the already strong momentum of financial market reforms at the national level in order to jumpstart political integration at the European level. The Commission obviously did not invent the existence of the market in the financial sector, nor could it claim to be a first mover in this policy area. The EU served as a locus of coordination because the Commission decided to support a trend that was happening anyway. Many national authorities had already come to terms with the necessity of reforms. The Commission participated in and accelerated a process of financial rationalization as a platform to obtain further institutional changes in areas where change was going to be more difficult.

BRINGING THE EUROPEAN UNION INTO THE PICTURE

The 1980s acceleration of financial market reform in Europe contrasts with the inertia of financial market regulation until then. During most of the post–World War II period, the nerves of finance were nationally contained and intimately linked to the forms of industrial development peculiar to each European state.[2] On a continent haunted by the memory of the Great Depression and the ensuing war, the consensus was that finance must be kept subservient to the needs of each national economy. The national containment of finance has also been described as a fundamental principle of Europe's compromise with the United States on "embedded liberalism."[3] Capital controls, in particular, shielded national economies from the potentially destabilizing forces of international finance.[4] By the mid-1980s, however, national restrictions on mobile capital began to crumble. Britain undertook dramatic financial liberalization, soon to

2. For treatments of the relationship between financial structures and economic development, see Shonfield, *Modern Capitalism*, and John Zysman, *Governments, Markets, and Growth* (Ithaca: Cornell University Press, 1983).

3. The term was coined by John Ruggie. For discussions of the postwar Western economic order, see Richard Gardner, *Sterling-Dollar Diplomacy in Current Perspective* (New York: Columbia University Press, 1980), and Ruggie, "International Regimes, Transactions, and Change." A survey of this literature can be found in Eric Helleiner, *States and the Reemergence of Global Finance* (Ithaca: Cornell University Press, 1994).

4. Helleiner, *States and the Reemergence of Global Finance*, chap. 2.

be followed by France, Italy, and other European countries. The advent of the single market completed the pan-European process of market reforms initiated at the national level. European reforms started with capital liberalization and quickly affected banking, securities, insurance, and pension funds. After more than thirty years of lethargic activity at the European level, the pace of financial reform was very sustained.

Explanations abound for the reform process that convulsed Western financial markets beginning in the 1980s. The main focus of scholarly debate is the relative importance of broad economic, institutional, and ideational determinants of change. One group adopts a utilitarian perspective and identifies the technological evolution of modern finance and the growing costs of administrative controls as the main cause of financial reforms.[5] Their main contention is that, in a world of increasingly mobile capital seeking liquid and profitable investment opportunities, states have been under strong economic pressure to liberalize their capital markets. With advances in telecommunications and the development of sophisticated financial instruments, financial liberalization was inevitable. A second group of scholars has argued from an institutionalist perspective that domestic and international institutional variables crucially shaped financial reforms.[6] These scholars question the conventional wisdom about the unstoppable power of global finance, suggesting instead that the 1980s were a period of "reregulation." "Deregulation" and "big bangs" were simply the latest hype in a process of financial internationalization and reregulation. Cutting across the basic divide between utilitarian and institutionalist interpretations of financial reforms, some scholars also stress ideas as important catalysts of financial reforms.[7] These analyses generally emphasize the ideational repercussions of historical events and economic or political trends,

5. For examples of this type of argument as applied to finance, see Ralph C. Bryant, *International Financial Intermediation* (Washington, D.C.: Brookings Institution, 1987); Frieden, "Invested Interests"; Michael Loriaux, *France after Hegemony* (Ithaca: Cornell University Press, 1991); Richard O'Brien, *Global Financial Integration* (New York: Council on Foreign Relations, 1992); John B. Goodman and Louis Pauly, "The Obsolescence of Capital Controls: Economic Management in an Age of Global Markets," *World Politics* 46 (October 1993); Paulette Kurzer, *Business and Banking* (Ithaca: Cornell University Press, 1993); David M. Andrews, "Capital Mobility and State Autonomy," *International Studies Quarterly* 38 (June 1994); Richard Herring and Robert Litan, *Financial Regulation in the Global Economy* (Washington, D.C.: Brookings Institution, 1995); Barry Eichengreen, *Globalizing Capital* (Princeton: Princeton University Press, 1996).

6. See, for example, Moran, *Politics of the Financial Services Revolution*; Geoffrey R. D. Underhill, "Markets beyond Politics?" *European Journal of Political Research* 19 (1991); Michael Moran, "The State and the Financial Services Revolution: A Comparative Analysis," *West European Politics* 17, no. 3 (July 1994); Ethan B. Kapstein, *Governing the Global Economy* (Cambridge: Harvard University Press, 1994); Andrew C. Sobel, *Domestic Choices, International Markets* (Ann Arbor: University of Michigan Press, 1994); Helleiner, *States and the Resurgence of Global Finance*; Vogel, *Freer Markets, More Rules*; Jonathan Story and Ingo Walter, *Political Economy of Financial Integration in Europe* (Manchester: Manchester University Press, 1997); Daniel Verdier, *Moving Capital* (Cambridge: Cambridge University Press, 2002); Layna Mosley, *Global Capital and National Governments* (Cambridge: Cambridge University Press, 2003).

7. See, for example, Loriaux, *France after Hegemony*; Moran, *Politics of the Financial Services Revolution*, esp. the conclusion; Moran, "The State and the Financial Services Revolution"; Vogel, *Freer Markets, More Rules*, esp. chap. 2.

such as the end of the Bretton Woods regime of fixed exchange rates, the maturation of U.S. financial power, or the 1970s context of macroeconomic slowdown and the surge of neoliberal economic policies.

Although the academic debate about the globalization of finance and its effects on national governments has been extremely lively, the particular sequence of events leading to EU-level reforms has not attracted much attention. Many scholars consider the EU political-regulatory sphere as a peripheral venue for the broader drama of financial reforms. For example, Michael Moran asserts that the EU-level process of financial services liberalization is a "sideshow" in relation to the U.S.-initiated "financial services revolution."[8] According to Moran, "Focusing on the financial services revolution as a European phenomenon . . . is to view the changes through a distorting glass in which marginal events on the continent of Europe are grotesquely magnified." Although Moran correctly emphasizes that the sheer weight of the U.S. financial sector overshadowed the changes in Europe, his sweeping statement is nonetheless questionable. After all, the process of EU-level financial liberalization not only occurred within the regionwide context of the single market program but it also went faster and arguably further than in both the United States and Japan. According to Daniel Verdier, the United States "owes its leading position to the absolute size of its economy and the wealth of its citizens, not to financial regulation."[9] By contrast, the European Union's financial reforms were, in the eyes of two experts, "the most ambitious effort to date . . . in various directives issued in connection with its single market initiative."[10] As the sequence of financial integration unfolded, the EU dimension of Europe's financial reforms became increasingly important.

The EU must be brought into the picture because the Commission's political strategy acted as a political accelerator of institutional change. Without the EU, national financial reforms would have been, in all likelihood, slower, more incremental, and less coherent than they have been. Commission officials did not invent anything new; they picked up the banner of market reform, prolonging and complementing an existing movement of national financial reforms. As a result, the single market agenda operated as a crucial articulation between market push and political choice, between the economic pressures against existing regulations and the perceived need and political demand for regulatory reform. Far from being conceived as antagonistic, the dismantling of existing regulations and the process of reform developed in parallel throughout the 1980s and 1990s. Commission officials acknowledged both the economic forces sapping outdated regulations and the political desire for new means to control financial flows. They sought to open up the various national

---

8. Moran, "The State and the Financial Services Revolution," 176.

9. Verdier, *Moving Money*, 2.

10. Herring and Litan, *Financial Regulation in the Global Economy*, 3; see also Carter H. Golembers and David S. Holland, "Banking and Services," in *Europe 1992*, ed. Gary Clyde Hufbauer (Washington, D.C.: Brookings Institution, 1990).

financial systems of Europe, while creating an EU-wide minimum framework of financial regulation. These reformist efforts accelerated the tide of change much beyond what would have occurred without it.

The reformers used the idea of the market as a constraint in two ways that can be analytically distinguished, even though they are often difficult to disentangle in empirical analysis. First, the constraining dimension of the market served as a frame to refocus actors' expectations on an increasingly predominant worldview. Insofar as there was a "pure" ideational logic at work in the reform process, actors focused first and foremost on the idea of the market as a constraint. The legal principle of mutual recognition, which some scholars depict as a crucial "focal point," played a comparatively minor role and emerged later as a result of a trial-and-error process.[11] Commission officials capitalized on a prevailing sentiment, shared by a broad audience of policymakers, that existing restrictions on financial markets had become obsolete. Since financial liberalization was going to happen anyway, it was more productive to be at the vanguard of financial modernization than to wage a rearguard battle in favor of old-style financial interventionism and administrative controls. Importantly, financial modernization was increasingly seen as a welfare-enhancing endeavor and no longer as a danger. Financial markets, once freed from unnecessary political and administrative interference, would grow in volume and increase the supply of capital available for governments as well as for industry.

Second, and just as important, the idea of the market served as a cue to mobilize an increasingly active political coalition without which reform would have been impossible. This second facet of the idea of the market as a constraint was important because the task of retooling and rationalizing national institutional frameworks was a political challenge. Much interest- or idea-centered scholarship concerning European integration takes capital mobility into account, yet underestimates the broader challenge of financial liberalization.[12] Although the perception of the market as a constraint was widespread among financial actors, its implementation was bound to run into opposition from entrenched actors in the financial establishment. Institutionalist scholars often recognize that challenge but tend to overestimate its impact. Although Commission officials took political realities into account, they did everything they could to push the envelope of reform. Their legislative proposals were self-consciously tailored to a political clientele of reform-seeking actors, especially among finance ministry officials, national regulatory authorities, and big European banks. These actors often found it convenient, each for their own self-interested reasons, to rally under the banner of market reforms.

---

11. On the focal point logic, see esp. Garrett, "International Cooperation and Institutional Choice."

12. Andrew Moravcsik's structural interest–centered analysis denies any importance to Commission-sponsored capital liberalization initiatives. Kathleen McNamara's idea-based analysis, although critical of structural determinism, is equally silent on the politics that led to the new era of capital mobility in Europe. See Moravcsik, *Choice for Europe*, and McNamara, *Currency of Ideas*.

As a result of its underlying political strategy, the EU process of financial reform was neither a simple case of market push nor of member states reasserting political control. On the one hand, certain national characteristics of Europe's mosaic of financial systems have proved resilient, even in the face of pan-European regulatory frameworks. In an industry in which economies of scale are often difficult to secure, many regulatory standards, policy practices, and niche markets have remained entrenched. On the other hand, the boundaries between national financial systems have been blurred. The effects of complete capital mobility, a hallmark of the single market, have been huge. With the benefit of single-license EU legislation and later of the euro, financial actors have also become more inclined to venture outside their domestic markets. The EU-wide legal-regulatory framework has become increasingly elaborate and a primary consideration in the governance of national financial sectors. This does not mean that the institutional characteristics of EU national financial systems have deeply converged, but it does suggest that EU rules have been more concrete and less open to outright avoidance strategies. After thirty years of purely theoretical existence, the European dimension of financial markets has finally become a tangible reality.

THE TIDE OF NATIONAL AND EUROPEAN FINANCIAL REFORMS

Although financial reforms clearly started at the national level, the European directives on the liberalization of long-term capital movements and on UCITS (mutual funds, or Undertakings for Collective Investments in Transferable Securities, in Brussels lingo) cautiously opened the way for new legislation that prolonged ongoing national-level changes. With the June 1988 Capital Movements Directive—universally hailed as the first major single market reform—the European reform process acquired a new momentum. Subsequent directives liberalized banking, through the Second Banking Directive; securities, through the first and second Investment Services Directives (ISDs); and insurance, through two successive "generations" of insurance liberalization directives. These key directives were complemented by a host of standard-setting directives on accounting, capital requirements, and liquidity. This section highlights the two most sweeping items of the European-level reform process, the liberation of capital movements and the so-called single-license directives.

Financial Modernization

The tide of European-level reforms started at the national level. By the mid-1980s, all the member states with significant financial sectors were engaged in financial modernization. The first front was the dismantlement of national controls on the cross-border mobility of capital.[13] That flurry of dismantling

---

13. On the dismantlement of national capital controls, see Goodman and Pauly, "Obsolescence of Capital Controls," and Helleiner, *States and the Reemergence of Global Finance*, chap. 2.

activity markedly contrasts with previous inertia in this area. Since the early 1960s, the European Commission had made numerous unsuccessful attempts to realize the "common financial area" that the Treaty of Rome cautiously mandated.[14] As a result, Europe's Common Market had come to mean a relative freedom of movement for goods and labor yet with an almost complete lack of cross-border capital mobility. By the mid-1980s, however, the context had changed at the member state level. Britain, Germany, and the Netherlands lifted their capital controls in the late 1970s and early 1980s. Germany, as chief advocate of fiscal discipline within the European Monetary System, was eager to see its partners do the same. Instead of revaluing the German currency periodically against other "inflationary" currencies in the system, the German government preferred to submit its policies to the daily test of "market discipline." Many member governments were also concerned about the decreasing effectiveness of capital controls over cross-border flows in an era of instant communication and increasingly sophisticated financial engineering. Thus, significant political and economic forces were pushing the member states toward capital liberalization.

The second front of financial modernization at the national level was financial services. Britain followed the United States and was the first member state to liberalize its financial regulatory framework. In 1986, the Thatcher government decreed a "Big Bang" at the London Stock Exchange when it abolished fixed commissions on share trading and market restrictions, opening the market for financial services to a multitude of new entrants.[15] France underwent what was in a sense an even more dramatic conversion because it started from a remarkably closed financial system. Until the mid-1980s, French finance was a complex corporatist system under tight state supervision, including restrictive credit-control policies (*encadrement du crédit*) and foreign exchange controls. Until the mid-1980s every attempt to liberalize the French financial sector had been frustrated.[16] Starting in 1984, however, the French finance ministry engineered a top-down modernization of national financial market structures.[17] Suddenly, the French government liberalized the whole system, enabling it to quietly drop many of its longstanding objections to financial liberalization at the European level. With three key member states (Germany, Britain, and France) now agreeing to undertake financial reforms, European initiatives could continue in the direction of a single financial area.

14. The 1957 Rome treaty called for freedom for capital movements "to the extent necessary to ensure the proper functioning of the common market" (Article 67).

15. On the British Big Bang, see esp. Moran, *Politics of the Financial Services Revolution*, and Vogel, *Freer Markets, More Rules*.

16. See, for example, Zysman, *Governments, Markets, and Growth*, 149–63.

17. Philip Cerny, "The Little Big Bang in Paris: Financial Market Deregulation in a Dirigiste System," *European Journal of Policy Research* 17 (1989); Jacques Mélitz, "Financial Deregulation in France," *European Economic Review* 34, nos. 2–3 (May 1990).

New Exit Options: The Liberation of Capital Movements

The liberation of capital movements was the result of two landmark directives adopted in 1986 and 1988. The freedom of capital movement directives effectively created new exit options for financial market players, backed with the full force of European law. Investors—including non-Europeans—were suddenly better able to shift their financial resources across borders and to operate freely across European financial markets in search of the best profit opportunities. The movement was launched in May 1986, barely three months after the Single European Act was signed by the member states, when the European Commission issued an ambitious programmatic document calling for complete freedom of capital movement.[18] A directive that liberalized long-term capital flows soon followed. The much more daring second step, the liberation of *all* capital movements, was finally taken in June 1988, including short-term and monetary transactions.[19] The German presidency was, along with the Commission, the most ardent proponent of full capital movement liberalization. After thirty years of domestic capital restrictions that had survived despite the freedom of capital mandated by the Treaty of Rome, the directive called "for the implementation of article 67 of the Treaty."

The effects of capital liberalization were far-reaching. For most member states (except Britain, Germany, and the Netherlands, which had already lifted their capital controls), the liberalization of capital movement meant governments' economic policies would become increasingly subject to the verdict of footloose financial actors. In addition, national financial establishments would need to compete more effectively with contenders like London's very open and dynamic financial marketplace. In France, for example, the liberation of capital movements removed the cornerstone of a once extensive financial framework of credit and capital controls. The state's control over monetary aggregates and capital allocation was diminished, since monetary policy would have to rely almost exclusively on the control of interest rates.[20] For debt-prone Denmark or deficit-prone Italy, easing capital restrictions meant a more constrained exercise of their monetary and fiscal autonomy. Some scholars have argued that all these governments, by initially sticking to "obsolete" policy instruments, were trying to buck an irresistible trend, thus hurting their own credit on capital markets.[21] Yet from a government's perspective, the decision to abolish wide-ranging and convenient financial prerogatives for the long-

18. "Agenda for a Liberation of Capital Movements," May 23, 1986, COM (86) 292.

19. "Council Directive 88/361/EEC of 24 June 1988 for the Implementation of Article 67 of the Treaty," *Official Journal of the European Communities*, L 178 of July 8, 1988. For detailed content analyses, see Vassili Lelakis, "La libération complète des mouvements de capitaux au sein de la Communauté," *Revue du Marché Commun* 320 (September–October 1988); Peter Oliver and Jean-Pierre Baché, "Free Movements of Capital Markets between the Member States: Recent Developments," *Common Market Law Review* 26 (1989).

20. "Réussir l'intégration financière européenne," *Le Monde*, September 9, 1986.

21. See esp. Goodman and Pauly, "Obsolescence of Capital Controls."

term benefit of a better reputation in global capital markets was not an easy one to make. Despite its radical nature, the 1988 directive met surprisingly little overt opposition and was passed unanimously in June.

Extraterritorial Privilege for European Banks: The Second Banking Directive

Capital liberalization was widely interpreted as a clear political signal in favor of the European financial space and for the EC 1992 single market platform more generally. Once that roadblock was removed, the task of building the legal and regulatory framework for a single financial space could begin. This was done according to the blueprint set out in the white paper of 1985, which combined two well-publicized principles: the "mutual recognition" of national regulations, and the "harmonization of essential requirements."[22] The principle of mutual recognition meant that each member state should recognize the right of any financial institution based in another member state to operate strictly according to the rules of its country of origin (the principle of "home-country control").[23] The ultimate goal was to create a "single license" for doing business, delivered in any member state yet valid throughout the Community. This single-license approach went much further than the international legal norm of free trade, which merely calls for granting national treatment to foreign-based corporations. While national treatment means that foreign firms are allowed to operate under the same rules as domestic firms, a single license means that foreign firms are allowed to conduct business in a host country according to the rules of their country of origin. In some cases, these home-country rules happen to be less constraining than the rules applicable to domestic firms in the host country. Thus, in effect, European firms operating abroad under home-country rules could obtain *better* than national treatment, which amounted to a kind of extraterritorial privilege vis-à-vis domestic firms.

In addition, the harmonization of essential requirements meant that a minimum level of common regulation had to be decided at the European level. This was translated into several directives that established regulatory benchmarks, such as the common systems of reserve requirements that European financial institutions were legally required to apply to their assets. The harmonization of essential requirements went hand in hand with mutual recognition. According to the single-license model, member states must authorize any financial institution previously licensed by its home authorities in accordance with the agreed minimum essential requirements. This approach did not build from scratch, since there was already a 1977 ("first") banking directive guaranteeing freedom of establishment for credit institutions across Europe. Yet the member states' endorsement of the two principles of mutual recogni-

22. Georges S. Zavvos, "L'acte bancaire Européen: Objectif et conséquences," *Revue d'Economie Financière* 4 (1989).

23. For an in-depth discussion of the mutual recognition approach in the financial sector, see Sidney Key, "Mutual Recognition: Integration of the Financial Sector in the European Community," *Federal Reserve Bulletin* (September 1989).

tion and harmonization went much further than the earlier directive. The objective was to strengthen the foundations of a genuine European financial space.[24] The resulting legal-regulatory framework was meant to enshrine, at the European level, a set of widely accepted rules and to prevent complex national rules from conflicting with market competition.

The Second Banking Directive (SBD) was the most resounding success of the single-license approach spelled out in the white paper. Yet the first single-license approach in the financial sector was passed quietly in 1988 and concerned mutual funds and other collective investment schemes. With the much more consequential problem of creating a single license in banking, the Commission and the Council followed a similar approach but agreed early on, in order to hasten the legislative process and avoid endless bargaining, that the new banking directive would apply only to the banking sector, that is, to a strictly defined group of "credit institutions." The SBD was hailed by Commissioner Brittan as a "formula for the largest and most unified banking market anywhere in the world."[25] The Commission's proposal was passed smoothly a few months later in an atmosphere of near consensus.[26] In broad terms, the objective of creating a "single banking license" as the harbinger of a European financial space was not contested, and finding a way to achieve it did not pose any major political difficulty.[27]

As part of the SBD agreement between the member states, the single banking license was to be flanked by two technical directives on "essential harmonization": the Own Funds Directive and the Solvency Ratio Directive.[28] The most important disagreements between the member states were on solvency ratios, the ratio of a bank's turnover to its capital assets. Although the member states broadly agreed on the necessity of minimal regulation through the use of solvency ratios, there were some disagreement as to their desirable levels. Germany, whose reserve requirements standards were tighter than those of

24. A communication elaborated by the Commission in late 1987 was the first document that coined this objective: "Creation of a European Financial Space," COM (87) 550.

25. "EC Cements Another Stone in Single Market Structure: Europe's Banking Services," *Financial Times*, June 21, 1989.

26. Council Directive 89/646/EEC of December 1989.

27. One mildly controversial issue was the insertion of a safeguard clause in the directive, providing for a relaxation of the mutual recognition requirement in instances where the "general good" was jeopardized. Commission officials viewed the clause as a necessary evil to ensure the directive's approval by the Council. See, for example, S. Katz, "The Second Banking Directive and the General Good Clause: A Major Exception to the Freedom to Provide Services," *CEPS Research Report* no. 9; Karel Lannoo, "The Single Market in Banking: A First Assessment," in *The Single Market in Banking: From 1992 to EMU* (*CEPS Research Report* no. 17, June 1995). The Commission later issued guidelines to prevent member states' abuse of that clause. See esp. Commission Interpretative Communication, "Freedom to Provide Services and the Interest of the General Good in the Second Banking Directive," June 26, 1997.

28. Technically, of course, there were three directives: the SBD, the own funds directive, and the solvency ratio directive. But the important fact was that the SBD embodied a consensus both on mutual recognition via home-country control and on harmonization via solvency ratios. After that, there was a need to define own funds, hence the Own Funds Directive, as a prerequisite for defining solvency ratios through the Solvency Ratio Directive.

other countries, wanted high ratios, whereas Britain and France traditionally had lax bank solvency standards.[29] Each country's national financial authorities had relied on the discretionary use of capital requirement rules as an indirect way to control monetary aggregates. Thus, the regulatory fixing of reserve requirements at the European level threatened to diminish the member states' degree of freedom. In the end, a compromise was reached on 8 percent as a minimum solvency rate. The compromise was helped by the directive's extensive definition of credit activities, which favored Germany's universal banks. The figure of 8 percent also happened to correspond to the level agreed on by the Basel Committee on Banking Supervision.[30] The important difference, however, was that the Solvency Ratio Directive was a legally binding piece of European legislation that concerned all European banks, whereas the Basel Capital Accord was a nonbinding international convention on regulatory guidelines and concerned only banks with an international dimension.

One Size Fits All: Insurance, Investment Services, and Pension Funds

The remarkably swift adoption of the SBD gave a huge boost to the credibility of the 1992 project and to the single-license model. When the model was applied to the rest of the financial sector, however, things became more difficult and the results were mixed. It took more than three years for the Council of Ministers to negotiate the First Investment Services Directive, originally introduced by the Commission in December 1989. In the meantime, two generations of insurance liberalization directives were muddled through with less trouble, but their effects have been mitigated by the persistence of various restrictive national rules. The legislation on pension funds remained in limbo for a long time. By the mid-1990s, the progress of financial reforms started to slow down. In view of the increasing difficulties in establishing the single market for financial services, the Commission issued its Financial Service Action Plan in 1999, later adopted by the member states in 2000.[31] The Lamfalussy process (named for Alexandre Lamfalussy, who chaired the Committee of Wise Men), established in 2002, was supposed to foster a single market by way of European financial integration benchmarks rather than binding legislation. But progress remained uneven, and Frits Bolkestein, the Dutch free-marketeer who was internal market commissioner from 1999 through 2004, repeatedly

29. "Banking without Borders: The New Worldwide Capital Adequacy Rules," *Financial Times*, July 19, 1988.

30. The Basel Committee is made up of central bankers from industrialized countries. It was established to formulate international standards and guidelines in the area of banking supervision. The committee meets regularly in Basel, Switzerland, at the seat of the Bank of International Settlements. For a history of the 1988 Basel Capital Accord, see Kapstein, *Governing the Global Economy*, chap. 5.

31. Commission Communication, "Implementing the Framework for Financial Markets: Action Plan," COM (1999) 232 final (May 11, 1999). See Elliot Posner, "Stock Exchange Competition and the NASDAQ Bargain in Europe," in *With US or Against US? European Trends in American Perspective*, ed. Nicolas Jabko and Craig Parsons (Oxford: Oxford University Press, 2005).

expressed his dissatisfaction with the slow pace of progress toward a full-fledged single market in financial services.

The difficulties started with the draft Investment Services Directive, submitted by the Commission to the Council as early as December 1989. Markedly different national regulatory and industry structures made the harmonization of essential requirements extremely controversial. Roughly speaking, two regulatory models prevailed. One was the "quote-driven" financial market model, best exemplified by the London Stock Exchange. All transactions were conducted through registered dealers acting as intermediaries between buyers and sellers of financial services. The second was the market model followed by most Continental countries in which transactions were primarily "order-driven." All transactions were concentrated on an official stock exchange operating as a unique corporate intermediary between buyers and sellers. Securities were exchanged through an auction mechanism that set a single price in real time according to the volume of supply and demand. The debate on the ISD, departing from the relatively abstract consensus on a single license, quickly focused on the problem of how to reconcile such differences under a single-license regime without putting some actors at a competitive disadvantage. The context of the negotiations did not help, since this was a time when the French and Italian stock exchanges were steadily losing business to SEAQ International, the London-based screen system for trading foreign equities (SEAQ stands for Stock Exchange Automated Quotations).[32] Thus, behind the apparently arcane debate about market structure loomed important and potentially costly implications for whichever member states would be required to adjust their regulatory standards and business practices.

In the end, a diplomatic yet somewhat awkward compromise was worked out and adopted by the Council under a qualified majority in June 1993.[33] France joined the group of member states that voted in favor of the directive, while only a few Continental member states, including Belgium, continued to oppose it. Under the directive each member state could mandate that all securities transactions by resident investors and carried out by resident investment firms be conducted according to the system prevailing at the national level, unless the investor gave clear instructions to the contrary. Not surprisingly perhaps, the directive had limited effects. On the one hand, the continental stock exchanges underwent a major technical modernization effort. Spurred by various European initiatives following the ISD, London, Frankfurt, and Paris entered a race and a game of strategic alliances for creating the most attractive euro-denominated market platforms.[34] On the other hand, the new regulatory

32. According to the *Economist*, SEAQ International's market share reached one-third of all trades in French blue chips in 1990 and one-half in 1992. See "Needed—More Matter, Less Art: Pan-European Share Markets," *Economist*, December 8, 1990; "Trading Places," *Economist*, January 11, 1992.

33. A detailed analysis of the directive can be found in Benn Steil et al., *The European Equity Markets* (London: Royal Institute for International Affairs, 1996), chap. 4.

34. Steve Weber and Elliot Posner, "Creating a Pan-European Equity Market: The Origins of EASDAQ," *Review of International Political Economy* 7, no. 4 (Winter 2000).

framework did not enable the Commission to genuinely ensure a "truly integrated financial industry."[35] Despite the introduction of a host of new legislative measures under the Commission's 1999 Financial Service Action Plan, including a second Investment Services Directive in 2004, it remained difficult to achieve a genuine integration of national markets for investment services.

Likewise, in the area of insurance, the idea of a single license was gradually translated into European law, with fewer political problems than the ISD but also with fewer practical effects. The first stumbling block was removed not by a directive but by a December 1986 European Court of Justice ruling against German, French, Irish, and Danish attempts to restrict the sale of "foreign" insurance policies. The Court ruling was ambivalent, in that it distinguished between the insurance of "large risk" (i.e., industrial-scale risk, meaning essentially the insurance of cargo ships) and the insurance of "mass risk" (i.e., the type of insurance available to individual customers). The Court ruled that the sale of foreign insurance policies did not ensure a satisfactory degree of consumer protection for "mass risk." The so-called second-generation directives, in 1988 and 1990, therefore modestly extended the single-license approach only to insurance for "large risk" and insurance buyers that would actively seek to buy insurance from a foreign insurance company (the principle of "own initiative" in the directive). Then it progressively moved on to "mass risk," and in June and November 1992 the Council of European finance ministers (EcoFin) quietly passed a third generation of insurance directives. Still, the single market for insurance remained limited because the tax treatment of insurance policies—an essential component of insurance marketing strategies—was not harmonized at all. The task of tax harmonization, which was originally an important axis of the single market program, became a low priority and any European tax policy remains subject to unanimity voting at the Council of Ministers. Although a shift to majority voting was again discussed in the drafting of a "constitution for Europe" in 2002–04, some member states—especially Britain—fiercely opposed it and the idea was quietly shelved.

As for the single license for pension funds, it quickly stalled and remained in limbo throughout the 1990s. In 2003, the Pension Funds Directive was finally adopted, but it was not a full-fledged single-license directive because the member states retain the capacity to organize national pension funding schemes as they wish and to drastically limit the extent of market competition. For example, an individual cannot opt out of a national pay-as-you-go system and entrust all of his or her retirement money to a foreign pension fund, unless the member state of residence offers that possibility. This is obviously different from the situation in which individuals can freely choose to move their banking business away from a national bank if they prefer to use the services of a bank located in another member state. From the beginning of the process, it was clear that any pension fund directive would run up against the

35. Posner, "Stock Exchange Competition and the NASDAQ Bargain in Europe," 213.

cross-national divergence in the mechanisms of pension financing.[36] The differences between national schemes for funding pensions were so deep that it was extremely difficult to achieve a consensus on the modalities of an internal market. In the case of securities markets, each member state displayed a natural tendency to defend its own system as the best. But above all, these issues could not be disentangled from the sensitive distributive politics of the welfare state. Even in the face of growing demographic and fiscal pressures on public pension systems, there was limited movement toward a unified European retirement policy system.[37] While the idea of a single license for pension funds was strongly supported by big insurance companies, the negotiations repeatedly stalled in this area in the absence of a minimum consensus on the future of pension financing. In sum, the main effect of the EU debate on pension funds was not to create a truly integrated market for such funds but to spur the member states to carry out pension reforms.

THE POLITICS OF ACCELERATION

Political strategy played an important role in European-level financial reforms. The Commission and its allies did not create the reform impetus, but proreform actors worked hard to accelerate existing trends and to reinforce the dynamic of the reforms. Pro-reform actors exploited this pro-market wind in order to get European-level financial reforms going, but they also resorted to hard-nosed alliance politics to consolidate the reforms.

The Wind of the Market

The idea of the market as a constraint significantly contributed to the snowballing of EU-level reform, both because it was prevalent in the broad ideational context of mid- to late-1980s Europe and because it was promoted by the European Commission. A crucial first ingredient to the positive reception of European-level financial reforms was the broad context of the mid-1980s. Prominent member states had started to implement such reforms at the domestic level, *before* the Commission came up with its own proposals. Financial policymakers in the member states had become increasingly aware that reforms were needed to adapt an increasingly "obsolete" regulatory framework to the unprecedented magnitude and rapidity of cross-border financial transactions.[38] The failure of the early 1980s French socialist experiment had triggered considerable rethinking about allocating finance in the economy ac-

---

36. Pension systems can be either need based, income based, or occupation based, and they can be financed by repartition or by capitalization. See Karel Lannoo, "The Draft Pension Funds Directive and the Financing of Pensions in the EU," *Geneva Papers on Risk and Insurance* no. 78 (January 1996).

37. Bruno Palier and Philippe Pochet, "Toward a European Social Policy—at Last?" in Jabko and Parsons, eds., *With US or Against US?* 253–73.

38. See, for example, Goodman and Pauly, "Obsolescence of Capital Controls."

cording to political or administrative priorities. This deep current of attitudinal change brought liberal economic ideas to a high point among European government elites. By 1986, many of Europe's member states (including Germany, the United Kingdom, and France) were governed by right-of-center coalitions that pursued assertive liberalization agendas.

While "liberalization" and "deregulation" and, later, "globalization" became buzzwords, an important reason was that the concrete meaning of these words remained somewhat unclear. Because many member governments tried to modernize their financial systems at the domestic level, some state actors who had long resisted any European-level liberalization, such as the French Ministry of Finance, increasingly adopted a market-friendly reformist outlook. While the British example of financial Big Bang represented for many actors a paragon of financial modernity, the German model of universal banking also exerted some attraction.[39] In fact, European-level reforms were not exclusively inspired by the British example. For example, the Second Banking Directive implicitly embraced German-style universal banking as the future of European banking. While national financial establishments were internally divided on the concrete meaning and implementation of financial liberalization, few of their members were willing to wage a large-scale opposition campaign to resist what they perceived as the dominant wind of change. The few remaining critics of financial reform were seen as archaic supporters of a closed and antiquated system of nationally oriented finance that did not work any longer, and their political influence quickly became marginal.

There was actually a two-way street between national reforms and European reforms—an equation that a state-centric view of the European policy process often tends to obscure. On the one hand, the Commission increasingly internalized the idea of the market as a constraint, a view that had gained so much currency in the member states. The British and French financial reforms were a direct source of inspiration to the 1985 white paper on the internal market.[40] On the other hand, the domestic advocates of financial liberalization were looking for ways to consolidate their reforms. In that context, EU-level initiatives aimed at furthering financial liberalization were welcome. Commission officials knew it, which is why they were able to propose particularly bold reforms at the European level. As Delors recounts in his memoirs, he often pointed out to his staff that "the wind is blowing and it is blowing hard."[41] The European political context of financial reforms was particularly ripe for a European initiative, which in turn helped validate the need for financial liberalization on the Continent. Commission officials latched on to this dominant

---

39. This was the case not only in Germany but also in other continental European countries, especially France. On the prestige of the German model in 1980s France, see Jonah D. Levy, *Tocqueville's Revenge* (Cambridge: Harvard University Press, 1999), chap. 7.

40. See Ministère de l'Economie et des Finances, "La réforme des marchés financiers français," *Notes Bleues* 250 (October 21–27, 1985); Mélitz, "Financial Deregulation in France."

41. Delors, *Mémoires*, 203 (my translation).

liberal economic discourse as a means to implement the EC 1992 agenda in the financial area.

Yet it would be misleading to believe that the whole Commission was opportunistic or, on the contrary, united around the idea of liberalizing finance. Three commissioners—Jacques Delors, Lord Cockfield, and Leon Brittan—promoted financial reforms most vigorously in the late 1980s and early 1990s. Their personal agendas provide a fairly accurate sounding of the diverse motivations that brought Commission officials together behind a common political strategy of reform. Delors primarily envisioned the reform process as a way to reinforce the integrity of a "European financial space" and the building of a "political Europe," which he consistently distinguished from a "mere free trade area." He justified the speedy liberation of capital movement because "in terms of synergy and dynamism, this is the central decision. [It] draws all other things along, it is this that leads to a reassessment of financial services in our economies, 15 percent or more of total value added, it is that that gives us our say in the world in discussions with the Americans and the Japanese on debt, on financial flows, it is this that allows us to envisage passing from the EMS to enlarged economic and monetary union."[42] Delors was ambivalent about the inherent desirability of financial deregulation, yet he accepted the political logic of liberalization as part of a strategy to give the single market its initial impetus and visibility.[43]

In contrast to Delors, Lord Cockfield and especially his successor Leon Brittan, the two British commissioners nominated by Thatcher, were strongly committed to a liberal reform agenda for European finance. Brittan's views emerged in a controversy over the "reciprocity clause" originally inserted in the Second Banking Directive. The strong wording of this clause fostered a conflict, primarily with the United States, which feared that the single market would turn into "Fortress Europe."[44] Within the Commission, this issue of reciprocity revealed fundamental disagreements over what stance Europe should take vis-à-vis the outside world.[45] The clause called for reciprocity in market access for financial services between Europe and its trade partners. It reflected the idea—favored by Cockfield as well as Delors—that Europe's single financial space should not only be governed by the principles of a free market but should also become a clearly bounded political entity. For these two men, Eu-

42. "Undimmed Ambitions for Unity in Europe—Interview with Jacques Delors, President of the European Commission," *Financial Times*, March 14, 1989.

43. Interviews with former Delors aides, Brussels, June 17 and July 2, 1997. Speaking of capital liberalization, Delors wrote in his memoirs that "the progress of an economically integrated Europe could only take place if we accepted some imbalances." See Delors, *Mémoires*, 203. According to Grant, "Delors' support for the white paper led him to swallow larger doses of deregulation, for instance on insurance, than he felt comfortable with. Thatcher, by contrast, liked financial liberalization more than anything else in the document." See Grant, *Delors*, 70.

44. For a detailed account of this controversy, see Kapstein, *Governing the Global Economy*, chap. 5; Philippe Vigneron, "Le concept de réciprocité dans la législation communautaire: L'exemple de la deuxième directive bancaire," *Revue du Marché Commun*, no. 337 (May 1990).

45. "Brussels to Clear Air on Reciprocity," *Financial Times*, April 13, 1989; Kapstein, *Governing the Global Economy*.

rope had to be capable of obtaining reciprocal treatment from its trading partners in return for its openness to the outside world. For the sake of preserving Europe's good relationship with its U.S. partner, Brittan succeeded in toning down the reciprocity clause considerably. A true free-marketeer, Brittan even expressed the hope that the European model would push the United States to liberalize its own financial markets and shed its internal (state-to-state) barriers to trade in financial services.[46] Europe's financial liberalization program was thus only one step in the pursuit of a global liberal agenda.

Forging Ahead with Financial Reform

After the promarket strategy became internalized by the European Commission, the idea of the market as a constraint was mobilized to bolster the 1992 agenda. Not only had the "need" for financial liberalization become a widely shared assumption that could be exploited at the European level but the Commission also provided a pragmatic and apparently neutral agenda for concretizing this assumption. Measures of financial liberalization figured prominently among the three hundred proposals, yet they were cast in the form of technical proposals. Liberalizing the financial system was seldom presented as an end in itself. It was consistently sold as a means to achieve a single financial space without borders, the ambitious objective that had received explicit political approval at the highest level. National financial authorities saw that the Commission's approach could work, because it seemed reasonable and modest. Rather than trying to add a complex layer of bureaucratic regulations, the Commission's approach was to remove "obsolete" regulations and have minimum standardization. This, in turn, was in line with the perceived need for an economically liberal, minimally interventionist approach to financial markets.

The Commission's decision to inaugurate the implementation of its 1985 white paper by promoting pan-European capital liberalization gave a crucial political impetus to the 1992 project. As early as 1986, the Commission's leadership manifested its intention to forge ahead with capital liberalization.[47] In conjunction with the German presidency in the first half of 1988, the Commission and especially its president raised the freedom of capital movement to a top strategic priority of the single market. Nobody in the Council of Ministers seriously argued against this directive.[48] Within six months, the 1988 capital

---

46. "Brittan Challenge on US Banking: Open Up Your Market to Competition, Urges EC Commissioner," *Financial Times*, May 3, 1989.

47. In a May 1986 communication to the Council, the Commission proposed to carry out this process in two stages: see COM (86) 292 final. See also Delors' expression of satisfaction and encouragement of further progress after the first capital liberalization directive (for long-term capital movements) was passed in November 1986: *Financial Times*, November 18, 1986.

48. Interviews with member state officials and Commission officials, Brussels, June 17, July 1, September 9, October 6, and October 7, 1997. According to one official, the Council even briefly considered the idea of a one-line directive that simply stated that after a certain date all capital movements were to be free without qualification.

liberalization directive was drafted and unanimously adopted by the Council of Ministers almost without discussion—after three decades of limbo. According to a national expert who sat on the Monetary Policy Committee, "The Commission had come up with an ambitious, far-reaching program which went considerably beyond what most member states seemed prepared to contemplate."[49] The white paper was both daring in its advocacy of a single market for financial services and remarkably prudent on the specific topic of liberalizing financial movements.[50] The only firm legal basis for capital liberalization remained Article 67 of the Rome treaty, mandating freedom of capital movements within the Community "to the extent necessary for the proper functioning of the Common Market."[51] Given the thirty-year-long history of intergovernmental haggling over previous capital movement directive proposals, it was unclear whether much could be achieved in this area in the absence of strong programmatic provisions or an explicit legal basis in the treaties.

From the perspective of Commission officials, the liberation of capital movement was a good horse to bet on, both for political and for economic reasons. First, the member states could not really oppose the principle of this directive without appearing to contradict their unanimous endorsement of the white paper in the form of the recently finalized Single European Act.[52] Second, it was a common concern of financial authorities that the various forms of capital controls were becoming increasingly porous, costly in terms of macroeconomic policy credibility, and ineffective at curbing cross-border capital flows in times of currency crisis.[53] The rationale for retaining capital controls had not disappeared, since they arguably represented an important guarantee for the stability of the European Monetary System.[54] In fact, Commission

49. Age Bakker, *The Liberalization of Capital Movements in Europe* (Dordrecht: Kluwer Academic, 1996)

50. The white paper only called for "greater" freedom for capital movements, as a precondition for improving the efficiency of financial service allocation within the Community and the convergence of national economic policies within a context of "monetary stability." It clearly fell short of recommending a *complete* liberalization of capital movements. See *Completing the Internal Market*, COM (85) 310, pp. 33–35.

51. The white paper *Completing the Internal Market* acknowledged this problem: "Contrary to the Treaty provisions concerning the free movement of goods and services, the principle of free capital movements is not directly applicable. Any progress in this direction implies an extension, by way of directives, of the community obligations last specified in 1960 and 1962" (paragraph 130, pp. 34–35).

52. A 1988 Commission-sponsored expert document on financial integration pointedly asserted: "The realization of this objective [i.e., the free provision of financial services throughout the Community] and more generally the logic of a European financial system without borders leads inexorably to the dismantling of all restrictions to capital movements." See Commission of the European Communities, *Creation of a European Financial Space* (Luxembourg: Office for Official Publications of the European Communities, 1988), 19.

53. Goodman and Pauly, "Obsolescence of Capital Controls."

54. For the economic argument that capital controls were central to exchange rate stability within the EMS, see Francesco Giavazzi and Marco Pagano, "Capital Controls and the European Monetary System," in *International Monetary and Financial Integration*, by Donald Fair and Christian de Boissieu (Dordrecht: Martinus Nijhoff, 1988); Francesco Giavazzi, *The European Monetary System* (Cambridge: Cambridge University Press, 1988); Daniel Gros and Niels Thygesen, *The European Monetary System* (*CEPS Paper* 35, 1988).

officials had long acknowledged and shared these concerns, which is why they had often cautioned against an unruly liberalization of capital movements.[55] Yet it was also increasingly clear that capital liberalization was occurring anyhow, in a rampant form. By 1988, many thought it best to go with the flow than to continue to reinforce porous boundaries with blunt and counterproductive instruments of control. In this sense, a consensus by default emerged in favor of freeing capital movements.

Although the 1988 capital liberalization directive was passed unanimously, capital liberalization was not a foregone conclusion at the outset. A number of state officials realized the extent and the momentum of liberalization only quite late in the process. By that time, turning the clock back on financial liberalization would have meant repudiating the entire character and logic of the European renewal since the mid-1980s. In this regard, it is worth quoting Hubert Védrine, the longtime diplomatic adviser to Mitterrand:

> The pressure of the "Community milieu" is so strong that after one, two, or three Council meetings, the majority of the member states, if they agree, almost always manage to obtain what they want from a resisting party. . . . For a country to sit tight on its position against all others, it is really necessary that the national interests at stake be vital, in a literal sense.[56]

More specifically on France's reluctant acceptance of capital liberalization, Védrine added: "We were not in a position to refuse it—we would have been completely isolated."[57] According to Jacques Attali, another adviser, Mitterrand told his cabinet ministers that capital liberalization was a "medication" that France had to "swallow" in order to avoid being considered as the European Community's "bad student."[58] In the end, the 1988 directive was an occasion for a typical round of European horse-trading between the member states, but the deal that was reached was beside the point.[59] The important fact is that no single finance minister was willing to go against what many considered to be the movement of history.

The Second Banking Directive experienced a similar fate for similar reasons. The Commission's underlying model for the single market in banking was one where big universal banks would compete on a regional basis within

---

55. See, for example, Tommaso Padoa-Schioppa [then director general of DG II], "European Capital Markets between Liberalization and Restrictions" (1982) reprinted in *Money, Economic Policy and Europe* (Luxembourg: Office for Official Publications of the EC, 1985).

56. Hubert Védrine, *Les mondes de François Mitterrand* (Paris: Fayard, 1996), 400 (my translation).

57. Ibid., 416.

58. Jacques Attali, *Verbatim III, 1988–1991* (Paris: Fayard, 1995), 323.

59. Two additional items were necessary to reach a political compromise: an escape clause authorizing the establishment of capital controls in the event of a major currency crisis and a quid pro quo commitment to work toward a regionwide withholding tax on capital income, requested by the French. The escape clause was so restrictive as to make it virtually irrelevant, and the idea of a withholding tax was buried about a year later when it nearly provoked a tax revolt in Germany.

and outside their traditional domestic markets. As one Commission official put it:

> The extremely fast changes that occurred within the financial sector have completely modified the traditional banking landscape. It was inevitable that de-specialization and disintermediation would affect the regulatory framework of the Community. That is why, as soon as it started working on this question, the Commission had wanted to revise this definition [of credit institutions] in such a way as to include a broader range of activities. . . . In addition, the adoption of the system of mutual recognition will contribute to the general acceptance of universal banking.[60]

Commission officials defended their proposed directive in the name of German-style universal banking. Then they defended the idea of a minimum solvency rate set at 8 percent, which corresponded to the recommendation of the Basel Committee. This was not coincidental; the Basel process provided added external leverage—against German misgivings, this time. Commission officials invoked the necessity of achieving a common European position in order to be able to assert itself in global multilateral fora (especially the Basel Committee). The argument that Europe must meet the challenge of "extremely fast changes" in the financial sector was effective and little contested.

From the outset, the Commission's plan was to create a domino effect across the financial sector—not to solve all problems at once, but to "create an integrative dynamic, even if this leads to temporary imbalances."[61] Starting with the banking sector, officials in the Directorate General for Financial Services (DG XV, at the time) hoped to extend the single-license model to the whole financial sector. Interestingly, the well-publicized trilogy of 1992 reforms—mutual recognition, home-country control, and harmonization of minimum requirements—only emerged as a politically powerful liberalization recipe at a relatively late stage. Although these principles figured explicitly in the 1985 white paper, the 287 agenda items in that program each involved technical measures, and it was not clear how they would fit in with the Commission's general approach. The UCITS Directive was the first to use the method of mutual recognition in the financial sphere, serving as a preliminary political test before the SBD.[62] As late as 1989, officials in charge of financial liberalization within the European Commission's financial services department were surprised by the enormous political success of the SBD.[63] They therefore attempted to extrapolate this recipe in other areas. For example, the First Investment Services Directive was originally intended to tackle the problem of

---

60. See Zavvos, "L'acte bancaire Européen: Objectif et conséquences" (my translation).
61. See COM (87) 550 final, the original proposal for a "European financial space" presented by the Commission in 1987. This idea of "temporary imbalances" was central to Delors' thinking.
62. Interview with Commission officials, Brussels, March 23, 1997.
63. Interview with Commission official, Brussels, September 23, 1997.

liberalizing financial intermediaries, as was explicitly laid out in the 1985 white paper. After the success of the SBD, however, these original plans were dropped in favor of a single-license approach, with the hope of replicating that political success.

In other words, this extrapolation of the single-license approach was driven by a political calculation rather than by a "focal point" agreement on how best to establish a single market. The story of insurance liberalization—first the liberalization of "large risk" insurance, then of "mass risk"—shows that Commission officials were willing to pick and choose from the Court's legal arguments, availing themselves of whatever legal grounds they could claim to support the single-license approach.[64] The ISD was different and more difficult to broker through the Council, as it divided financial establishments along national lines. This was an area where cleavages run along, rather than across, national boundaries (e.g., the competitive struggle between national stock exchanges). Therefore, Commission officials cautiously adopted the view that the directive should let the two prevailing types of market structures—dealerized and auction—compete on their relative merits in a pan-European single-license system. But even here, Commission officials continuously exerted political pressure, by presenting the deadlock over the ISD as a major stumbling block on the way to a single market in financial services.

Consolidating European Regulatory Reform

Although the path of financial reform until 1992 can easily appear as fast and relatively smooth, reform proponents had to engage in hard-nosed alliance politics. The favorable context and growing demand for EU-level regulatory changes would never have been sufficient to produce such a remarkable reform momentum. Like any far-reaching movement of change, the process produced winners and losers and therefore it was necessary to defeat or win over the actors who stood to loose from it and, more generally, to prevent the risk of a political backlash. The reformers' belief that their reforms could work was not enough unless they could muster sufficient political support to overcome the unavoidable opposition. In particular, there were two prominent sources of potential opposition to EU-level financial reforms—national regulators and niche market actors. Over time, however, the Commission's political strategy broke the logic of institutional inertia and obtained these actors' support for, or at least tacit consent to, the reform process. The market rationale of financial liberalization was not only relatively coherent and compelling but it also presented the dual advantage of serving the interests of a growing political clientele and of providing honorable exit or retooling options for the losers.

---

64. Interview with Commission officials, Brussels, March 23, September 11, 1997. See also Key, "Mutual Recognition": "The EC Commission has in effect extended the Court's public interest test [i.e., the legal requirement that any restrictions be justified by a clear public interest] to apply also to host country restrictions on services provided through branches" (606).

The first apparent surprise of the European reform process was that it continuously enjoyed the support of national regulators. The Commission's proposals easily could have been perceived as threats to the national regulators' turf, because they aimed both at easing the financial regulation of national markets and at strengthening the EU-level regulatory framework. The increase in European regulatory competence was remarkable. According to a Commission official, "In matters of banking regulation, the only competent bodies were the national authorities until a few years ago. . . . This situation is being modified [through] the creation of a big unified European financial market and the globalization of international financial markets."[65] As one national regulator put it, "From now on, the framework within which national legislation may be adopted is determined by the European dimension."[66] The question, therefore, is why national regulators did not mobilize to prevent this European turf expansion.

National regulators did not see the growth of EU regulation as a zero-sum game between the Commission and themselves, for three main reasons. First, Commission officials put themselves forward not as competitors but as EU-level regulators by default. They consistently repeated that they were in the business of regulation only to harmonize standards when necessary.[67] They closely aligned their proposals with those of the Basel Committee on Banking Supervision or the International Organization of Securities Commissions (IOSCO). Second, national regulators were encouraged by the prospects of greater regulatory coordination. They became involved in the Commission's reform endeavor through the various expert and national committees operating at the international or regional level.[68] Commission officials welcomed the involvement of national regulators, in part because they did not have the technical expertise necessary to assert themselves as exclusive regulators at the Eu-

65. Paolo Clarotti, "La coopération administrative entre organes de contrôle bancaire dans la CE," *Revue de la Banque* (October 1993), 583 (my translation).

66. See Jean-Louis Duprat, "Co-operation between Regulating Bodies in the European Union," speech to the Eura-CD Seminar, April 20, 1994 (p. 6 of transcript, my translation).

67. Geoffrey Fitchew, then director-general of DG XV, expressed this as follows:
We in the Commission are in the business of regulating financial institutions for two reasons. First, because we are under an obligation to ensure that the opening of the Community financial market does not put at risk either the stability of the banking system or the protection of consumers. Second, because all too frequently it is the differences in Member States' regulatory systems which are the main obstacles to cross-frontier competition. One man's prudential regulation is another man's trade barrier.
See Geoffrey Fitchew, "The European Regulatory and Supervisory Framework," in *Financial Institutions in Europe under New Competitive Conditions*, ed. Donald Fair and Christian de Boissieu (Dordrecht: Kluwer Academic, 1990), 28.

68. For example, in the banking sector the Banking Advisory Committee and the Contact Group brought together national supervisory authorities to provide technical input to the Commission in drafting directive proposals and to implement them in a cooperative manner. Article 14 of the Second Banking Directive explicitly provides for the establishment of multilateral collaboration between the different national regulators. On the growth of international regulatory coordination, see Jean-Louis Duplat, "Co-operation between Regulating Bodies in the European Union," speech to the Eura-CD Seminar, April 20, 1994. See also Clarotti, "La coopération administrative entre organes de contrôle bancaire."

ropean level.[69] Third, national financial authorities remained responsible for regulating the financial sector above the "minimum" European level. European directives were framework laws that left national authorities to meet the objectives in whatever manner they deemed appropriate at the domestic level. Regulators knew that they would be part of the process of turning European legislation into national laws.

Substantively, the Commission's program also carried the reassuring promise of a certain balance between deregulation and reregulation.[70] On the one hand, the Commission's program involved straightforward deregulation, as it eliminated or streamlined a number of national regulations. The goal was to liberalize Europe's financial markets and to have them operate more freely, under the smallest possible number of rules. Many Commission officials (especially in the Commission departments in charge of financial services and competition) hoped that regulatory convergence on the "minimum harmonization" benchmarks specified in European directives would occur over time, through a market-driven process of regulatory competition.[71] On the other hand, the Commission responded to national demands for reregulation of the financial sector. It took into account the growing awareness that financial transactions needed to be better regulated to prevent money laundering.[72]

---

69. See, for example, the following acknowledgement by a Commission official: "It is absolutely clear that the Commission does not have the necessary experience to elaborate technically valid proposals for banking matters and that by necessity it must resort to the assistance of experts from the regulatory authorities and from the national administrations within the framework of ad hoc working groups." See Paolo Clarotti, "Le rôle des organes supranationaux en matière de réglementation bancaire," *Revue de Droit Bancaire et de la Bourse* no. 9 (September–October 1988), 154 (my translation).

70. For an insider's view of the Commission's role in drafting regulatory requirements that accompany regionwide deregulation in banking, see Paolo Clarotti, "Le rôle du processus d'intégration communautaire dans la dérégulation en matière bancaire," *Revue de Droit des Affaires Internationales*, no. 7 (1986).

71. Interview with Commission officials, Brussels, June 10, September 11, 1997. See, for example, the opinion expressed by Commission official Georges Zavvos:
The directive proposal leaves a free choice for the member states to be more restrictive [than minimum European standards] toward national banks. But such a situation is liable to provoke "reverse discrimination." Even if it is legal, it is very likely in practice that competitive forces will force the authorities of the most restrictive countries to align themselves on this deregulation at the Community level. (my translation)
See Golembe and Holland, "Banking and Securities": "The assumption is that mutual recognition will lead to regulatory convergence. . . . The core of essential regulations and standards, if adopted throughout the Community, should both forestall an unmitigated 'race to the bottom' and provide a target for regulatory convergence" (68–69). See Story and Walter:
The multiple decisions of producers and consumers seeking to arbitrage the rents derived from each regulatory system would substitute for the elusive search for harmonization, and provide an incentive for governments to link their public policies to each other. In other words, the new approach was predicated on allowing business to exploit to the maximum the diversity of the European state system. (*Political Economy of Financial Integration in Europe*, 16)

72. The 1991 fraudulent bankruptcy of the Bank of Credit and Commerce International, a Luxembourg-based bank involved in international money laundering, created a great political stir. This was expressed at the EU level by the enactment of a directive, the Post-BCCI Directive, aimed at improving transparency in the accounting standards of banks. On the BCCI scandal, see Kapstein, *Governing the Global Economy*, chap. 7.

Rising concerns about the need to retain some measure of control over liberalized financial markets in order to prevent the spread of financial crises also spurred a renewal of regulatory activity in the area of prudential supervision.[73] The Commission not only gave official support to these efforts but its single market agenda carried the promise of greater coordination in the definition of "harmonized minimum requirements." The move to the EU level of regulation was a way for national regulators to cooperatively preempt the challenges of regulating increasingly internationalized financial activities.

The second constituency that the Commission had to take into account to ensure the political success of its reforms was financial actors. Ostensibly, the Commission's agenda was merely to establish a level playing field among financial actors across the single market. But this was politics—not cricket. The deregulatory aspects, which enabled internationally oriented financial players to shift capital and services within a unified European space, were no small tasks. Relatively weak financial players did not see these reforms as particularly advantageous, and some felt threatened in their markets. For example, small French brokerage firms (*agents de change*) that collectively possessed—until December 31, 1992—a monopoly over stock market transactions were in jeopardy. Likewise, Germany's politically powerful regional savings banks (*Landesbanken*), which were not allowed to conduct business beyond regional boundaries, did not have anything to gain.

To support its reforms, Commission officials relied on a minority of internationally active financial players. A small number of European banks sailed with the "wind of change," attempting to gain market share by moving into the new high-value-added securities segments of the financial industry and away from traditional lending and relationship banking. Economies of scale or scope are difficult to secure in the financial sector.[74] The most dynamic actors were therefore not always the biggest and most powerful, and thus achieving reforms that pleased them was not a foregone conclusion. For example, the small Dutch and Belgian banks were at the forefront of internationalization. These banks were aggressively expanding their service offerings, since profit margins on bank loans were being squeezed by heightened competition between banks and the availability of new investment options in equity markets.[75] These corporate strategies were widely seen as the logical response to industry trends of "decompartmentalization," "disintermediation," and "securitization." This explains why a minority of dynamic, internationalized financial institu-

73. Organization for Economic Cooperation and Development, *Prudential Supervision in Banking* (Paris: OECD, 1987).
74. That is why the economic rationale for mergers between banks and insurance companies was often questioned and, more generally, why the shape of the future "financial conglomerates" seemed uncertain. See, for example, "Europe's Bancassurance Beasts," *Economist*, October 17, 1992.
75. For overviews of these trends, see Organization for Economic Cooperation and Development, *Banks under Stress* (Paris: OECD, 1992), and Alfred Steinherr, introduction to *The New European Financial Marketplace*, ed. Steinherr (London: Longman, 1992).

tions had become opinion leaders in their respective national banking associations.[76] They were in a position to exert political pressure on national governments not because of their sheer resources and power but because governments were unwilling to let their most dynamic banks lose ground or defect to other member states.

It was not long before a vanguard of European financial players and opinion leaders, spearheaded by international banks, started to support the European program of a single financial area. The process of decompartmentalization meant, among other things, that financial products available on the markets were becoming increasingly close substitutes. For example, insurance products were increasingly considered a form of financial equity and were sold by banks, in direct competition with insurance companies. Therefore, the implementation of the Capital Movements Directive and the Second Banking Directive promised to put huge competitive pressures on actors that operated in nonliberalized segments of the financial sector. The intent of Commission officials to develop a financial environment conducive to universal banking not only enjoyed a natural constituency among leading European banks but it also generated further political pressure in favor of liberalizing other segments of the financial services industry.[77] There was a clear domino effect of financial reforms after capital liberalization. The desire of the most dynamic financial industry actors to develop their activities and to cope with increased stress in their environment placed them in a situation analogous to that of national regulators.

Substantively, the most dynamic industry actors were particularly fond of the Commission's approach because they saw it as the promise of "one-stop shopping" when it came to regulations. Unlike national regulators, they also pushed Commission officials to deregulate as much as possible on a European scale. What they really liked about the 1992 program—and a key reason why they supported it—was *de*regulation, not reregulation.[78] From this perspective, the Commission's promotion of universal banking, that is, the regionwide provision of the broadest possible range of financial services, served a coalition-building purpose. For example, on the issue of access to securities markets in the Investment Services Directive, the Commission took the view that it should be as broad as possible without endangering the stability of the financial systems.[79] Such proposals rallied strong support from and active lobbying by the whole banking sector. From the banks' perspective, the fact that they would

76. Interviews with banking executives and Commission officials, Brussels, June 5, June 10, July 2, 1997 and Paris, July 22, 1997.

77. Interview at the Banking Federation of the European Union, Brussels, July 2, 1997.

78. Interviews with banking executives and at the Banking Federation of the European Union, Brussels, July 2, and Paris, July 22, 1997. See the 1996 Annual Report of the Banking Federation of the European Union: "The Banking Federation is of the opinion that the scope for a Host Member State to invoke rules justified by the general good must be kept to the minimum. Member States must be prevented from using such rules to re-establish protectionist barriers within the Single Market" (38).

79. Interview with Commission official, Brussels, September 23, 1997.

have to comply with a new regulatory requirement, the Capital Adequacy Directive, was a small price to pay for unlimited access to securities markets. They also knew that, once European directives were passed, the argument of preserving a "level-playing field" vis-à-vis foreign banks, combined with increasingly credible threats of defection, would help them lobby their national financial authorities for of a "strict" transposition of European rules into national legislation. On the losing end of the reform process, many financial actors accepted the logic of European reforms once it became futile to resist. All the financial players who thrived from their legally privileged market access or protected niches feared the competitive intrusion of universal banks into their comfortable livelihood. Some of these actors, like Germany's regional banks or the banking branches of national postal service, were entrenched in their respective national political systems. But the international banks' increasingly credible threats of defection significantly tipped the political balance in favor of reform. A resistance strategy against European reform was increasingly seen as too risky, which in turn generated incentives to accept the discomfort of reform. For example, France's securities brokerage firms obtained a long transition period before the scheduled end of their monopoly over securities transactions in 1996, which then allowed them to sell out to large French banks eager to gain early access to the Paris stock market. Beyond a certain point, then, the market constraint acquired the character of a self-fulfilling prophecy and therefore its own interest-driven dynamic. Some actors such as the German regional banks remained reticent until the end, but they were outgunned by the political momentum of reform.[80] Many actors joined the ever-longer bandwagon of financial liberalization, so that it becomes difficult to distinguish instances of actors succumbing to genuine persuasion from opportunistic and interest-driven behavior.

CHANGING PERCEPTIONS OF NATIONAL INTERESTS

The success of the Commission's reform proposals unquestionably depended on their acceptance by state officials who evaluated these proposals through the lens of "the national interest." Thus, there were clear limits on the Commission's degree of freedom in pursuing financial liberalization. As we will see, however, perceptions of national interests in finance considerably evolved over less than a decade—much more than we would expect if looking only at material factors. After the early enthusiasm about the "re-launching" of Europe, many member governments started to have mixed feelings about European reforms. But these reforms cannot be interpreted merely as a backlash of national interests, since perceptions of national interests themselves changed as

---

80. As one Commission official put it, "They could not quite say that they were opposed to European integration and to the single market." Interview with Commission official, Brussels, June 10, 1997.

a result of EU reforms. This EU-induced evolution of national interests makes it problematic to treat national interests as a key explanatory variable of EU reforms.

The 1990s Backlash against Market Reforms

In the 1990s, many state officials began to resent the reformist initiatives coming from Brussels. As long as governments were pushing for financial reform at the domestic level, as in the mid-1980s, the Commission's reform proposals were welcome. But by the turn of the decade, the tide of liberalization had acquired its own dynamic and had begun to go further than some of its domestic proponents would have wanted. Like Britain, both France and Germany had been key supporters of some of the Commission's main initiatives. France's modernization of its financial system had been a key inspiration for the single market program, while Germany was especially active in supporting capital liberalization. That is why these two countries' misgivings deserve closer analysis.

Germany's support of EU reforms soon became lukewarm when it became clear that Germany's cartelized and decentralized financial markets were lagging behind its main European competitors, especially Britain and even France. Although Germany had lifted its capital controls as early as 1981, it had not modernized its financial markets. By taking up the banner of capital liberalization, the German government had entered a broader logic of financial liberalization that had unforeseen consequences. In the mid-1980s, the German "model" of bank-based industrial development was widely perceived as a robust alternative to British-style liberalized financial markets.[81] This model rested on the involvement of universal banks not only in the financing but also in the management and strategic decisions of industry. But as London gained market share at the expense of Germany's regional stock exchanges, big German universal banks went on a shopping spree to increase their presence across the Channel. In 1989, the acquisition by Deutsche Bank of the British investment bank Morgan Grenfell had a major political echo. For the first time, the growing movement of bank defection stirred serious concerns at the federal level about the future of "Finanzplatz Deutschland." Many realized only then that the German model was not airtight in a new environment of mobile capital.

To make matters worse, Germany was repeatedly isolated at the Council of Ministers in the discussion of several EU financial reform proposals. Doing away with some of the most mundane and apparently technical idiosyncrasies of the German model carried important political implications. For example, the threat of lower capital requirement standards struck at the heart of the re-

---

81. On the problems of Germany's coming to terms with EU-level regulatory pressure, see Susanne Lütz, "The Revival of the Nation-State? Stock Exchange Regulation in an Era of Globalized Financial Markets," *Journal of European Public Policy* 5, no. 1 (March 1998).

liance of Germany's monetary policy on monetary aggregates, constantly reasserted by the Bundesbank.[82] Germany's isolation on this issue put the German government under considerable political pressure. Similarly, the insider
trading directive was widely regarded by most member states as predominantly
technical and an obvious step toward the single financial space. Yet Germany's
regulatory standards were notoriously weak in this area, as was revealed by its
isolation on the issue of insider trading. The regulation of insider trading required politically sensitive adjustments in German bank-industry relations.
Therefore, the German government dragged its feet for a long time on this
particular directive and became increasingly wary of European financial reforms in general.

France soon joined the chorus of discontent against the financial reform
proposals on the issue of the Investment Services Directive. French finance
minister Pierre Bérégovoy publicly announced that the Commission's proposals were unacceptable because the British system did not offer the same guarantees of transparency and investor protection as the Continental system of
auction markets.[83] Most of the member states on the Continent had centralized systems of order-driven equity trading operated by traditional and relatively closed stock exchanges. Yet London's order-driven market, SEAQ International, posed a competitive threat by virtue of its sheer size and growing
market share, thus making it hard to find rules for cross-border trade that
everyone could agree on. The Portuguese presidency was keen to obtain a
compromise and no single member state was willing to undermine the process
and thus pass for a "bad" European.[84] But the French decision to settle for a
compromise rather than jeopardize the entire prospect of a directive was a
Pyrrhic victory for the Commission.[85] Resilient differences in financial and
regulatory structures prevented the emergence of a robust compromise that
would enable a true integration of national securities markets. Despite important economic and political pressures to conclude the ISD negotiations, the
directive only provided a minimal framework for the coexistence of the two
systems.

After the bitter row over the Investment Services Directive, French officials
clearly had second thoughts about the desirability of European financial reforms. Yet France's rebellion against Brussels was clearest in the area of pension funds liberalization. France's pension system rested almost entirely on a
"pay-as-you-go" system. Since most of French pensions were paid out of the
public pension-funding scheme (Sécurité Sociale), private pension funds were

82. "Bundesbank Chafes at Cooke Report: Reactions to a Common Definition of Capital," *Financial Times*, March 15, 1988. For an analysis of postwar German monetary policy, see John B.
Goodman, *Monetary Sovereignty* (Ithaca: Cornell University Press, 1992), chap. 3.
83. "International Equity Issues: Many Rows on the Way to Market," *Financial Times*, November
21, 1990.
84. Interviews with member state and Commission officials, Brussels, September 26, 1997.
85. Interview with member state official, Brussels, October 7, 1997.

practically nonexistent. The French government feared that a single license for pension funds would undermine the system and deliver an untapped French market into the hands of British pension funds. The Commission's directorate in charge of financial services was increasingly accused of being "too liberal" and suspected of catering to the economic interests of the British.[86] Having failed to secure the Council's approval of a single-license directive for pension funds, Commission officials attempted to implement their proposal by dint of competition law. Expressing its dissatisfaction with the Commission's activism on this issue, France challenged it in court and the European Court of Justice subsequently ruled in favor of France and against the Commission.[87] The Court's ruling against the Commission underscored the fact that this issue remained politically explosive in member states.

More generally, the rising French and German protests underscore the impression of a backlash of national interests against European market reforms. As the 1992 objective faded into the past and conflicts of interest came back to the fore, member governments no longer hesitated to thwart Commission proposals. The inherent sense of urgency associated with the completion of the internal market before December 31, 1992, obviously lost some of its force after this date. By that time, the cumulative dynamic from capital movement liberalization to wholesale liberalization in all segments of the financial sector started to founder. The Commission's attempts to go beyond the 1985 white paper's agenda were often coldly received in the member states, which were no longer willing to consistently go along with the Commission's proposals. Even the British were somewhat disillusioned with the prospect of a single financial space, as the City faced not only an economic downturn but also a counteroffensive from continental stock exchanges. By the mid1990s, Commission officials began to seek other avenues of activity in the financial sector, especially in the area of consumer protection under Italian commissioner Emma Bonino. Financial liberalization was still officially pursued, especially under Dutch commissioner Frits Bolkestein, but with less fervor than in the late 1980s.

The Problematic Role of National Interests

To ascribe the slowdown in EU reforms to a backlash of national interests is tempting, yet it overlooks the impact of the European Union on changing perceptions of national interests. An interest-centered explanation of reforms would imply that the EU reforms adopted from the mid-1980s through 1992 were clearly in the national interests of the member states and that this state of affairs changed after 1992. In fact, this claim is extremely dubious. From the

---

86. According to several interviews both outside and within the Commission, the Commission's proposals were often suspected of a pro-British bias because both the commissioner in charge, the director-general of DG XV, and a number of key DG XV officials were British.

87. Judgment of the Court of March 20, 1997; French Republic v. Commission of the European Communities Case C57/95.

beginning, prospects of financial liberalization jeopardized the status of some powerful national actors. These actors could have mounted a defense of the status quo under the banner of the national interest much earlier than they did. The fact that this did not happen and that domestic preferences changed all across Europe needs to be explained rather than taken for granted. Preferences changed because perceptions of the national interest evolved as the single financial area began to materialize. With capital movement liberalization and the EC 1992 perspective, the balance of political forces was tipped in favor of financial liberalization. The very notion of national interests acting as a key explanatory variable of EU reforms is therefore problematic. The examples of Germany and France are, again, particularly illuminating in regard to this EU-induced redefinition of national interests.

A first major impact of EU reforms was the consolidation of national reforms that would not have been so far-reaching without the European Union. This is perhaps clearest in French financial reforms. The fact that market reforms in finance were increasingly adopted at the European level no doubt facilitated domestic reforms, after decades of abortive attempts to liberalize French finance.[88] France's financial liberalization was in the interest of big national banks and insurance companies that had become increasingly European or even global. It was also connected with France's increasing integration into global financial flows and with its membership in the European Monetary System. Some scholars have therefore argued that market forces pushed in favor of financial liberalization in France.[89] But others have argued that credibility concerns in the face of international economic pressures were not paramount in the 1980s liberalization movement and the redefinition of France's interests by its government.[90] The financial system overhaul hurt some well-entrenched interests in the French economic establishment. From this perspective, France's "little Big Bang" was successful not because of overwhelming economic pressures but because the French state threw its weight behind the reforms.[91] The utilitarian reliance on national economic interests as the key driver of France's rapid liberalization is therefore questionable.

Whether France's financial reforms would have been consolidated in the absence of the EC 1992 European horizon is an open question. Although France's decision to liberalize its financial sector preceded the European movement of financial reforms, the consolidation of France's liberalization

---

88. For a history of these abortive attempts, see Zysman, *Government, Markets, and Growth.*

89. See esp. Helen V. Milner, *Resisting Protectionism* (Princeton: Princeton University Press, 1988); Loriaux, *France after Hegemony;* and Goodman and Pauly, "Obsolescence of Capital Controls."

90. Levy, *Tocqueville's Revenge;* Cerny, "Little Big Bang in Paris."

91. On the phasing out of the stockbrokers' monopoly, see Cerny, "Little Big Bang in Paris." Cerny makes the interesting remark that the *agents de change*, whose monopoly over stock exchange transactions was terminated only on December 31, 1992, had been created as venal offices by Louis XIV in the seventeenth century and had survived all of France's political revolutions.

may have required the glue of European-level financial reforms.[92] In this regard, not all of France's mid-1980s liberal financial reforms survived the test of time. The decartelization of France's financial industry and the removal of capital controls remained unquestioned. But other financial reforms were later reversed. The system of preferential credit allocation (*prêts bonifiés*) was partially reinstated, as was France's traditionally high level of taxation of corporate profits. The most enduring reforms were often those codified in European law through the Capital Movement Directive and the "single-license" directives, such as SBD, ISD, and such. Gone was the time when French banks—public or private—were called *les enfants du Trésor* (Treasury's children) and protected from competitive pressures in exchange for their support of the government's financial and monetary policies. The private banking sector now perceived a clear interest in furthering the Commission's initiatives in favor of a level playing field.[93] This became evident when the European Commission's competition policy officials worked to minimize the amount of state aid that was going to be injected to rescue the state-owned Crédit Lyonnais. In their negotiations with the French government, Commission officials' best allies were Société Générale and other big private French banks that did not hesitate to side with the Commission against French government officials.

The second major impact of European reforms is that they often went much further than national governments would have wanted them to go. The snowball dynamic of European reforms was so overpowering that it induced changes in perceptions of national interests. Here the example of Germany is most interesting because Germany's financial liberalization had started much earlier than France's, with the liberation of capital movements in 1981. Yet, when negotiating European legislative proposals, German officials did not merely engage in the defense of German national interest strictly conceived. They also became increasingly ambivalent about the robustness of the German model of bank-industry relations in the face of global and European economic pressures.[94] Ironically, the German government had contributed to unleashing a change in the perception of German national interests through its support of capital mobility directives. In Germany, the state-owned postal service and regional savings banks used to be in direct competition with private sector banks in draining cash deposits, yet they retained a quasi monopoly over certain services. In the 1990s, however, the cartel-like structure of German finance eroded and some businesses such as Deutsche Bank and the insurance

---

92. Levy also cites the failure of France's pursuit of the slowly eroding German model of "banque-industrie" as a main reason for the default choice of free-market reforms. See Levy, *Tocqueville's Revenge*, chap. 7.

93. François Léonard de Juvigny [Association Française des Banques], "Les pouvoirs public français et les résistances à la création d'un marché bancaire intérieur unifié," in Fair and Boissieu, eds., *Financial Institutions in Europe under New Competitive Conditions*.

94. Interviews with Commission and member state officials, Brussels, March 23, June 10, September 9, 1997. See also Lütz, "Revival of the Nation-State?"

company Allianz became truly international, thus putting further pressure on the German model. Of course, the emergence of a European legal-regulatory framework did not automatically lead to the disappearance of national financial specificities. The German financial sector remained significantly decentralized, even after the advent of EU financial reforms. Information asymmetries enabled the regional banks to fully exploit the benefits of Germany's decentralized political system.[95] Yet the European agenda of financial liberalization and regulatory pressure on member states to fulfill their commitments certainly helps explain the rapidity of financial reforms across Europe and the relative shift in the perception of German interests.

Financial reform in Europe in the 1980s and 1990s occurred at such a dramatic speed over a relatively brief period of time that it is difficult to isolate particular sets of causes. Some scholars argue from a utilitarian perspective that economic pressures carried the reform movement, while others tend to view financial reforms in institutionalist terms as a set of reregulatory state actions in response to these pressures. In this chapter I have tried to bring the European Union, and especially the European Commission's political strategy, more squarely into the picture. I do not pretend to have definitively settled the debate between utilitarian and institutionalist scholarship on what was probably an overdetermined phenomenon. The European-level reform process originates both in the deregulatory push of economic forces and in the reregulatory thrust of politicians to deal with such developments. From this perspective, conventional explanations should be seen as complementary rather than mutually exclusive. Rather than attempting to prevent the tide of liberalization, European state officials generally chose to accept the logic of deregulation and, at the same time, to reregulate what they thought could and should be reregulated. This is where the Commission's political strategy intervened— at the juncture between market developments and state aspirations to maintain control. Commission officials consistently acted to lock in the forces in favor of financial reform and to channel them in the service of its 1992 agenda.

What I have done in this chapter is to demonstrate four aspects of a complex reality. First, I have argued against the flattest version of the utilitarian claim, that is, that one need only look at how economic forces filter through in various levels of European decision making. The European Commission did not merely act as the faithful "agent" of member governments confronted with economic pressures and objective changes in material interests. Instead, the Commission's political strategy played a crucial role in the process of financial reform. The Commission formulated and successively pursued, at the very core of the 1992 program, its own agenda of financial reforms, going further than most member states would have been willing to go on their own. At a time when control instruments were in global disarray and when British and U.S. fi-

95. Verdier, *Moving Capital.*

nancial market deregulation programs were in full swing, the context was undoubtedly ripe for European financial reform initiatives. But, while the Commission's liberal reform agenda clearly benefited from this context, it also reinforced that context and built quite original reforms on this basis. Commission officials exploited the widespread perception of the market as a constraint and rallied a small but dynamic clientele of public and private actors. Altogether, the proreform coalition led by the Commission broadly set the terms of the debate and the orientation of financial reforms.

Second, I have shown that the institutionalist themes of incremental evolution and unintended consequences can be misleading. Financial reforms cannot be explained simply in terms of exploiting the "gaps" of a developing EU institutional framework. Of course, there were certain elements of institutional continuity. For example, the relatively lesser success of the single-license approach for investment or insurance services was partly due to the greater resilience of national differences in these sectors relative to the more homogenous and internationalized banking sector. Regulatory reform in the European financial sphere was complex and thus could not have occurred in an institutional vacuum. Yet this should not obscure the fact that institutional change did occur at an accelerated pace. Capital controls were completely dismantled, and banks and many other financial actors suddenly obtained a green light to operate across Europe—these were no small changes. Institutional differences in the structure of markets and the representation of interests may help to explain why liberalization occurred faster in some sectors than others, but they can hardly account for the overall momentum of reform. The multiplication of European financial reforms must be assessed not only in terms of institutional continuity but also as a genuine departure after three decades of inertia.

Third, I have shown the snowballing dynamic of a political strategy premised on the idea of the market as a constraint. In the context of the EC 1992 objective, the advocates of financial reforms consistently built on the widely perceived inevitability of ongoing trends in the financial sector among corporate actors and policymakers. Led by European Commission officials, a proreform coalition turned the idea of the market as a constraint into a rationale for accelerating the pace of reforms and for making the EU-level financial regulatory framework more market friendly. First the reformists secured the sweeping Capital Movements Directive that locked the financial sector into a competitive dynamic. Then they pitched many of their proposals to the European banking industry as a constituency for single-license reforms. Finally, they played up other financial actors' demands for a level playing field with the banks. To the extent that there was a successful domino effect, it was largely the result of that idea-based political strategy. Of course, the variation in the degree of liberalization is important and cannot entirely be ascribed to the reformers' political strategy. Yet the variation probably would have been even more pronounced in the absence of the domino effect. The main reason for the bandwagon behind European financial reforms is that many actors were induced to redefine their material interests in ways compatible with EU-level reforms.

The fourth thing I have tried to demonstrate in this chapter is that there were limits to this reformist political strategy in a changing ideational context and with increasingly reluctant member state officials. The member states agreed above all to reinforce the coordination between different national political and regulatory authorities in the governance of finance. They did not agree to increase the treaty-defined prerogatives of the Commission. The Commission eventually suffered from being seen as an overly bureaucratic organization and a believer in across-the-board liberalization. Over time, such perceptions had deleterious effects on the process of EU-level financial reforms. Despite the advent of EMU at the turn of the twenty-first century, the spillover effects on the integration of financial markets and on the reform process were relatively modest. My focus in this chapter on political strategy as a determinant of reform is therefore justifiable only within certain political boundary conditions. The member states clearly remained broadly in charge of setting the agenda and the pace of its progress. When they managed to agree on a common goal (e.g., freeing capital movements), directives were passed and progress was made. When they had conflicts over goals (e.g., establishing a single license for pension funds), there was a stalemate. The reformers were able to carry the day only as long as they were able to lead the way in changing perceptions of national interests.

We can only speculate about what would have occurred in the absence of the political strategy developed by the European Commission. The most likely counterfactual scenario is that of a lengthy, backlash-ridden, and protracted period of financial reforms. Without the Commission's 1992 deadline, domestic actors who were opposed to financial liberalization would have been more vocal and probably more effective at blocking reform, especially in the member states in which reforms required the most dramatic adjustments. As a result, Europe's national financial industries may well have continued to evolve relatively insulated from one another and the EU probably would have lagged farther behind the United States in financial integration. Such counterfactual conjectures are, by definition, highly speculative. To better understand what is missed by conventional approaches and to see the value of the concept of political strategy, we need to address other areas of reform where economic pressures were less demanding and where institutional inertia played a comparatively greater role. In fact, the greatest impact of EU financial liberalization may have been that it spurred reforms in other areas where the tide of change was not nearly as powerful as in the financial sector.

SIX

The Market as a Norm

In June 1996, the Council of Ministers unanimously adopted a legislative text calling for a gradual liberalization of electricity supply in the European Union. Behind the façade of unanimity and the moderate tone of the intergovernmental compromise, the agreement represented a major step at the end of an overdrawn and rough negotiation process—almost four years after the "1992" inauguration of the single European market, and nine years after the original proposal for an internal energy market for electricity. It set a mandatory timetable for the progressive entry of new competitors into a previously closed electricity supply industry and for an unprecedented availability of consumer choice for big (industrial) electricity consumers. Two years later, in 1998, a copycat text was passed that liberalized the European gas sector. And in June 2003, new laws were adopted mandating a full liberalization of the energy sector by 2007—for both gas and electricity and for all categories of consumers.

Although the practical consequences of the 1996 electricity directive remained uncertain at the time, the passage of this legislation was a surprising reform and a watershed for public utility regulation in Europe. Until the 1990s, the electricity supply industry was highly entrenched in each country's political economy. Since the early years of European integration, member states had been notoriously eager to preserve national autonomy in the energy sector and had quietly filed away numerous proposals for a comprehensive European energy policy. The 1985 white paper on the internal market barely even mentioned energy. Typically, the early 1990s scholarship on the topic of the internal energy market saw it as an illustration of "the limits of 1992."[1] That the objective of an "internal energy market" was progressively grafted onto the single market agenda in the 1990s is remarkable. Why member states finally

---

1. For earlier skeptical views about the prospects of electricity liberalization, and liberalization in general, see Stephen Woolcock et al., *Britain, Germany, and 1992: The Limits of Deregulation* (New York: Council on Foreign Relations, 1991), and Stephen Padgett, "The Single European Energy Market: The Politics of Realization," *Journal of Common Market Studies* 30, no. 1 (March 1992).

agreed to a gradual form of liberalization of the electricity supply deserves a careful explanation.

A key factor in change was the European Commission's pursuit of its integrationist agenda through using the market as a norm. Advocates of European-level liberalization appealed to this norm by saying that energy supply was economically "inefficient." As a normative model, the market is first and foremost a promise of superior efficiency. As defined by economists, efficiency (or, more specifically, Pareto efficiency) is reached when individual welfare gains from trade are maximized. The appeal of this norm is not simply a matter of the ideology of self-interested actors. In advanced industrial societies, it is hard to argue against the pursuit of efficiency. The market appears almost like a state of nature and is rarely recognized as an overtly normative vision. Yet it is possible to isolate the normative appeal of the market in sectors or policy areas where the market is *not* an overwhelming substantive force or constraint. The internal energy market is especially illuminating as a control case against the utilitarian explanation of the European Union's quiet revolution in markets and technological change.

Because the functional rationale for energy liberalization was objectively not as obvious as it was in a sector like finance, the politics of institutional change can be highlighted very starkly. Significant change occurred in the highly entrenched institutional framework within which the industry was embedded, that is, precisely where it was to be least expected. The advocates of the single market in the 1980s and 1990s used this norm to draw up reform proposals for sectors where competitive forces were not initially present, like the electricity supply industry. They fought a long battle of ideas, but over time they managed to shift the normative underpinnings of sectoral organization. In strictly utilitarian terms, the economic rationale for market reform was weak. In institutionalist and constructivist terms there was virtually no institutional development or learning process at work prior to the initiatives of liberalization advocates. Thus, the investigation of the driving forces of change in the electricity sector casts a very useful light on the causal dynamics of the European Union's quiet revolution. The market manifested itself not as a competitive pressure or as a best practice but as a normative weapon in a political battle of ideas.

The outcome of this battle was a process of controlled liberalization under EU oversight. Energy liberalization did occur *and* the process was gradual and carefully monitored by political actors. Depending on the perspective that we adopt, then, the cup can appear as either half empty or half full. It would be rash to describe energy liberalization as an unstoppable tide, but it would be equally misleading to minimize its significance. It is therefore very important to explain both terms of this liberalization equation. The European Union, and especially the European Commission, stepped into energy politics and regulation by becoming the watchdog of liberalization. Because the new legislation basically mandated a radical reorganization of a highly institutionalized sector of the economy in many member states, there was no guarantee that the member states would fully live up to their commitments. Once the process was under way, however, many sectoral actors wanted to operate in a predictable environment, and governments were under increasing pressure to play by the new rules. Precisely because the process was slow and because good will could not be taken for granted, the oversight role of the European Union was solidly established in an area previously organized at the national level and beyond the scope of market competition. In this chapter I offer a strategic constructivist explanation, as against alternative modes of explanation in terms of interests, ideas, and institutions.

REFORMIST ACTION IN A STATIC ENVIRONMENT

The EC 1992 process in the electricity sector took place against the background of a long period of sectoral stability in all the member states. Electricity supply was organized everywhere in Europe according to the public utility model. In that electricity supply was network-bound and widely regarded as a natural monopoly, regionally or nationally based electricity companies usually enjoyed exclusive concessions in the public domain. They took care of the production, transportation, and distribution of electricity within their allotted areas of operation. Competition was absent and there was a preference for national autonomy in the supply of energy sources. Furthermore, the level of uncertainty in this sector was relatively low. Because electricity is a relatively simple and well-established basic commodity, the industry is not subject to erratic changes in demand or fast technological change. Its investments are highly capitalistic and carefully planned on a medium- to long-term basis. This is not to say that there were no important supply shocks and technological innovations in the 1980s and 1990s, especially with the considerable decrease in real-term oil prices and the advent of low-cost technology for gas-fired and combined cycle power generation. Yet these trends had been progressing slowly, and in overall energy utility portfolios their effects can only be felt over the long run. Thus, the sudden emergence of a legal-regulatory framework for sectoral competition at the European level represented a major departure from traditional ways of thinking and of doing business in this sector.

In the wake of the EC 1992 initiative, actors pushed for the liberalization of electricity supply. The market was branded as a normative ideal in a sphere where it had previously been almost absent. Typically, electricity liberalization has been explained in terms of the evolution of actors' interests, historical trends, paradigmatic shifts, and institutional development. By contrast, my explanation grants pride of place to the promarket militancy of political actors in and around the European Commission. Starting from an initially very static situation, these actors have managed to reshape the debate about and eventually the structure of European electricity supply. The process of liberalization followed a particular logic that resulted from the implementation of a particular strategy of action invented by the European Commission in the mid-1980s. The movement of economic liberalization in Europe needs to be understood as part of this innovative political movement, rather than in terms of external structuring factors—such as ideas about economic efficiency and competitiveness, the interplay of national interests, or the weight of institutions.

There is an important sociological subplot underlying the story of electricity liberalization, that of the construction of electricity policy as a "field" of European policy, with its own set of dominant actors, purposes, and practices. In this process, the negotiations and conflicts of interests took on important symbolic as well as material aspects. The role of Commission officials was central to the dynamics of field construction. Commission officials crystallized the internal energy market debate around a nexus of institutional norms and practices. These are in flux, however. Far from always shaping interests in a uniform manner, they acquire a multifarious dynamic of their own. These cognitive elements can be seen as complementing interest-driven behavior and orienting it, especially as they help to shape inherently fluid interests in a situation of uncertainty. But they are best understood as a set of cognitive elements that can be ordered and mobilized by political actors. Although the normative elements of field construction can be analytically isolated, strategic action gave a crucial purposive orientation to that sociological dynamic.

For the European Commission, liberalization became not only a policy goal in itself but also a means to further regional institutional integration. European Commission officials in Brussels tackled the task of reorganizing the field of electricity policy in Europe. They relied heavily on the acquired force of certain symbolic constructs, including that of evolving legal norms. They compensated for their obvious lack of material power and resources by developing a coherent panoply of normative arguments in favor of liberalization and by carefully constructing alliances within the domestic political arenas of the member states. Over time, they effectively eroded the dominance of well-entrenched domestic interest groups in the member states. They developed important alliances at the national levels and built political momentum that considerably enhanced the initially dim prospects of liberalization in the electricity sector and in the energy sector more generally.

This does not mean that Commission officials made no mistakes or that they obtained everything they wanted. In their efforts to fundamentally change the norms of energy supply, Commission officials encountered important difficulties and opposition. Within the Commission itself, not everyone was equally convinced of the virtue of a more open and competitive electricity supply industry. The Commission's early proposals were not well received by most member states. There were long moments of inertia and stalemate in this process. As difficulties arose, the Commission was led to modify the content of its liberalization proposal. This explains why the eventual compromise solution, however significant, is not as "liberal" as some Commission officials would have liked (especially within the Competition Directorate, DG Competition). Over time, however, the Commission's political strategy did alter the terms of the debate. The Council of Ministers never completely withdrew its support for building an Internal Energy Market. In this context, the Commission was able to retain the initiative and make sure that its proposal remained the only game in town. Thus, the Brussels negotiation process continued and was able to reconfigure the field of electricity policy across Europe. Despite the important odds against electricity liberalization at the outset, this reconfiguration made it possible for the Commission's revised proposal to eventually gain the support of the Council and to prevail over an increasingly marginal opposition.

By tracing the steps that led to the 1996 directive, we can see the importance of political strategy in driving institutional change. Market forces were not as omnipresent in the dynamics of reform as they were, for example, in finance. Although the advocates of electricity reform consistently appealed to market rationality, their success cannot be explained by the sheer push of economic interests or the alleged diffusion of a free-market consensus. Unlike the financial sector, for which the arguments of market reformers were increasingly borne out by self-reinforcing market dynamics, the "objective" reasons for electricity liberalization were not nearly as pressing as in finance. To identify economic interests as the key factor behind liberalization ignores the important economic interests that were radically antagonistic to liberalization. Likewise, very few sectoral actors were convinced at the outset of the inherent superiority of the market as a norm of sectoral organization. To understand what caused electricity liberalization, we have to look at the nuts and bolts of the decision-making process that led to the adoption of the 1996 directive.

Electricity liberalization is not an isolated example, however. A number of collective services that used to be provided exclusively by public or semipublic corporations in each member state were demonopolized and liberalized. A comprehensive examination of all these examples is obviously beyond the scope of this chapter. Yet there are striking similarities to the unfolding of European-level liberalization processes. Unlike financial reforms, European reforms of collective services largely preceded the evolution of national regulation.[2] Most evidently, the liberalization of the natural gas sector was modeled

2. There is a large volume of secondary literature and research on the liberalization of European collective services, including Peter Cowhey, "Telecommunications," in *Europe 1992: An American Perspective*, ed. Gary Clyde Hufbauer (Washington, D.C.: Brookings Institution, 1990); Reinhard Ellger, "Telecommunications in Europe: Law and Policy of the European Community in a Key Industrial Sector," in *Singular Europe*, ed. William James Adams (Ann Arbor: University of Michigan Press, 1993); Wayne Sandholtz, "Institutions and Collective Action: The New Telecommunications in Western Europe," *World Politics*, no. 45 (January 1993); Hervé Dumez and Alain Jeunemaître, "Political Intervention v. L'Etat de Droit Economique," *Essays in Regulation*, no. 5 (Oxford: Regulatory Policy Institute, 1994); Volker Schneider, Godefroy Dang Nguyen, and Raymund Werle, "Corporate Actor Networks in European Policy-Making: Harmonizing Telecommunications Policy," *Journal of Common Market Studies* 32, no. 4 (December 1994); Edith Brenac, "L'exemple des télécommunications," in *Le tournant néo-libéral en Europe*, ed. Bruno Jobert (Paris: L'Harmattan,

on the electricity directive. While objective reasons for introducing competition in sectors such as telecommunications were more salient than with electricity, market pressures alone would not have been sufficient to bring about full-fledged liberalization. The reliance on a network infrastructure was a crucial and unavoidable aspect of service provision in telecommunications, railroad transportation, and postal services. The market forces that pushed in the direction of liberalization were generally less powerful in these sectors than in a sector such as finance—except maybe in some segments of the telecommunications sector. Thus, the case of electricity has a more general significance for understanding other processes of liberalization at the European level.

THE SAGA OF ELECTRICITY LIBERALIZATION

In substance, the 1996 European directive mandating "gradual liberalization" laid the basis for an internal energy market for electricity.[3] Until that directive, only the legally designated utilities in the member states had monopolistic rights to engage in the supply and commerce of electricity. Typically, third parties (i.e., nonchartered electricity producers, consumers, or distributors) did not have direct access to the grid and were not allowed to contract with suppliers or customers of their choice. The directive changed the status quo not only by mandating a certain level of "third party access" (TPA) to the electricity networks, but also by ending the monopoly rights for the construction of power lines and power stations.[4] In the first phases of market opening, only certain "eligible" customers were involved, and the task of defining eligibility criteria is left to the discretion of national legislatures.[5] To defuse and postpone possible disagreements in implementing the European legislation, the Council set the relatively remote date of 2006 for a review of progress toward the objective of an internal energy market.

1994); Susanne Schmidt, "Commission Activism: Subsuming Telecommunications and Electricity Policy under European Competition Law," *Journal of European Public Policy* 5, no. 1 (March 1998); David Levi-Faur, "On the 'Net Impact' of Europeanization: The EU's Telecoms and Electricity Regimes between the Global and the National," *Comparative Political Studies* 37, no. 1 (February 2004): 3–29.

    3. Directive 96/92/CE of the European Parliament and of the Council concerning common rules for the internal market in electricity, *Official Journal of the European Communities*, January 30, 1997.

    4. Third party access means that networks are open to third parties, with freer entry on the supply side and the possibility for customers to choose among a variety of electricity producers.

    5. Only big industrial customers consuming more than 100 GWh per year were initially to be considered eligible. But the member states may also designate other consumers—even household customers—and electricity distributors as eligible. To provide for an equivalent degree of liberalization in all the member states, the directive required the member states to conform to certain quotas at each stage of market opening. These quotas were based on the EU-wide annual consumption profile of various categories of industrial consumers (1999: >40 GWh; 2000: >30 GWh; 2003: >9 GWh). As a consequence of these incremental quotas, the member states had to gradually open their markets from around 25 percent of national consumption in 1999 to around 33 percent in 2003.

A first difficulty resides in assessing the significance of that text. In hindsight, the 1996 electricity directive was not only an isolated attempt to marketize the energy sector. But only the future evolution of the European energy sector will tell us whether it was a landmark blueprint for change or a parenthesis between two periods of nonmarket sectoral organization. Some skeptical observers noted that the result of the 1996 compromise was to legitimate rather than remove obstacles to market competition in various countries. Advocates of liberalization within the European Commission and elsewhere believed nonetheless that, once the directive was implemented at the national level, market forces would be unleashed and would push the electricity supply industry in the direction of greater openness. Several member states (Finland, Germany, Spain, the Netherlands, Sweden, and the United Kingdom) quickly indicated that they would move far beyond the minimum thresholds and that they intended to fully open their markets. There is no doubt that the electricity directive contains a great degree of flexibility and has been described as "à la carte" when compared to other more sweeping examples of EU-level reforms. It delineated a careful and incremental schedule of market opening that was initially limited to particular segments of the market. Despite these limitations and in view of subsequent events, the directive now appears as a fundamental reform that hardly anybody expected in 1992 when the first Commission proposals were submitted.

The path to the final text of the directive in 1996 was neither straight nor uneventful. The directive proposal was introduced by the European Commission in 1992. This Commission initiative was in itself a surprising development and the result of a rather convoluted process. Although liberalization in the electricity sector was only part of a broad movement of market-building encapsulated in the 1992 objective, that sector was deliberately left aside in the white paper on the internal market. In the mid-1980s, a common energy market was not high on the agenda. On the contrary, there were bitter memories of failed attempts to build a common energy policy, since the early days of the European Community and through the oil shocks of the 1970s.[6] Under the goad of a 1986 Council resolution, however, a piecemeal approach to electricity liberalization began to emerge. In 1988, the European Commission introduced a green (working) paper on the internal energy market, proposing price transparency and freer transit of electricity across borders.[7] Two directives were to be adopted, in 1990 and 1991, to fulfill these significant yet rela-

---

6. Euratom, which was originally designed as the spearhead of a European energy policy, did not live up to the expectations of its early supporters such as Jean Monnet. One analyst concluded, at that time, that there was a "general agreement that energy policy must be ranked as one of the Community's major failures" (Padgett, "Single European Energy Market," 55). For a historical perspective on European electricity policy, see Janne H. Matlary, *Energy Policy in the European Union* (London: Macmillan, 1997).

7. Commission of the European Communities, *The Internal Energy Market*, reprinted in *Energy in Europe*, special issue (Luxembourg: Office for Official Publications of the European Communities, 1988), 17–18.

tively modest goals.[8] However vaguely defined at that stage, the Commission's objective of liberalizing the electricity sector triggered important reactions from both sectoral and state actors: In 1989, the member states' utilities and associations set up a trade association in Brussels—Eurelectric—with a mandate to defend their common interests. Also, the German and French governments passed a joint communiqué at their summit of November 1989 that included a protocol on energy policy, in which they tried to set strict boundaries on liberalization—they accepted the principle of "free transit" of electricity across Europe, but only if it was mediated and controlled by the utilities; and they declared their opposition to the new concept of third party access as exemplified by the British electricity deregulation program.

In the early 1990s, it was far from clear that electricity liberalization would continue beyond the fairly limited steps that had already been agreed upon. Any attempt to further liberalize this sector was risky, if only because of the predictable political opposition to this process. After airing in 1991 a first concrete proposal for TPA and some internal hesitations about the best method to implement it, the Commission decided not to act under its discretionary competition law prerogatives, that is, by way of an Article 90 (now Article 86) directive. Instead, in 1992 it submitted a first directive proposal subject to the Council's and the European Parliament's approval (under the new codecision procedure as defined by the Maastricht treaty).[9] Yet, in the face of opposition by important players, the proposal soon appeared moribund. Many observers interpreted the Maastricht treaty, which reasserted national prerogatives over energy policy, as an important setback for proponents of a European energy policy, including electricity.

As it turned out, however, the liberalization process in electricity did not stop there. The member states at the Council expressed their intention to proceed with liberalization and the relevant actors continued to negotiate on this issue. The Commission's proposal was the object of heated negotiations and numerous important amendments by the Council of Ministers from 1993 to 1996. The enlargement of the European Union to include Sweden and Finland in 1994 gave a second wind to the idea of third party access, while Germany and the Netherlands incrementally adopted official positions much more favorable to liberalization. The French government mandated the Ministry of Industry to set up an expert commission to draft a report with policy recommendations on governance of electricity in France.[10] Following this report, France proposed its own brand of liberalization, the "single buyer" (SB)

---

8. Council Directive 90/377/EEC (June 29, 1990); Council Directive 90/547/EEC (October 29, 1990).

9. The Commission's directive proposal is reproduced in *Official Journal of the European Communities*, March 14, 1992.

10. The report was drafted and published in January 1994 by the French Ministry of Industry as Ministère de l'Industrie, Rapport du groupe de travail, *La réforme de l'organisation électrique et gazière française* (Paris: Ministère de l'Industrie, 1994); hereafter, the Mandil Report.

concept. While accepting the principle of market competition for electricity generation, the proposal reaffirmed the role of monopoly utilities as the sole operator of the technical networks for transportation and distribution of electricity. This new proposal did not satisfy the Commission, but the Council decided to fudge the issue and mandated that the SB proposal be drafted into legislation in conjunction with TPA.

For a while, the anti-TPA stance was unexpectedly reinforced by two European Court rulings that leaned in favor of the French principle of *service public* (public interest), the 1994 Corbeau and Almelo decisions. In March 1995 the Commission issued a Council-mandated report comparing the TPA and SB systems, concluding that the two systems could be adopted in conjunction only if they guaranteed "equivalent results" in terms of market opening. But the question remained politically sensitive and negotiations kept stalling. The increased powers of the European Parliament under the codecision procedure also created new hurdles in the policy-making process. At the Kohl-Chirac summit of December 1995, the French and German governments had agreed to maintain cohesion and not let each other be outvoted in the Council on the issue of electricity liberalization. The prospect of an end to the saga of electricity liberalization looked even bleaker then, since the French and German governments held diametrically opposite positions on the most contentious aspects of the proposal. Until very late in the process, it was not clear that there would be any genuine liberalization of electricity supply, let alone one acceptable to all parties. Many had almost given up hope of ever reaching agreement on the Commission's proposal.

The situation dramatically changed in the first half of 1996, when France and Germany came up with a compromise proposal that lifted the most important political obstacles to the directive. Based on the existing directive proposal, the governments of these two protagonist states negotiated a common solution to the remaining disagreements. The text of the directive was accepted and unanimously adopted by the Council of Ministers on June 21, 1996. The Council resolution was then sent to the European Parliament and passed with almost no amendments in December 1996. The dominant sentiment at the time of the second reading at the European Parliament was that the carefully crafted compromise resulted from a fragile political balance; any further amendments would thwart the chances of a directive ever seeing the light of day.

THE RESHAPING OF AN INSTITUTIONAL FIELD

There are four broad components in the strategy of electricity reform developed by its proponents, especially within the European Commission. First, they cautiously incorporated the energy sector into the 1992 reform agenda, thus opening a path in the forest of institutional obstacles that stood in the way of reform. Second, they undertook to reshape the expectations of the main actors of European electricity supply in such a way as to present the process of liberalization as an inescapable movement. Third, they resorted to a variety of more typical carrot-and-stick tactics that were available to them. Fourth, they proved ready to sacrifice the purity of their liberalization objectives for the sake of reaching compromise. The pragmatic development of this strategy explains both the extent and the limits of the electricity reform achieved by its proponents.

Opening a Path

With the single market program, the European Commission was suddenly upgraded from a marginal to a potentially central player in determining the organizational characteristics of various sectors of the European economy. Yet the Commission faced a series of difficulties that were the result of constraining institutional legacies and circumstances. The single market objective built on a series of technical proposals for market opening—the white paper on the internal market—but they did not specify the full range of economic activities to be covered by the single market. The Commission's formal powers remained weak, except in certain domains such as competition policy.[11] In addition, the Commission's sectoral objectives were not always congruent with the new objectives expressed in the single market program. Adjustments had to be made on a sector-by-sector basis, and this was not necessarily easy.

On energy issues, the Commission's thinking (as expressed by the Directorate General for Energy) was marked by a policy legacy that was more marked by interventionism than by liberalism.[12] Although the European Community had been involved in energy policy since the early days of the European Coal and Steel Community in the 1950s, there was no exclusive Community competence in energy policy. Historically, European policy objectives consisted of sheltering the energy sector from short-term market uncertainties and enhancing the security of supply. These goals had been promoted first through the European Coal and Steel Community for the provision of coal and later through Euratom for the promotion of nuclear power. The Commission's limited formal prerogatives had not been sufficient to formulate a comprehensive European energy policy, and Commission initiatives in this area had been consistently thwarted by divergent national energy policies, especially in response to the 1970s oil shocks.

In the face of such obstacles, Commission officials' attempts to capitalize on the EC 1992 agenda were not certain to succeed. The first step was to get a green light from the Council for the establishment of an internal energy market, which came in 1988 in the form of a Council request to draft a proposal. Although energy was not one of the areas covered by the white paper, the Cec-

11. David Allen, "Competition Policy: Policing the Single Market," in *Decision-Making in the European Union*, ed. Helen Wallace and William Wallace (Oxford: Oxford University Press, 1996).
12. On the ambiguities of European energy policy, see Francis McGowan, "Conflicting Objectives in European Energy Policy," in Crouch and Marquand, eds., *The Politics of 1992*.

chini Report contained a section about the "costs of non-Europe" in the energy sector. As a matter of principle, most member states favored reducing these costs. France, in particular, was eager to secure European export markets for its surplus nuclear power. This was based not on a grand design of Europe-wide corporate expansion but on the immediate and well-understood self-interest of its public utility, Electricité de France (EDF), whose staff participated in drafting the Cecchini Report.[13] Thus, by engaging the drive toward an internal energy market at the Council of Ministers, France probably triggered, albeit involuntarily, a broader process of liberalization.

Following the Council's request, the college of commissioners mandated DG Energy to draft a comprehensive working paper on energy liberalization.[14] That document reflected the ambivalence of many Commission officials in charge of energy toward an internal energy market. Although the green paper did not close the door to the internal energy market, it listed so many obstacles that it seemed unlikely that the Commission would proceed very far. Energy officials did not want to alienate the electricity supply industry. Opponents of large-scale structural change in the electricity sector generally felt comfortable in their claim that energy policy was a national prerogative, and this was reinforced by a 1992 provision of the Maastricht treaty that required unanimous votes for issues of Europe-wide energy planning.

After the first and least contentious steps toward creating the internal energy market (the Transit Directive and the Price Transparency Directive), proponents of a more rapid and radical liberalization were gaining ground within the Commission. In particular, the position of Commissioner Leon Brittan and his Commission staff in charge of competition policy was boosted by the Court of Justice's early 1990s rulings in favor of the Commission's use of Article 90.3 to bring about competition in telecommunications. DG Competition began attacking some special conditions awarded to certain interests, by stigmatizing the special electricity contracts granted to public sector or big firms in various countries. Some breaches of European competition law were relatively easy to point out, and this was the area in which the Commission's enforcement powers were most extensive. Meanwhile, the opponents of liberalization were slow to react to developments at the European level. For a long time, they did not have the mandate, the collective action capacity, or the expertise to issue counterproposals at the European level.

In the long run, however, an agenda of electricity liberalization based only on the application of regular competition law was bound to reach certain limits. Liberalization could probably not have been carried through in relatively short order simply by applying competition law formulas. Utilities were quick

---

13. Later France turned against liberalization, when it became clear that electricity liberalization threatened its national monopoly and technical adjustment capacities. The EDF strategy was gradually clarified over time in the late 1980s, as it became apparent that the internal energy market was not going to be only about the interconnection of national electricity grids.

14. Commission of the European Communities, *The Internal Energy Market*, 1988.

to redress the most glaring distortions of competitive pricing between their customers, and in many cases the discontent of large electricity consumers in the face of high electricity prices could be appeased with the help of special discounts ("sweetheart deals"). As for the possible use of Article 90, it was unclear that the European Court of Justice would support an aggressive enforcement strategy by DG Competition. The risk of alienating the member states on a politically sensitive issue such as energy policy was important, whereas the need for more competition was much less obvious, from a technological viewpoint, than in telecommunications.

The novelty of the electricity liberalization project was that it potentially went far beyond merely striking down trade barriers between member states. The member states would have to agree on common rules of electricity supply organization, which was virtually impossible—precisely because of the absence of a common structural framework of electricity supply—unlike telecommunications where all member states started from a similar model, since telecommunication services were provided by a single national entity that was usually in charge of postal services as well. In trying to create a single market for electricity, the Commission had to depart dramatically from legal principles and rules of thumb such as "mutual recognition" and was led to propose a coordinated cross-national reform of the organization of electricity supply.[15] Thus, the implementation of this agenda was bound to be challenged and possibly overturned, unless the Commission could build support for its agenda and, crucially, persuade potential opponents to accept its terrain of battle. This would not have worked if the Commission's agenda had not been attached to a broader strategy of changing the political-economic environment of electricity supply.

Reshaping Actors' Expectations

To advance the internal energy market, Commission officials started to fundamentally reshape the context of expectations within which actors articulated their interests and strategies. The first step was to work out what strategy the Commission wanted to adopt. Traditionally, DG Energy was careful not to offend national utilities and governments and more reluctant to use competition law to create an internal market for electricity. But around 1990 the internal dynamics of the Commission changed. The new Portuguese commissioner for energy, Antonio Cardoso e Cunha, moved strongly in favor of liberalizing the electricity sector. Perhaps fearing that Brittan, his very active British colleague

---

15. Commission of the European Communities, *Energy in the European Community* (Luxembourg: Office for Official Publications of the European Communities, 1991). The internal energy market objective was broken down into several subgoals: getting rid of economically inefficient subsidies, especially those to noncompetitive national coal industries; breaking the monopolistic structures that allowed excessive slack in utilities and the extraction of rents on social welfare; promoting decentralized and market-driven technological innovation, especially technologies of energy efficiency, combined cycle, and renewable energies.

for competition, would capture the initiative on the internal energy market, Commissioner Cardoso moved radically in favor of electricity liberalization and formed a special internal energy market task force that reported directly to his cabinet—over the head of DG Energy's staff, which normally would have been in charge of drafting the directive proposal.[16] Once the college of commissioners resolved the procedural issue by excluding the idea of an Article 90 directive, that task force was wholly in charge of drafting and amending the Commission's proposal.

To induce state and sectoral actors to gradually accept the Commission's proposal, it was necessary to make these actors believe that preserving the status quo was out of the question and to convince them that it was in their best interest to negotiate a compromise. In the European political climate of the mid-1980s, the idea of an internal energy market was acquiring political momentum. The problem for Commission actors was to find the Achilles' heel in the electricity sector's institutional armor. The price differential problem was a good candidate. It figured prominently in the Commission's agenda for electricity liberalization.[17] This was a politically sensitive issue in the context of an emerging single market, especially in countries where electricity prices were high, where the governments were subject to pressure from big electricity-consuming industries that they might relocate to low-price regions of Europe. The price of electricity varied within as well as between countries. In each national context, electricity supply has been subject to a number of economic, regulatory, and political incentives and constraints.[18] Everywhere in Europe, electricity rate structures, somewhat like tax structures, had been the object of governmental intervention and had favored certain categories of producers and consumers. Complex patterns of cross-subsidization prevailed, ranging from subsidies to favored domestic industries (e.g., regional and industrial development subsidies in France) to "clean" or declining energy sources (e.g., environmental regulations and coal subsidies in Germany). Different national models of economic infrastructure and development across Europe, structured around different policy objectives, were largely responsible for the important price differentials for any given category of consumers.

16. Interview with Commission official, Brussels, September 22, 1997. Cardoso's activism did not fare very well among DG XVII bureaucrats and in the energy industry. See, for example, a very skeptical view on TPA by two Commission officials "expressing their own personal views": Guy de Carmoy and Gerard Brondel, *L'Europe de l'énergie: Objectif 1992 et perspective 2010* (Luxembourg: Office for Official Publications of the European Communities, 1991).

17. For an agenda of change set by the Commission, see Commission of the European Communities, *Energy: A Challenge for Europe and the World* (Brussels: Commission of the European Communities, 1992), 7–8.

18. The following passage from the French Mandil Report departs dramatically from the document's otherwise technocratic style: "Electricity and gas systems are not only rational constructs but are also the fruits of history, geography, and geology. . . . There is no reason whatsoever for gas and electricity distribution to take the same forms in a country (Germany) that was built as a federation of towns and in one (France) that owes its existence to the centralizing will of the Capetian kings."

It is important to understand that technical methods of calculating prices and costs often incorporate what organizational sociologists call "ceremonial" elements.[19] Such elements not only play the functional role of market signals but also serve the purpose of enhancing the legitimacy of various energy-planning concepts. The apparently neutral cost-accounting and price-setting techniques used in the sector do not reflect economic factors only. Economic efficiency is obviously an important consideration, but there are also other concerns such as security of supply, public service obligations, environmental concerns, and the like. This explains in large part the conundrum of cost and price structures in the electricity sector. The fact that the Commission decided to examine these structures as a "test case" for the internal energy market fits nicely with the sociologist's notion that technical expertise is often used to delegitimize ceremonial elements. A harmonization of energy price structures would involve a direct questioning of the cost-accounting elements that are not directly warranted by efficiency-based considerations.

The Commission's decision to first investigate energy price structures was politically astute. Although many pricing techniques could have been criticized as incoherent or archaic, their underlying energy-planning concepts were so highly institutionalized that a frontal attack would have failed. From the beginning, therefore, the European Commission singled out price differentials as the single most important rationale for liberalization reforms.[20] More surreptitiously, Commission officials often cast the utilities as monopolistic rent-seekers, whose cushy rents would be hurt if there were competitors in the supply of electric power.[21] The existence of monopolistic rents implies that regulators are "captured" by the utilities and that the regulated prices are excessively favorable to the industry on a systematic basis. Although this accusation was hard to prove, it made intuitive sense. The argument that utilities were protecting their cushy rents was not overly developed, but it underlay proliberalization discourse as a politically useful characterization of the utilities.

This proliberalization offensive also echoed timely concerns and broad political objectives, such as the necessity of liberating national economies from their "sclerosis" while preventing a race to the bottom and a relocation of national industries. Commission officials constantly referred to other models of liberalization as the vanguard of modernity—especially British precedents of liberalization in electricity and gas, and the precedent of European telecommunication—to justify electricity liberalization. They also raised the specter of "regulatory competition" at the expense of high-price countries. It was argued

19. Meyer and Rowan, "Institutionalized Organizations."
20. Commission of the European Communities, *Internal Energy Market*, 17–18.
21. See, for example, the speech by Energy Commissioner Cardoso e Cunha, "The Unavoidable Future" (April 1992), in Commission of the European Communities, *Energy in Europe* 19, July 1992 (Luxembourg: Office for Official Publications of the European Communities, 1992). The commissioner characterized the structures as monopolistic or oligopolistic and thus naturally bent on "protectionism": "If I were in charge of one of the monopolistic undertakings in the energy sector I would very likely do exactly as they do" (5).

that, in the absence of sectoral competition, prices would remain high, and this would provoke the relocation of energy-intensive industries and discourage their emergence. This argument was especially salient for Germany, especially after the publication of a much-discussed 1993 parliamentary report about the situation of Germany as a site of industrial production ("Standort Deutschland") in the global economy.

The utilities' first arguments were purely defensive. They warned that public service obligations would disappear if sectoral liberalization occurred. They pointed out the failures of electricity liberalization in the United Kingdom, where a TPA formula had been pioneered rather unsuccessfully. They argued that the United States, after contemplating liberalization in the 1970s and 1980s, had retreated from the idea and had decided to keep its regional monopoly structure. Yet the utilities were on shaky political ground due to the highly technical and sometimes counterintuitive nature of their arguments. In the 1980s context of "market-oriented" reforms, the traditional electric utility structure of Europe appeared particularly lackluster. Due to a variety of historical and technical as well as political legacies, the industry seemed to be mired in antiquated and parochial patterns of strategic and technical thinking—to say nothing of its complex management structures. Defensive arguments were sailing against powerful political winds on many of these issues.

Much against their will, the utilities were drawn into an economic and political debate with the proliberalization advocates. They began to seriously consider the practicality of the TPA option. In 1989, they created Eurelectric, an industrial lobby based in Brussels, in charge of elaborating counterproposals. The lobby first came up with an alternative model to the TPA model of electricity liberalization. In defending the status quo, they called it the "industrial model" and presented it as the only "pragmatic" solution of "regulated competition"—implying that the other one was utopian.[22] Whether this model was indeed "pragmatic" or not, it was not pushed by a coherent and stable coalition of interest groups. There was little in common between the different national utility structures that the antiliberalization lobby moved to oppose. The "industrial model" was invented and put forward in the face of external pressure and, therefore, many actors' reactions were negative.

At that point, the European debate on liberalization had acquired a dynamic of its own. The utilities probably contributed to this dynamic by engaging in the debate for fear of being left out of big decisions that affected them. The big German utilities, in particular, were under considerable political pres-

22. Eurelectric, "Quelle forme de concurrence pour le secteur électrique en Europe: Position des membres continentaux d'Eurelectric," March 21, 1991. The "continental members of Eurelectric"—that is, everybody except the British—signed this position paper, in which the model of electricity deregulation is said to rest "on the ideology of 'small is beautiful' " (11). This same phrase can be found on page 2 of a conference paper—"Electricity Monopoly vs. Competition?"—delivered by two EDF executives, Pierre Lederer and Jean-Paul Bouttes, at the *Financial Times* World Electricity Conference (London, November 12–13, 1990).

sure. By 1994, the German government had moved squarely in favor of electricity liberalization, with the economics minister, Günther Rexrodt, taking a strong proliberalization stance both in the European and the national spheres. Meanwhile, in the course of the first reading of its proposal by the European Parliament, the Commission had been induced to modify it so as to make it more acceptable to the German utilities.[23] In such circumstances, the big German utilities that belonged to Eurelectric calculated that unless they took a more positive attitude toward liberalization they would run the risk of being squeezed between the politically well-protected municipal distributors (*Stadtwerke*) and their would-be foreign competitors.[24]

Faced with the mitigated success of the notion of an "industrial model" and given the fragility of the supporting coalition behind it, Eurelectric decided to abandon its obstruction strategy in 1994. This was, as one analyst put it, a recognition that the "internal energy market debate was not going to go away."[25] The report can also be seen as a tactical bargaining move by the French, that is, a way to gain some influence over the modalities of liberalization. After the breakdown of the Eurelectric compromise, the national opponents of TPA adopted diverging positions. The big German utilities called for all-out liberalization for everybody, including the dismantling of their potentially threatening rival EDF in France, whereas the French Ministry of Industry elaborated its single buyer proposal as an explicit alternative to TPA under the subsidiarity principle. This proposal accepted the idea that some measure of liberalization was warranted, although not as mandated by the TPA proposal.[26]

In a spirit of compromise, the Council of Ministers mandated that the SB proposal be studied in conjunction with the TPA proposal.[27] Confusion reached a climax as the Commission and national officials in charge of negotiating the terms of the directive were asked to combine two abstractly defined models of market liberalization. From a technical viewpoint, combining the

23. The Commission adopted a modification originally sponsored by the association of big German electricity consumers (VIK) and relayed by members of the European Parliament, especially the Belgian *rapporteur* of the energy commission, Claude Desama. It guaranteed that network access would be mandatory but subject to contractual agreement between the parties (i.e., "negotiated access" instead of "regulated access"). According to several interviewees, the purpose was to make TPA more palatable to German utilities. Subsequently, the Commission's proposal was renamed "negotiated TPA." Interviews in Brussels, December 12, 1996, March 18, 1997, March 19, 1997.

24. Interviews with German utility executives and government officials, Brussels, October 22, 1996; Essen, March 14, 1997, September 9, 1997.

25. Janne H. Matlary, "Energy Policy," in Wallace and Wallace, eds., *Policy-Making in the European Union*.

26. The argument was that the utilities would lose the technical control of the network infrastructure, resulting in a loss of productive efficiency. The single buyer concept means that, while independent power production ceases to be a monopoly, the transport and distribution of electricity remain the responsibility of a single network operator. Thus, the operator continues to act as an intermediary between producers and customers.

27. Meanwhile, the TPA proposal had been modified and renamed "negotiated TPA." There was now some room for the negotiated, instead of mandatory, access of third parties to the network.

two proposals into a single liberalization project did not make much sense.[28] This instruction, however, was a sure sign that the debate had moved into the political realm of European decision making. The reformers within and outside the European Commission had won the most difficult battle.

Carrots and Sticks

The reshaping of the normative field of electricity regulation cannot be described as a smooth process orchestrated by enlightened reformist actors. Important political aspects of the directive emerged over time in the course of a bumpy bargaining process. Actors that were under political obligation to find some common room for an internal energy market agreement continuously fought one another and struck deals in order to avoid a collective loss of face. The evolution of the Commission's internal energy market initiatives provides a good illustration of this process. To some extent, Eurocrats discovered their preferences regarding the internal energy market through promarket action. Spurred by the success of the single market program, they used a relatively abstract cognitive and procedural framework, embodied in a competition law, in writing the first electricity policy proposals.[29] The Commission first claimed that electricity was not a "special" commodity and that the internal market for electricity fit squarely within the single market agenda. In the face of political opposition to Commissioner Cardoso's 1992 proposal, the Commission's proposals were stalled for several years. When a new energy commissioner, Christos Papoutsis, took office, he ignored the bad blood and rallied DG Energy officials to the task of designing an internal energy market based on a modified version of Cardoso's proposals. From that point on, the Commission as a whole could use its experience of Brussels politics, its unique albeit limited European energy policy mandate, and a combination of expertise both in energy policy (DG Energy) and competition law (DG Competition). The Commission's position evolved and opened up more room for compromise, as reflected in the final outcome.

With the benefit of hindsight, two well-used types of political tactics can be distinguished in the development of the Commission's strategy. First, the Commission used a variety of carrots and other positive inducements to find allies among key state actors, especially within the Council of Ministers. A majority within the Commission decided to pursue the internal energy market through directives endorsed by the Council, rather than through generic competition law. That was a smart move because the member states believed they retained

28. Conjoining the single buyer and TPA proposals would have meant that utilities retained responsibility for operating the network while losing their ability to coordinate the generation of power with the capacities of the transportation network.

29. The draft directive on TPA unveiled in 1991 by the Commission was inspired by the principles of competition law, and few of its provisions appear to have been made on the basis of sector-specific considerations. Many observers report, sometimes critically, the legalistic bent of the Commission.

the upper hand in building an internal energy market. The Council began by passing two directives mandating the free transit of electricity across borders and price transparency for industrial customers. There was clear support for these directives from important constituents, especially electricity-exporting countries (including France) and the majority of the electricity supply industry. The Council's direct involvement was important insofar as it opened the way for more important developments. The Council took many years to reach a final compromise, and along the way the debate often seemed completely bogged down. Yet each meeting of energy ministers invariably reiterated the Council's official support of the internal energy market and thus supported the Commission's position, even when its proposals did not go through.

Increasingly, the Commission was also able to rally the support of well-established actors at the substate level. While potential competitors to incumbent utilities did gain a certain measure of influence in the process of liberalization, their voices remained marginal, both because they had no foothold in the electricity supply industry and because they were fairly skeptical about their prospects of entering this market. By contrast, industrial consumer groups of electricity began to emerge and became politically active across Europe. This new interest group activity did not precede the directive proposal, however. It evolved largely in response to and in support of the directive proposal. Such groups existed both at the national level and at the European level, where they belonged to a federative entity called the International Federation of Energy Consumers (IFIEC) with its seat in Brussels. The most important group at the national level was probably the German Verband Industrielle Energie- und Kraftwirtschaft (VIK). VIK and other consumer groups were made up of German industrialists, often led by heavyweight corporate actors such as the German chemical company BASF, which were united mostly against the high electricity prices in Germany.[30] Other consumer groups such as UNIDEN in France were present in countries where electricity prices were not as high. In such cases, industrialists were looking for ways to increase their "bargaining room" for negotiating delivery contracts with the monopolistic utilities.[31] The impact of these groups was at first relatively weak, as they could hardly match the political clout of utilities such as EDF in France.[32] Yet these actors gained legitimacy over time and were increasingly able to convey their reformist message in support of the European liberalization process to politicians and government officials.

Second, the Commission made tactical use of the stick of competition law. One possibility was that the Court might reach procompetitive conclusions in the long-standing case brought by the Commission (under Article 169, now Article 226) against national import and export monopolies. Another possibility

30. Interview with VIK official, Essen, March 14, 1997.
31. Interview with UNIDEN official, Paris, September 29, 1997.
32. Interview with French government official, Paris, April 18, 1997.

was for the Commission to use its exclusive prerogative under competition law (under Article 90, now Article 86), if all else failed, as a basis for creating the internal energy market. The Commission never abandoned these threats, which proved to be a powerful goad during intergovernmental negotiations. Member state actors knew that, if no progress was made, there was a nonnegligible risk that the internal energy market would emerge anyhow, as a result of a legal rather than a political process. In the member states, an increasing number of people sided with the Commission's proposals, especially within the closely connected social networks of national competition authorities.[33] Despite a situation of apparent deadlock in 1992 and continuous difficulties in the bargaining process, there was progress, as reluctant member states reasoned that it was in their best interest to compromise.

Whether this was actually the case, however, is a debatable point. The agenda of economic liberalization was still relatively new and fragile. The treaties were notoriously ambivalent on the exact field of application of European competition law, especially concerning public undertakings.[34] Therefore the case law, which was relatively slim on large-scale industrial organization and reform, took on an extraordinary importance. Existing case law strongly suggested that the Luxembourg judges considered the internal energy market central to the achievement of European integration. Judging from judicial precedents (especially in the telecommunications sector), the Court seemed strongly inclined to help the Commission attain its market-building goals. The judicial uncertainty was therefore too high for member states to run the risk of clinging to the status quo.[35] State actors preferred to seize the initiative in the multilateral arena of the Council, where each member state could at least contribute some input, rather than leave the problem to the judicial arena over which they had no direct control.

The Commission used the internal energy market objective as a rallying call, but it carried its proposal well beyond the strict least-common-denominator interest of the member states. It modified the original proposal to make it palatable to a maximum number of member states, while holding firm on the principle that some degree of competition must be forcefully introduced in the electricity sector. Once the debate was firmly set in Brussels, Commission officials invented a whole battery of technical arguments of a legalistic nature about how to introduce competition. The fact that they rarely asked the "why" question in a systematic way did not seem to matter. They had

33. Interview with DG Competition and French competition officials, Brussels, March 10, 1997, Paris, April 18, 1997.

34. This ambivalence reflects the compromise quality of many substantive provisions about the nature of the Common Market in the Treaty of Rome, which were often the result of political compromises between national negotiators. For example, the very strong procompetitive provisions of Article 90.3 are preceded by Article 90.2, which is, in essence, an escape clause from Article 90.1. On the political roots of the mix of liberal and not-so-liberal provisions in the Treaty of Rome, see Ernst B. Haas, *The Uniting of Europe* (Stanford: Stanford University Press, 1968), esp. 19–31.

35. See, for example, the Mandil Report, 21.

time on their side and the legal aspects already gave the negotiators plenty of work to do. The Commission's arguments were congruent with the legal procedures and negotiation context dominant in Brussels' politics, including at the Council of Ministers. Thus, the Council's decision to include both TPA and the SB system in the draft directive is not overly surprising. Although this was distressing to the drafters of the original directive, it provided a way to defuse conflict and to make progress toward the final directive.

At the end of the day, a substantial measure of economic liberalization was achieved, despite all the odds against it. The national governments' position papers evolved from a full-scope but abstract support for the internal energy market to a more limited and gradual but concrete and real version of economic liberalization. The realization of an internal market was the only objective that remained endowed with a high degree of legitimacy throughout the process. As the discussion became more concrete, the debate became more technical, but it remained loaded with political objectives. The evolution of the French government position was typical: it first advocated full liberalization, seeing the immediate benefits of freer transit for electricity exports; then it backed down and became much more circumspect, without however capsizing the negotiations. The initial binary choice set for structuring the electricity supply industry—the status quo ante vs. full-fledged liberalization—disappeared along the way, as both alternatives became politically proscribed.

The Commission's success was in creating a political momentum in favor of liberalization. First achieved in the name of the EC 1992 objective, it continued beyond that date. Periodically, the European Council unanimously renewed its support of the Commission's plan to create an internal energy market—despite intense disagreements between member states about the meaning and substance of the internal energy market. The reasons for this unanimous support varied across member states. Some fully supported the Commission's approach (Britain), whereas others moved from reluctance to support (Germany). Yet the crucial point is that not a single member state was willing to take responsibility for obstructing the establishment of a much-heralded internal energy market. Because the Commission held the formal monopoly of legislative initiative, those member states that opposed certain provisions of the directive proposal were progressively cornered into a defensive strategy (especially France). With the majority of the Council consistently supporting the objective of an internal energy market, critics gradually lost political credibility.

A Compromise Outcome

In the end, while the two methods (TPA and SB) mandated to organize electricity supply were left optional, the 1996 directive specified that all member states must attain "equivalent results," that is, competition in electricity supply for eligible customers. In the final text, the Commission was confirmed as the single agency in charge of monitoring the implementation of the directive and reporting on its progress. The much fought-over Article 3.3 states that "the interest of the Community includes, inter alia, competition with regard to the eligible customers." Most remarkably perhaps given the continuing feud over the directive, the member states voted unanimously in favor of the final draft directive. Of course, saving face required everyone to claim victory at the end. But national positions on liberalization have evolved considerably over time, largely as a result of the Commission's action. However we define "liberalization," the June 1996 directive clearly held the promise of a certain degree of genuine change in this direction and made the mere continuation of the status quo very unlikely. In this sense, some form of electricity liberalization, which had been very unlikely at the outset, was now squarely on the European agenda.

The limits of the directive, however, were equally apparent. These limitations stemmed mostly from the compromise nature of the directive and the new political climate of the mid-1990s. The Commission was forced to water down its original proposal several times along the way. First, it backed down from its early preference for Big Bang liberalization, as envisioned by competition commissioner Leon Brittan, in favor of a more gradualist strategy. Then, in building a coalition and winning over potential adversaries, especially during the first reading of the proposal in 1994 at the European Parliament, the Commission had to accede to not-so-liberal demands for a more restricted and "negotiated" version of TPA. After a period of initial confusion, actors in the field found ways to lobby the relevant actors both at the national and the European level. The main outcome was that the Council systematically delayed its decision on TPA, and typically requested from the Commission some further elaboration of its proposals.[36] At various points during the negotiation process, member state initiatives—for example the decision to go along with both the TPA and SB proposals, and the final bilateral negotiation between the French and the German government—took policy leadership away from the Commission.

As a result of this give-and-take process, the final directive was much less liberal and homogenous than DG Competition and some member states would have liked.[37] Due to the political bargaining between France and Germany, the proposed directive contained a reciprocity clause that may in the end slow down the development of a Europe-wide energy market since it can be used as a pretext for protecting national markets. Italy's long resistance to EDF's takeover of Montedison in 2001 confirmed this possibility. Furthermore, eligibility criteria excluded entire categories of electricity consumers, which were to remain "captive" for the foreseeable future.[38] A lot of leeway remained for member states to decide eligibility—at least until the rules were rewritten in

36. Council of Ministers, Meetings of Energy Ministers: Nov. 30, 1992; June 25, 1993; Dec. 10, 1993.
37. Several interviewees described the resulting process as "liberalization à la carte."
38. Even at the last stage of implementation of the 1996 directive by 2006, only 40% of all consumers would be "eligible" to choose their electricity providers. The June 2003 directive later accelerated this schedule by mandating an opening of the electricity market for all business consumers by July 2004 and for all individual consumers by July 2007.

June 2003. In sum, the principle of liberalization was partially accepted, but the traditional utility structure for the management of the technical network was only gradually reformed. The 1996 directive itself was already clear on the member states' dual intent of reregulating as well as liberalizing the sector, as indicated by its very title: "Directive concerning common rules for the internal market in electricity."

Beyond the completion of energy liberalization in 2007, the normative trend of sectoral regulation remains sketchy. One likely scenario is the consolidation of connected but distinct national energy markets dominated by oligopolistic actors. But other scenarios are also possible. In 1996, the Commission issued a communication on "services of general interest in Europe," leaving much more room than in prior proposals for national definitions of "public service obligations."[39] Subsequently, at the request of the French government, the Amsterdam Treaty of 1997 added a new provision to the list of general principles contained in the first part of the Treaty of Rome, recognizing the "place occupied by services of general economic interest in the shared values of the Union as well as their role in promoting social and territorial cohesion."[40] The 2004 constitutional treaty went even further in the same spirit, since it recognized the need to secure funding for these "services of general economic interest."[41] As liberalization and changes in collective service provision begin to affect the lives of European citizens (including electricity consumers and utility employees) they may become more politicized. Future battles over European energy regulation will not simply reflect conflicting national interests per se but will increasingly echo political struggles over the definition of the public interest. Disruptions or even reversals of liberalization remain possible, especially if sensitive issues such as job protection or the enforcement of public service obligations are involved.

A CRITIQUE OF CONTENDING EXPLANATIONS

While interests, ideas, or institutions certainly played a role at various points in the process of electricity liberalization, to focus on these variables misses what is arguably the main underlying dynamic of the story—the unfolding of a political strategy whose goal was precisely to short-circuit the normal interplay of interests, ideas, and institutions. The comparative advantage of a strategic constructivist approach is obvious in this case, since the other causal dynamics do not strongly point in the direction of reform. Unlike the finance case, interpreting the case of electricity liberalization centered on the development of a political strategy does not require a counterfactual argument. A comparison

---

39. European Commission, "Communication of the Commission: Services of General Interest in Europe" (Luxembourg: Office for Official Publications of the European Communities, 1996).

40. Amsterdam Treaty, Article 7d.

41. Treaty establishing a Constitution for Europe, Article III-122.

of contending explanatory perspectives is sufficient to highlight the crucial importance of political strategy.

Interests

The most traditional type of explanation would emphasize the causal impact of *interests*, either sectoral or national. Explanations in terms of sectoral interests have a distinguished pedigree in regional integration studies, going all the way back to neofunctionalist theory. They stress the impact of particular interest groups on pluralistic decision-making processes. In the case of electricity liberalization, such an explanation would seem particularly appropriate, since certain easily identifiable economic interests appear to be in a position to benefit from liberalization. While all big industrial buyers of electricity now face the prospect of a choice of suppliers, some electricity producers that wish to increase their market share may also benefit from liberalization. On the face of it, it would seem that some big industrial players, including big industrial customers but also the biggest and most powerful utilities in Europe, would be in good position to benefit from liberalization. In the event of full-fledged liberalization, the big industrial customers will be in a strong bargaining position vis-à-vis the utilities to obtain electricity at cheaper rates, while the most efficient and/or biggest utilities will likely be able to compete successfully with new entrants and may even capture new markets. And indeed, at various moments since the beginning of the negotiations, big customers have generally been in favor of introducing more competition, and big utilities have declared themselves in favor of a certain degree of liberalization.

As it turns out, however, most utilities opposed rather than favored liberalization during the 1990s. They saw it as a risk to their adjustment capacity and, potentially, to their market position and notoriously high profit margins.[42] All in all, vested interests in the status quo, traversing the whole electricity supply industry, pushed strongly in favor of existing equilibria and against liberalization. When the incumbent utilities—through the mediation of their Brussels lobby, Eurelectric—officially declared themselves in favor of liberalization, this was more the result of tactical opportunism than because they wanted it to occur.[43] Likewise, on the consumer side, while some industrial consumers pay very high electricity rates in certain countries (especially in Germany), this was not a new concern. Until the mid-1980s, the industrial consumers' long-standing desire for cheaper rates had never threatened to upset the very structure of the electricity supply industry. An explanation in terms of interest group politics begs the question of why these interests were suddenly able to prevail at the European level. Furthermore, the big consumers' desire for cheap electric-

---

42. Some European Commission officials, including Energy Commissioner Cardoso, have accused the utilities of oligopolistic rent-seeking behavior. Although it remains to be proved that rent-seeking is the sole rationale of industry lobbying, the utilities have a vested interest in the status quo.

43. Interviews, Paris, October 21, 1996, March 17, 1997; Brussels, March 18, 1997.

ity could be satisfied in many ways other than liberalization, for example in tougher price regulation of the utilities. Their support for the liberalization process was instrumental yet not crucial to the eventual success of the Commission's directive proposal. Thus, it is doubtful that the big consumers' interests were of such a pressing nature as to "explain" the drive toward liberalization.

One potential way out of this explanatory conundrum is to point to a potential shift in national interests in favor of liberalization. Germany, with its notoriously high electricity prices, is the obvious candidate here. Past a certain point, one could argue, expensive electricity undermined German competitiveness and the German state was bound to take up this problem and drive the process of electricity liberalization. By the same token, France would be the main obstacle to liberalization and would favor the status quo for reasons of national interest, because its electricity was cheaper and it exported electricity under the existing system. Yet it is once again unclear whether the dynamics of national interests was really tilted in favor of liberalization. In the absence of an intergovernmental consensus on how to reform electricity supply, the status quo was perhaps the most likely outcome. From the perspective of national interests, it is not at all clear that liberalization was a priori more likely than a continuation of the status quo. Besides, it took several years before most governments, including Germany, changed their positions on electricity liberalization. All other things being equal, electricity liberalization was not clearly in the cards by the mid-1980s.

On the whole, interest-based explanations do not withstand the test of time very well, and their conclusions must be periodically reevaluated as new events make them obsolete. This is surprising given that the electricity sector is relatively static over time. One would assume that this would be an ideal case for entrenched interests to constitute more powerful magnets or constraints. Yet this relative entrenchment of interests is precisely the problem. Insofar as powerful interest groups and potentially powerful national actors were going to be hurt, the pure dynamic of finding a least common denominator between objective national interests would have probably led to a stalemate.[44] It is difficult to single out any hard-and-fast "interests" that can be identified as the independent variable driving liberalization from beginning to end. In the face of relatively stable sectoral characteristics (slow-moving technology, small number of actors), a constant need to reevaluate the explanation is troublesome. The point is not that objective interests did not matter in the process. Yet an analysis of electricity liberalization that mainly tries to identify such interests runs the risk of being wrongheaded. Material interests were not absent, but they were not the key driving variable behind liberalization.

In the case in question, the Commission acted as the main engine of politi-

---

44. Indeed, one analysis of the process of electricity liberalization plausibly concluded that the process was going to fail due to a divergence of national interests. See Padgett, "Single European Energy Market."

cal change, fostering and leading, rather than bandwagoning behind, an interest-group coalition in favor of its liberalization agenda. The Commission's supplying of a new policy perspective, that is, the internal energy market, counted more in driving the process of liberalization than the interest-driven demands of its natural constituents, which remained quite static. The Commission's political strategy induced the relevant actors (the big industrial consumers and, later, the big electric utilities) to rearticulate their interests around the ever-more concrete prospects of liberalization. In explaining liberalization, therefore, the political strategy that consisted in channeling interests into a proliberalization process deserves top billing.

Institutions

Another category of explanation in political science foregrounds the institutional factors that shape both actors' interests and the range of possible outcomes. This approach would identify the institutional determinants of the process of liberalization. The presence of certain institutionalized procedures or expectations may have channeled actors' interactions, thus yielding identifiable patterns of reforms. For example, the evolution of the intergovernmental negotiation away from systematic anti-TPA obstruction could be the result of a convergence of actors' expectations and beliefs about some institutional method for building an internal energy market. Candidates for institutional determinants include the organizational characteristics of electricity supply (e.g., whether the former system rests on a centralized or a decentralized organization of electricity supply) and the set of institutional procedures or legal norms that underpinned European negotiations (e.g., the development of competition law subject to the principle of mutual recognition, or the dynamic of qualified-majority voting at the Council).[45]

To be sure, institutionalist explanations illuminate certain aspects of the electricity liberalization process. In particular, international and domestic institutional structures help to explain the moderation of the 1996 directive and some patterns of cross-national differences in its subsequent implementation. At the European level, the institutional dynamics of the negotiations also heavily influenced the substance of the 1996 directive. In particular, the incremental bargaining dynamics at the Council and more generally the historical and institutional environment of EU-level negotiations help explain the open-endedness (some would say the vagueness) of the electricity directive. Institutional inertia at the domestic level and cross-national differences are quite per-

---

45. For an explanation of the mitigated results of electricity liberalization in terms of Community case law, see Piet Jan Slot, "Energy and Competition," *Common Market Law Review* 31 (1994). For a similar argument cast in terms of an institutionally induced principal-agent logic, see Schmidt, "Commission Activism." For an argument about the embeddedness of electricity liberalization in domestic and European institutional frameworks, see Rainer Eising and Nicolas Jabko, "Moving Targets: National Interests and Electricity Liberalization in the European Union," *Comparative Political Studies* 34, no. 7 (September 2001).

sistent, despite the enactment of a common electricity directive. In fact, the open-endedness of the directive makes it potentially problematic to speak uniformly of a "European" process of electricity liberalization, when some national electricity markets are being opened much more widely and rapidly than others. Institutional determinants are helpful in explaining cross-national variation in liberalization outcomes.

Yet institutional determinants largely fail to explain the prior and main puzzle, namely the occurrence of electricity reform at the level of the European legislative framework. The problem with this type of explanation is that there were also important institutional dynamics that favored a complete status quo. At the industry level, utility-centered social and institutional networks and practices had been established over the years at the national level in each member state. Indeed, the developmental function of electricity supply, in addition to its territorially defined sphere of activity, had brought electric utilities into a close, sometimes symbiotic relationship with the political and administrative elite. In many instances, this was reinforced by the public or semipublic ownership of utilities. Internationally, the belief that cooperation, rather than competition, was the normal business practice in electricity supply, was partly the result of cross-national network socialization. The task of interconnecting national electricity grids had fostered social interactions within well-established international technical organizations, such as UCPTE (created in 1925) and UNIPEDE (created in 1951). The utilities conducted various forms of cross-national coordinated energy planning, including joint R&D projects. Finally, the latest addition to these network structures was the lobbying organization Eurelectric (created in 1989).

Although the shift to qualified-majority voting did somewhat change the rules of the game, this institutional factor was not sufficient in itself to generate a departure from the status quo and an agreed-upon idea of what the internal energy market should mean in concrete terms. There was no least-common-denominator, well-delineated, and agreed-upon rule or model available for electricity liberalization. Competition law was of little help, since almost everybody recognized that it did not provide an easy and ready-made way to build the internal energy market. No one actor was powerful enough to impose any particular institutional solution. This state of affairs did not fundamentally change after the adoption of new voting rules and other institutional reforms contained within the Single Act. Any agenda of institutional change had to proceed by iteration—and this could not be done without sacrificing legal purity. In themselves, the characteristics and legacies of competition law tell us little about the broader significance of liberalization in the electricity sector. Unless an attempt is made to explain why a particular institutional formula suddenly carried *more* political weight than others, it is impossible to understand the dynamics of the liberalization process. Objectively, there was no preset institutional basis for agreement on any particular formula of reform.

The strength of the Commission was its ability to use the norm of the market, in combination with legal arguments and threats of legal action, as a weapon in the political battle. This resulted much less from any secular evolution of European law than from a particular political strategy developed in the "thick" context of the 1992 project. For this reason, a strictly institutional perspective misses much of what is most interesting about electricity liberalization. The process of electricity liberalization epitomizes the importance of market rationality and the Commission's newly acquired aggressiveness on competition issues—not the institutional dynamic of competition law alone. In fact, the Commission displayed considerable restraint in its judicial initiatives in front of the European Court of Justice. Since individual member states wanted to achieve consensus—especially France and Germany—the risk of a backlash from the member states was ever present, even after the shift to qualified-majority voting. In the search for a compromise solution, DG Energy officials did not particularly care about preserving the legal purity of their arguments as long as they managed to advance the cause of their directive proposal. In the end, the Commission agreed to restrictive eligibility conditions in order to obtain French assent to its directive proposal. It even put up with a "reciprocity" clause that flew in the face of competition law principles, so as to consolidate German support. In both cases, the Commission did not hesitate to jockey its way toward a directive, even if that implied major distortions of its original proposal and of its policy principles.

Ideas and Paradigm Shifts

The last hypothesis that we will examine focuses on the role of ideas and paradigm shifts in technological evolution. In the case of electricity liberalization, it has been argued that, due to technological and market evolution, there occurred a change in actors' thinking, or a "paradigm shift," about optimal ways of organizing electricity markets.[46] This type of explanation stresses the causal role of "learning" and the evolution of dominant thinking about technological and market evolution. In constructivist scholarship, ideas are rarely presented as monocausal factors of change. Usually, they are singled out as key factors of institutional change alongside the evolution of interests or the developmental trajectory of institutions. Insofar as historically prevalent sets of ideas—paradigms—can be distinguished from actors' interests and from the institutional context within which these actors interact, they represent a different type of variable, whose explanatory power can be assessed separately.

A certain "shadow of the future" certainly became more widespread in the 1990s among many in the electricity supply industry, which could superficially appear as an example of a dominant paradigm. In particular, the combination of low gas prices and gradual technological progress (improvements in the

---

46. Matlary, "Energy Policy." Padgett's article implicitly makes a similar assumption by equating the common interest with the proposed liberalization.

technology of cogeneration) prompted a dash for small-scale decentralized power stations, such as gas-fired or combined cycle power stations. This seemed to raise the prospect of a different energy portfolio in the future and a greater recourse to market mechanisms to fine-tune supply and demand. Some also argued that, in the post–oil shock context of abundant energy resources, the specter of energy dependence had receded so far that the premium placed on energy independence as well as the preference for certain technologies (e.g., nuclear) should be considerably lower. Yet for the paradigm-shift story to hold as a valid explanation of energy liberalization, the view that liberalization would entail clear benefits must first be consensual among a majority of concerned actors. This is the point where a technology-based line of explanation encounters important difficulties. Although proponents of liberalization have typically—and not very surprisingly—adopted this view, it was hardly shared by all actors.

First, the economic foundations of the proliberalization argument appear somewhat fragile to many observers. A number of economists, in view of the nature of the electricity supply industry, tend to agree with the traditional view that important segments of the electricity supply constitute "natural monopolies." In the presence of market imperfection, it is generally recognized that the social benefits of certain monopolistic structures may outweigh their costs. An important body of literature on the topic of transaction costs in electricity markets suggests that there is a good case for maintaining a classic public utility structure, at least in certain crucial segments of the electricity sector.[47] In other words, there may be some elements of economic truth in the utilities' self-interested claim that they operate in a "special" economic sector. A second and perhaps more immediate concern is that power generation entails huge sunk costs, which cannot be easily recouped in a context of liberalization given the quasi-saturated European markets.[48] Liberalization is about the Europe-wide creation of a competitive market. A full-fledged market is not simply waiting in the wings to be unleashed. It seems certain that a large-scale transition to gas on a European scale would entail hefty adjustment costs—not to mention the industrial restructuring costs and the political costs of hurting certain well-entrenched constituencies.

47. This is due, in particular, to the high degree of asset specificity of high-cost investments; the market uncertainty stemming from the absence of reserves (since electricity cannot be stored); the pervasive situations of small-number bargaining and possibilities for opportunistic behavior, since electricity must be supplied in a coordinated manner to all customers on a continuous basis (this is a special problem if nuclear reactors are a large part of the supply system, in that they are economically profitable only when in continuous "baseline" operation). See Paul Joscow and Richard Schmalensee, *Markets for Power: An Analysis of Electric Utility Deregulation* (Cambridge: MIT Press, 1985); Paul Joscow, "The Role of Transaction Cost Economics in Antitrust and Public Utility Regulatory Policies," *Journal of Law, Economics and Organization* 7, special issue (1991). The underlying transaction cost approach is explained in Oliver Williamson, *The Economic Institutions of Capitalism* (New York: Free Press, 1985), esp. chap. 13.

48. This is very different from the situation in other sectors, such as telecommunications, where analysts recognize that the prospects of rapid demand expansion are high.

Furthermore, the presence of important market uncertainties makes it difficult to speak of a strongly dominant paradigm of electricity supply. Despite the "dash for gas" in certain countries such as Britain—a country that had important gas resources—representatives of the electricity supply industry remained generally cautious. Nobody really knew, given the obstacles (both political and technical) to cross-border electricity traffic, what the abolition of all trade barriers would really mean. Nobody knew how the general political context would evolve. The hot issues in the European energy policy debate after "deregulation" could easily become "sustainable energy" or "employment" or "public service obligations." Other major uncertainties included the evolution of energy portfolios after Chernobyl, global warming, and the level of oil reserves and prices. Nobody knew how these issues would affect the future organization of the electricity market, for example, what the future of nuclear energy and fossil fuels, including natural gas, would look like. Thus, on the whole, the assertion that there was an emerging consensus, or paradigmatic shift, in favor of decentralized fast-moving production technologies seems premature. Energy analysts and policymakers continued to strongly disagree on the "shadow of the future." It was not clear, even to the actors involved, whether liberalization would necessarily increase economic efficiency and lead to a paradigm shift in electricity supply.

This chapter has demonstrated the political utilization of the market as a norm. There was no fixed ex ante predictable definition of the "internal energy market" as mandated by the European Council in 1986. The configuration of the field of energy policy became the object of political struggles between various actors. The advocates of EU electricity reform relied on the market as a norm in two main ways. First, they invoked the efficiency gains of the market as compared to a monopolistic sectoral structure. They also relied on the threat of litigation before the European Court of Justice and on the power of judicial precedents, especially in the area of telecommunications liberalization. Over time, they turned the debate into a discussion of *how* to open the market that largely eluded the more fundamental question of whether such change was needed. Second, the reformers made sure that their proposals were acceptable to powerful actors, especially big electricity consumers, potential new industry entrants, and national competition authorities. Once liberalization was on track, incumbent utilities understood that they were shooting themselves in the foot by resisting change. At that point, they often decided to join the chorus of market advocates. These preferences, however, were expressed relatively late in the process of liberalization. They did not exist before the drive for liberalization and only contributed to its success on the margin.

Contrary to many expectations, then, a small number of comparatively weak Commission officials were able to considerably reshape the electricity sector. This enabled significant, albeit gradual, electricity liberalization. By appealing to Europe's single market program, Commission officials led other actors to change the ways in which they articulated their own interests and strategies. That political strategy fundamentally reshaped the area of electricity policy, thus short-circuiting the deeper but slower evolution of material interests, economic and legal-political institutions, and historically dominant ideas. This obviously does not mean that interests, institutions, and ideas were unimportant in the unfolding of events. Neither does it constitute a systematic refutation of all potential explanations based on one or a combination of these core concepts. It suggests that a number of potential outcomes—and perhaps the most likely one in terms of interests, institutions, and ideas—simply did not materialize. The fact that each of these concepts—interests, institutions, and ideas—could have just as easily explained the (counterfactual) occurrence of inertia as the (averred) occurrence of change further casts doubt on their explanatory power.

In particular, the norm of the market does not in itself explain the success of electricity reform. Commission officials were able to gain a political high ground, not despite but because they eventually sacrificed the purity of the original liberalization objective. This suggests a much more problematic connection than is generally recognized between market ideas and the progress of Europe's integration in the 1990s. Electricity liberalization is but one of several examples of collective service liberalization that occurred at the European level. Similar processes took place for natural gas, telecommunications, transportation, postal services, and other network-based industries. Yet the case of electricity starkly reveals the power of the political strategy of market building. Electricity was an area where the Commission's liberalization initiatives were originally unwelcomed by many member states. Within the Commission itself, the desirability of a marketization of energy supply was far from consensual. Even at the most controversial stages of the debate, however, the member states never withdrew their collective support or reneged on their fundamental commitment to the realization of an internal energy market. Liberalization carried the day because it proved to be a viable path, perhaps the only one realistically available at the time, to ensuring some convergence in the evolution of domestic energy sectors in Europe.

SEVEN

The Market as a Space

Although the single market and the euro were certainly the European Union's biggest achievements in the 1980s and 1990s, the European agenda was not limited to a narrowly conceived process of market liberalization and monetary unification. In that same period the European Union considerably expanded its regional development and economic assistance programs through the Structural Funds. A new policy domain was established at the EU level—EU "structural policy"—with its own objective of "economic and social cohesion" and a variety of instruments. In 1988, the European Union adopted a new six-year budget that doubled the funds available for these programs. This was followed in 1993 by another almost two-fold increase of Structural Funds for the 1994–2000 budget. EU Structural Funds were somewhat scaled down in 1999 in the context of budgetary consolidation, but they still represented more than 35 percent of the budget and thus remained the second largest budget item after the common agricultural policy. The Community's structural programs were also quickly extended to the new EU member states of central and eastern Europe.

To justify this expansion of EU policy capacity, European Commission president Jacques Delors and his allies presented the market as a space for economic development. Pro-European actors drew from the market repertoire, but this time the market was held out as a spatial category. To package the new policy as a developmental rather than a redistributive policy was a politically smart move. Structural policy was fully incorporated into the European Union's market-building program as a "flanking" policy (*politique d'accompagnement*). It gave something to the actors that objectively benefited from the redistribution of funds, without alienating the supporters of the free market. Although there was certainly a give-and-take element in the packaging of structural policy, a pure logic of bargaining fails to explain its peculiar nature and remarkable endurance. Likewise, structural policy was not simply an incremental next step on an evolutionary policy trajectory, or the work of political actors that wanted to counterbalance the free-market orientation of the single market program. Structural policy was an innovative policy that was acceptable to moderate fiscal conservatives and free-marketeers because its costs were relatively contained and because it was designed as a supply-side instrument geared toward the competitiveness of European regions. The promoters of Europe also presented the new policy as a minimum requirement to ensure the integrity of the single market and to prevent a political backlash. Because its main focus was on development rather than redistribution, structural policy enlisted the support of politicians on both the left and the right.

Ultimately, this invocation of the market as a space for development served as a platform for moderate fiscal and organizational expansion at the EU level. This outcome is ironic since it does not square well with a pure logic of market forces or ideology. On the face of it, the EU decision to subsidize regional development seemed to run against conventional understandings of the market as a sphere of self-help, free of government intervention. For political reasons, the case for structural policy thus combined—some would say confused—an economic and a social justification. The policy may be criticized for being a macroeconomic policy choice by default. In a sense, it performs the role of a negative substitute for policy options that have been consistently rejected by most EU member states since the mid-1980's, namely, the building of a social welfare state at the European level, or the fiscal-federalist idea of a common fiscal policy geared toward countercyclical actions. In the face of budgetary difficulties, the member governments were very reluctant to endow Brussels with a big budget. Capped at 1.24 percent of the European Union's GDP, the European budget has remained quite modest. Yet the member states did agree on considerable increases in expenditures, which was not in the cards at the outset.

A DEVELOPMENTAL POLICY

The expansion of EU Structural Funds has attracted considerable attention from students of EU politics. Most analyses are informed by one or a combination of three prevalent readings. In a first reading, the growth of interstate transfers should be seen as a series of "side payments" from the wealthier to the poorer member states in exchange for deeper market and monetary integration.[1] The creation of this new policy area was merely ideological makeup for self-interested bargains. A prime example is the linkage that Spain made during the Maastricht negotiations between its demand for a new fund (the Cohesion Fund) and its acceptance of the single currency.[2] In a second reading, the

---

1. Mark A. Pollack, "Regional Actors in Intergovernmental Play," in *Building a European Polity? The State of the European Union*, ed. Carolyn Rhodes and Sonia Mazey (Boulder: Lynne Rienner, 1995); Moravcsik, *Choice for Europe*, most explicitly 367, 374, and 446; and to some extent Gary Marks, "Structural Policy in the European Community," in Alberta M. Sbragia, ed., *Euro-Politics: Institutions and Policymaking in the "New" European Community* (Washington, D.C.: Brookings Institution, 1991), 191–224.

2. See, for example, Loukas Tsoukalis, *The New European Economy: The Politics and Economics of Integration* (New York: Oxford University Press, 1993), 243–46; Ross, *Jacques Delors and European Integration*, 152 and 182.

development of a new policy framework should be viewed as evidence of the "multilevel" institutional growth of EU governance.[3] As several scholars have pointed out, the periodic intergovernmental decisions to appropriate new funds every six years does not foreclose the slow evolution of the day-to-day policy process.[4] That process is not fully determined by the interests of state actors, as shown by the crucial introduction of a "partnership" principle that gave an important role to subnational as well as supranational actors in the 1989 reform of the Structural Funds.[5] Finally, a third reading analyzes "cohesion policy" as the embryonic "social dimension" of the European Union, as opposed to the (presumably) more economic projects of market and monetary integration.[6] Scholars who read the new policy through this ideological lens call it the "flagship of regulated capitalism" as against "neoliberal capitalism."[7] Likewise, those who believe that the European Union should be focused on free-market liberalism are generally wary of the redistributive effects of cohesion policy.[8]

Despite the burgeoning of lively academic controversies, scholars rarely delve into the paradoxical relationship between cohesion policy and the rest of the single market agenda. Most analyses oscillate between a utilitarian perspective (Structural Funds as "side payments"), an institutionalist perspective (cohesion policy as "multilevel governance"), and a constructivist perspective (cohesion policy as "regulated capitalism"). Meanwhile, most scholars essentially seem to accept a conventional view of structural policy as a form of redis-

3. Marks, "Structural Policy in the European Community"; Liesbet Hooghe, ed., *Cohesion Policy and European Integration* (Oxford: Oxford University Press, 1996); Stephan Leibfried and Paul Pierson, eds., *European Social Policy: Between Fragmentation and Integration* (Washington, D.C.: Brookings Institution, 1995); Barry Jones and Michael Keating, eds., *The European Union and the Regions* (Oxford: Clarendon Press, 1995); Johannes Lindner, "Institutional Stability and Change: Two Sides of the Same Coin," *Journal of European Public Policy* 10, no. 6 (December 2003): 912–35.

4. Pierson, "Path to European Integration"; Marks, "Structural Policy in the European Community."

5. Hooghe, *Cohesion Policy and European Integration*; Raffaella Y. Nanetti, "EU Cohesion and Territorial Restructuring in the Member States," in Hooghe, ed., *Cohesion Policy and European Integration*; Gary Marks, "Structural Policy and Multilevel Governance in the European Community," in *The State of the European Community*, ed. Alan W. Cafruny and Glenda G. Rosenthal (Boulder: Lynne Rienner, 1993); Brigid Laffan, "The Politics of Identity and National Order in Europe," *Journal of Common Market Studies* 34, no. 1 (1996): 81–102; Andy Smith, "The Sub-Regional Level: Key Battleground for the Structural Funds," in *Regions in Europe*, by Patrick Le Galès and Christian Lequesne (London: Routledge, 1998); Christopher Ansell, Keith Darden, and Craig Parsons, "Dual Networks in European Regional Development Policy," *Journal of Common Market Studies* 36, no. 3 (September 1997): 347–75.

6. Jeffrey J. Anderson, "Structural Funds and the Social Dimension of EU Policy: Springboard or Stumbling Block?" in Leibfried and Pierson, eds., *European Social Policy*; Nanetti, "EU Cohesion and Territorial Restructuring"; Robert Leonardi, *Convergence, Cohesion, and Integration in the European Union* (New York: St. Martin's, 1995).

7. Liesbet Hooghe, "EU Cohesion Policy and Competing Models of European Capitalism," *Journal of Common Market Studies* 36, no. 4 (December 1998): 457–77.

8. Giandomenico Majone, "State, Market, and Regulatory Competition in the European Union," in Andrew Moravcsik, ed., *Centralization or Fragmentation? Europe Facing the Challenges of Deepening Diversity and Democracy* (New York: Council on Foreign Relations, 1998).

tributive politics at the EU level (either as side payments, social policy that empowers multilevel governance, or regulated capitalism). This is surprising because many scholars acknowledge at the same time that the relationship between cohesion policy and the single market is complex. In the introduction to their seminal collection on European social policy, Leibfried and Pierson write that "the EU's social dimension is usually discussed as a corrective to market-building, but it has proceeded instead as part of the market-building process itself."[9] Jeffrey Anderson's chapter on the Structural Funds notes the impossibility of any European social policy that would be "either expensive or threatening to existing policy networks."[10] Even Hooghe and her colleagues, who study the European Union through the lens of partisan politics, acknowledge that "social considerations have not featured explicitly in the debate about regional policy."[11]

The question, then, is whether the near-universal scholarly understanding of cohesion policy as a redistributive policy really captures the paradoxical essence of the new policy. The architects of structural policy always claimed to be doing something new and quite different than straightforward redistribution. They argued that the single market was a space that had to be actively developed in the face of centrifugal forces. Some scholars have already pointed out the quasi-natural justification of the new policy in terms of the territorial basis of the European Union.[12] But the internal market itself, not only Europe, can be understood as a spatial category. The Commission officials who spearheaded the drive to reform EU structural policy wanted to fold existing EU regional and social policy programs into a more holistic developmental framework. "Structural policy" was an especially attractive label, because it legitimized some limited redistribution under a label that was increasingly popular among fiscal conservatives and free-marketeers who called for "structural reforms." The Commission's objective was to provide seed money for the development of public infrastructure and for improving microeconomic conditions on the supply side. Commission officials and their allies favored a decentralized pattern of policymaking, involving both public and private actors, to facilitate adjustment to market integration at the local level. In this sense, EU-level reforms of regional and social funds were integral to the market-building agenda.

The connection between market building and structural policy was not self-evident, however. The upgrading of structural policy reflected a broadly acceptable conception of Europe's single market as a self-contained space—

9. Leibfried and Pierson, eds., *European Social Policy*, 51.

10. Anderson, "Structural Funds and the Social Dimension of EU Policy," 127, in Leibfried and Pierson, eds., *European Social Policy*.

11. Liesbet Hooghe and Michael Keating, "The Politics of European Union Regional Policy," *Journal of European Public Policy* 1, no. 3 (1994): 370.

12. Anderson, "Structural Funds and the Social Dimension of EU Policy"; see also Smith, "Sub-Regional Level," about the birth of an "ideology of territorial development" within the Commission.

more than a laissez-faire free market but less than a full-fledged federal polity. This middle-of-the-road spatial understanding of the market was obviously not the object of a universally enthusiastic consensus. It departed from the liberal economic conception of the market as a separate realm from society and politics, without fully satisfying the latent demands for European social policies. But it was a view that free-marketeers could live with, if only to facilitate the political acceptance of market and monetary integration. As for the supporters of "social Europe," they considered it a step, albeit a small one, in the right direction. The architects of the new policy rallied a natural clientele of regional political actors. These actors were delighted to stress the notion of the market as a space, since they became the subunits at which level the policy was going to be implemented—with positive effects on their own economic resources and even on their political standing. But the promoters of structural policy also gained the support of moderate fiscal conservatives and advocates of the free market as well as supporters of social policy. All these actors paid lip service to the new policy—not simply because it was in their material interest, nor because they truly believed in it, but because the new policy provided an acceptable equilibrium point for different constituencies with divergent interests.

The development and future prospects of the new policy are better understood if we consider it as the outcome of a political dialectic, rather than as a social policy that dares not speak its name. In essence, "structural policy" geared toward "economic and social cohesion" was a balancing act that provided a way to surmount material and ideological cleavages. It appeared as a sensible new area for Community action from a political perspective and as a relatively benign counterpart to the single market. Some scholars have argued that it was a mistake to sweep political tensions under the rug.[13] But in this as well as in other policy areas the promoters of Europe had to cater to different constituencies. In practice, the new policy enabled a considerable reinforcement rather than a termination of the existing EU funds. These funds were reformed and largely reinvented under the umbrella of structural policy. Contrary to what one might have expected in view of its significant redistributive effects, structural policy was successfully incorporated into the market-building agenda of the 1980s and 1990s. Paradoxically, then, the inoculation of market ideas led to a rejuvenation of policies that were originally identified with Keynesianism. Starting in the late 1990s, however, the prospects of an eastward enlargement of the European Union raised new and potentially lethal questions for the future of structural policy. Although external circumstances have certainly clouded the prospect of any further expansion in the near future, the legacy of structural policy as it was established the 1980s and the 1990s is still in place. Furthermore, the European Union has always privileged incremental budgetary adaptation rather than dramatic partisan rever-

---

13. Petra Behrens and Marc Smyrl, "A Conflict of Rationalities: EU Regional Policy and the Single Market," *Journal of European Public Policy* 6, no. 3 (September 1999): 419–35.

sals.[14] If the past is any indication of the future, structural policy will not simply wither away because of challenges.

THE BIRTH OF A NEW DEVELOPMENTAL POLICY

A key to the political success of structural policy was that it self-consciously broke away from what had been the Commission's political and economic ideology during most of its existence, that is, a peculiar mix of federalism and Keynesianism. Of course, the fact that structural actions were seen as expressing the "social dimension" of Europe's single market was also important. But it was not the main selling point of the new policy. The original salesmanship of the new policy, as designed by President Delors, was premised on three elements. First, the Commission embraced a significant measure of fiscal conservatism (*rigueur*) as a precondition for change. Second, it harbored the policy as an indispensable flanking policy (*politique d'accompagnement*) that would ease structural adjustment in the new single market. Third, it relied on a constituency of regional actors (*forces vives*) whom it co-opted as partners in policy evolution.

Rigueur: *The Precondition of Reform*

When Jacques Delors was appointed president of the European Commission in late 1984, he faced European governments that were on the whole very reluctant to expand the Community budget. After two years of British prime minister Margaret Thatcher holding up budget negotiations, the Community had barely found a solution to this crisis, at the Fontainebleau summit of June 1984, in the form of a "rebate" on the British contribution. While Thatcher was particularly blunt about the Community budget ("I want my money back"), she was representative nonetheless of a change of atmosphere among European governments. Even in founding member states such as Germany, France, and the Netherlands, there was little inclination to massively increase the Community budget. In that political context, Commission officials were fully aware that an expanding "federal" budget at the Community level was not a realistic agenda for the foreseeable future.[15] In a period of protracted recession and budgetary difficulties in many member states, the mood was not favorable to fiscal expansion at the European level.

Delors took this reluctance into account early on and acted to rationalize the Community budget accordingly, as a way to reassure the member states.[16]

---

14. On the importance of *acquis communautaire* as an argument against fundamental revisions, see Michael Shackleton, "The Delors II Budgetary Package," *Journal of Common Market Studies* 31 (August 1993). For a general argument about budgetary incrementalism, see Aaron Wildavsky, *The Politics of the Budgetary Process* (Boston: Little, Brown, 1979).

15. Such a prospect was described to me by three Commission insiders as a "nonstarter." Interviews, European Commission, Brussels, September 16, 1997, October 7, 1997, and September 27, 2005.

16. Jacques Delors, *Mémoires* (Paris: Plon, 2004), 244.

He benefited from his aura as former French finance minister and initiator of the French Socialist government's turn to budgetary *rigueur* in 1982–83.[17] His rationalization of regional development spending with the creation of the Integrated Mediterranean Programmes in 1985 further established his reputation as a fiscally conservative socialist in Brussels. The main idea behind these programs was to better coordinate regional development policy in the Community's Mediterranean regions and to introduce a multiyear budget plan. Subsequently, he was able to use his credentials as an asset in the political debate about the European budget and the "Delors packages" of 1988 and 1993. The Integrated Mediterranean Programmes can thus be analyzed as a prelude to the reforms of the following decade. These programs had some redistributive effects, but they had an aura of fiscal discipline. Insofar as they provided a strict blueprint for budgetary outlays over several years, they allayed fears of a runaway Community budget.

What Delors decided to do then was to upgrade this programmatic logic into a generalized approach for all Community-sponsored development policies. The Integrated Mediterranean Programmes of 1985 generalized the principle of programmatic assistance. They mandated a greater involvement of European Commission officials in the allocation of funds at the implementation stage. Finally, they marked the first attempt to fold the European Regional Development Fund into an "integrated" logic of coordinated action with two other EC funds: the European Social Fund, which had existed since the 1957 Treaty of Rome and which was originally designed as a retraining and relocation program for laid-off workers, and the Guidance Section of the Agricultural Guarantee and Guidance Fund, which was an integral part of the Community's common agricultural policy yet specifically designed to support rural development initiatives. This task was continued with the Single European Act in 1986, when the objective of maintaining "cohesion" in the context of building the single market was formally inserted into the framework of Community treaties.[18] The Single Act renamed the European Community's three existing "funds" the Structural Funds. Although the new treaty did not authorize a merger between the three funds, it explicitly laid the basis for a comprehensive "structural policy" framework. The very terminology used to designate the policy reflected the new imperative of coherence. After the Single Act, Delors and his entourage spoke of a single "structural policy" geared toward the objective of "cohesion." "Structural policy" functioned as an

---

17. Even Thatcher was impressed by Delors' slashing zeal and therefore supported his first bid for the Commission presidency. See Grant, *Delors*, 58.

18. Since the Single Act, "economic and social cohesion" is listed in Article 2 of the EC Treaty as a generic Community objective. Article 130a specifies the meaning of this objective: "In order to promote its overall harmonious development, the Community shall develop and pursue its actions leading to the strengthening of its economic and social cohesion. In particular, the Community shall aim at reducing disparities between the levels of development of the various regions and the backwardness of the least favoured regions or islands, including rural areas." The related policy instruments are the object of Articles 130a through 130e.

umbrella for a variety of policies that were previously conceived as independent actions under the heading of three different funds.

The next big hurdle was for the Commission to come up with a budget proposal for 1988–94 that would be acceptable to the member states. This proposal took the form of the Delors I budgetary package.[19] The package proposed a doubling of Structural Fund money over five years, from 7.7 billion ecus in 1988 to more than 14 billion ecus in 1993 (measured in terms of 1988 prices). It refocused the allocation of funding onto five priority objectives, thus accelerating the shift from project-based to program-based assistance and officially eliminating the practice of quota-based budget allocation.[20] Delors presented the upgrading of Structural Funds and policies as a "minimum" set of necessary measures to preserve the integrity of the large internal market without borders.[21] An increased budget was depicted as a functional requirement for the full establishment of the single market.[22] Delors saw the budgetary package of 1988 as part of a "triptych" of reforms, along with the white paper on the internal market and the Single Act of 1986.[23]

Delors' budget proposal was bitterly fought by many actors. Within the Commission itself, the Delors package was "hotly debated."[24] Delors could count on the support of Grigoris Varfis and Manuel Marin, the two commissioners respectively in charge of regional policy and social policy. But the main reason for their allegiance to Delors' plan was the prospect of increased budgets in their policy areas. As for other commissioners, they tended to reflect the positions of their national governments. German and Dutch commissioners were against any massive increase in the Structural Funds, arguing that the recipient member states did not have the capacity to absorb the extra money and that the funds would become less effective. French commissioners reflected the French government's ambivalence toward the Structural Funds and its interest in price support rather than rural development through the Agricultural Guarantee and Guidance Fund. The Spanish, Portuguese, Greek, Italian, and Irish commissioners were strongly in favor of a big increase in the funds, reflecting the interests of their countries of origin.

19. A useful summary of these reforms can be found in Commission, *Guide to the Reform of the Structural Funds* (Luxembourg: Office for the Official Publications of the European Communities, 1989).

20. The objectives were (1) promotion of lagging regions with a GDP per capita of less than 75% of the Community average; (2) conversion of regions affected by industrial decline; (3) combating long-term unemployment; (4) facilitation of youth assimilation into the labor market; and (5a) agricultural infrastructure and (5b) rural development.

21. Interview with Commission officials about the 1988 Delors I package, Brussels, May 20, 1997, and June 27, 2001.

22. The title of the Commission's 1988 budget proposal was *Réussir l'Acte Unique* (Making a Success of the Single Act). The same linkage was made in 1993 between the new budget increase and the requirements of monetary union: the 1993 title was "From the Single Market to Monetary Union and Beyond: The Means to Match Our Ambition."

23. See Grant, *Delors*, 76–80.

24. Interview with Commission official, September 27, 2005.

After the Commission adopted the Delors package, the budget negotiations of 1987–88 were extremely difficult among the member states themselves, as is often the case.[25] Since the European budget is primarily negotiated at the intergovernmental level, member states naturally try to minimize their contributions and to maximize their returns from the Community budget. While utilitarian calculations obviously matter, they do not foreclose the possibility of reaching agreements that deviate from what we would expect in international bargaining driven purely by self-interest. Delors tried to neutralize individual member governments' opposition to his package. Britain was obliged to remain neutral because Thatcher had obtained her rebate. France was roughly satisfied once it became clear that the new budgetary package would not diminish agricultural expenditures. Yet the reluctance of net contributors to increase the EU budget seemed insuperable. At the Copenhagen summit in December 1987, the member states seemed deadlocked, and Delors was very disappointed.[26] After that failure, Delors asked German chancellor Helmut Kohl for his support as a condition for the success of the Single Act. With Germany agreeing to act as the main paymaster of the single market, the member states finally adopted Delors' proposal in February 1988.

Delors' record as a fiscal moderate and as a modernizer, both as French finance minister and as Commission president, certainly eased the acceptance of his rather ambitious budgetary package. Whether or not Kohl was truly convinced, he made a political decision to soften the German government's position in the negotiations and to accept the Delors package. It is difficult to argue that Kohl made this concession as a side payment to poorer member states that had agreed to open their borders to German products. By 1988, the white paper of 1985 and the Single Act of 1986 had already been agreed on, and the internal market was being implemented. Part of the explanation for Delors' success is certainly that his package saw the light at a time of renewed Euro-optimism. For European government officials in the core countries, even a two-fold increase in the Structural Funds was a reasonable price to pay for the single market. But the member states were also comforted by the Commission's pledge that this was not the beginning of an ever-expanding Community budget.

Politique d'accompagnement: *The Spirit of Reform*

In Delors' presentation of his reform and his budget proposal progress on the path of "economic and social cohesion" was constantly presented as a necessary step to ease the adjustment of lagging regions to a fully open internal market. Scholars who adopt an institutionalist perspective rightly stress that the Commission's structural policy under Delors did not start from a blank

25. For two well-informed accounts of the negotiations, see Grant, *Delors*, 77–80; Brigid Laffan, "The Big Budgetary Bargains: From Negotiation to Authority," *Journal of European Public Policy* 7, no. 5 (December 2000): 725–43.
26. See Grant, *The House That Jacques Built*, 78, and Delors, *Mémoires*, 238–40.

slate. According to one analyst, "The Commission's presentation of a policy model that acknowledged existing political realities in the Council eased the process of reevaluation among the member governments."[27] The origins of EU structural policy can be dated to the creation of the European Regional Development Fund (ERDF) in 1975.[28] In addition, structural policy was built on a well-established regional development policy tradition in postwar Europe.[29] The Community's development policy in the 1970s initially was a meager part of the EC budget—the ERDF budget was 257 million ecus in 1975, or 4.6 percent of the EC budget.[30] Furthermore, the label "Community regional policy" was misleading, since the money was distributed by member state officials according to a system of strictly defined "national quotas" determined at the European level. The ERDF was still "little more than an interstate transfer mechanism."[31] This began to change in the late 1970s and especially with the successive reforms of the mid- and late 1980s.[32] The first wave of experimental reforms began in 1979, when the Community created a "nonquota" section within the ERDF. This measure ensured that 5 percent of ERDF spending would be allocated to targeted areas according to a programmatic rather than a distributive logic. In a sense, Delors only continued along the track of a preexisting institutional development trajectory.

Yet the innovative character of the new policy, which was closely related to the single market initiative as a flanking policy, is crucial to understand its political success. First, the reforms of the 1980s and 1990s were firmly under the sign of fiscal conservatism. Although Delors' initiatives built on past attempts to increase the Community's control over regional development funds, they also marked a clean break with earlier dreams of a federal budget. In 1977, the Commission had authored the so-called McDougall Report, which advocated

27. Anderson, "Structural Funds and the Social Dimension of EU Policy."

28. The establishment of "regional policy" as a new policy domain was formalized in Community law. See esp. Commission, "Regulations Establishing a Community Regional Policy," *Official Journal* OJ L73 of March 21, 1975. For the prehistory of EU structural policy (before 1985), see H. von der Grohen, *The European Community: The Formative Years* (Luxembourg: Office for Official Publications of the European Communities, 1987), 81–83 and 214–16, and Harvey W. Armstrong, "The Role and Evolution of European Community Regional Policy," in *The European Union and the Regions*, ed. Barry Jones and Michael Keating (Oxford: Clarendon Press, 1995), 23–62.

29. On these intellectual origins, see Anderson, "Structural Funds and the Social Dimension of EU Policy" in Leibfried and Pierson; Nanetti, "EU Cohesion and Territorial Restructuring in the Member States" in Hooghe, *Cohesion Policy and European Integration*; Behrens and Smyrl, "A Conflict of Rationalities."

30. Between 1975 and 1987, the ERDF's budget increased relatively slowly, attaining 3.311 million ecus in 1987, about 9% of the EC budget. See Commission, *The Regions of the Enlarged Community: Third Periodic Report on the Social and Economic Situation and Development of the Regions of the European Community* (Luxembourg: Office for Official Publications of the European Communities, 1987).

31. Hooghe and Keating, "Politics of European Union Regional Policy," 372.

32. On these changes, see Commission, *Regions of the Enlarged Community*; Armstrong, "Role and Evolution of European Community Regional Policy"; Marks, "Structural Policy in the European Community"; Hooghe and Keating, "The Politics of European Union Regional Policy"; Anderson, "Structural Funds and the Social Dimension of EU Policy."

creating a major countercyclical fiscal redistribution scheme at the Community level.[33] Under Delors, the Commission basically repudiated these budgetary demands. Delors enlisted the support of the member states for a set of measures that ensured Community-level financial discipline in exchange for more centralized control by Brussels of the disbursement of Community funds. Unlike its predecessors, the Delors Commission signaled no intention of turning the EU budget into an instrument of active social or macroeconomic (fiscal) policy. Delors gave the member states repeated assurances that the increase in budgetary expenditures was not the beginning of an all-out drive to expand the Community budget. This fiscally conservative orientation remained unchanged over time, despite the significant increases in structural expenditures.

Second, the new policy initiative was packaged as strictly complementary to the market-building project. In this regard, the so-called Padoa-Schioppa Report of 1987 was an important inspiration for the Commission's structural policy. Written under the auspices of the European Commission and by a committee chaired by Tommaso Padoa-Schioppa, an Italian public finance expert, this report laid out very clearly the intellectual rationale for increasing structural expenditures. Padoa-Schioppa, who had been director general for economic affairs at the European Commission and who would later go on to serve as a member of the European Central Bank's executive board, could not be suspected of advocating massively redistributive social policies. According to the Padoa-Schioppa Report, market integration should be "flanked" with policies that ensured both "structural adjustment" and a "fair" distribution of the efficiency gains from market integration.[34] Clearly, the underlying rationale for these *politiques d'accompagnement* was to smooth out the process of economic integration. "Structural adjustment"—increasingly a code word for market liberalization—was desirable but should be conducted with a concern for "fairness" so that "poor regions" would also benefit from the economic gains of the single market. In the same vein as the Padoa-Schioppa Report, the Delors Report was issued in 1989, the product of the famous Delors Committee on Economic and Monetary Union, of which Tommaso Padoa-Schioppa was an active member; it reiterated the dual rationale behind structural expenditures.[35] Thus conceived, structural expenditures should be aimed pri-

33. Commission, *The Role of Public Finances in the Process of European Integration* ("McDougall Report") (Brussels, 1977).

34. Tommaso Padoa-Schioppa, "After the Single European Act: Efficiency, Stability, and Equity" (September 1987), in his *The Road to Monetary Union in Europe* (Oxford: Clarendon Press, 1994).

35. The Delors Report on Economic and Monetary Union explicitly links the imperative of structural adjustment and flanking policies: "History suggests . . . that in the absence of countervailing policies, the overall impact on peripheral regions could be negative. . . . The economic and monetary union would have to encourage and guide structural adjustment which would help poor regions to catch up with the wealthier ones." See Commission, *Report on Economic and Monetary Union in the European Community* (Luxembourg: Office for Official Publications of the European Communities, 1989), 22.

marily at alleviating the hardships endured by regions that were not accustomed to the competitive pressures of an open and unified market. Yet their primary raison d'être was to facilitate the marketization process—not to limit its effects.

Third, the important 1988 reform of the Structural Funds mechanisms reflected the minimally interventionist outlook of the new policy. Eligibility criteria and stringent grant application procedures were established. Structural Funds were not designed to function as social entitlements and their raison d'être was productive rather than redistributive. They were, in many ways, a form of self-help for the regions. Funding was limited and, in principle, it is granted by Commission officials to eligible regions on the basis of the technically assessed merit of their regional development plans. In addition, many of the budgetary rules required that local and state actors participate in the budgetary effort. In many cases, these actors were supposed to match a certain level of Community funding. Rather than providing comprehensive funding to turnkey development projects, the spirit of EU structural policies was to distribute seed money and to introduce dynamic incentives for autonomous regional initiatives. In the ideal scenario, EU structural funding enabled regional-level actors, preferably local public authorities and small and medium enterprises (SMEs), to lead their region into the single market and onto a path of accelerated growth.

Whether many actors genuinely subscribed to the developmental spirit of the new policy and bought Delors' plea about the pressing need for exactly this kind of policy is another issue. Given the importance of fiscal conservatism, structural reforms, and self-help principles at the core of the new policy, the identification of structural policy as the embodiment of "regulated capitalism" can be pushed only so far. In fact, many moderate fiscal conservatives and free-marketeers supported the new policy. As for the Commission, it cautiously refrained from advocating the buildup of a new policy for its own sake. To present the upgrading of regional policy as an integral part of the already approved single market program was less hazardous than to go for an entirely new policy initiative. Above all, the idea of structural policy was seldom presented explicitly as a "social policy." The policy of "cohesion" at the EU level was intended to diminish the gap between the "core" and the "periphery" of the European Union, rather than between the "haves" and the "have-nots" among individual European citizens. The innovative design of structural policy meant that it did not carry a loaded ideological meaning or compete with national efforts, unlike other ventures such as the Commission's technological programs. As it attracted little controversy, structural policy came to be seen as a benign complement to the single market.

Forces vives: *The Constituency of Reform*

While the Commission's case for structural policy reassured both the Left and the Right, it was also helped by an increasingly active coalition of regional actors that became the Commission's allies. To the extent that the underlying thinking relied heavily on private sector initiative and on supply-side reforms, it was roughly consistent with the political preferences of fiscal conservatives. But the reform of the Structural Funds was not simply a way to streamline expenditures in such a way as to please contributing member states. It also claimed to be embedded in a coherent framework of developmental thinking that gave more importance to local initiatives and private-sector involvement. Here again, the new policy bore the stamp of Commission president Delors.[36] The thrust of the 1988 reform was to encourage the local-level mobilization of what Delors called the *forces vives* (dynamic forces). As analysts have often noted, "the Commission sought to move from infrastructure projects to human capital, productive investment and indigenous development."[37] Structural policy incorporated the latest thinking about how to conduct developmental policy in a decentralized fashion.

For political reasons, the reform naturally appealed to many locally elected officials who called for decentralization. In 1986–88, as the Community was swiftly passing legislation for the single market of 1992, many local officials feared that they were surreptitiously losing some of their prerogatives. In particular, many politicians in Germany's *Länder* felt that the German federal government was effectively colluding with Brussels to create a "superstate" that would snatch power away from the regional level. Delors became aware of this uneasiness and decided to preempt the risk of a political backlash.[38] As part of the 1988 Structural Fund reform package, the Commission came up with a framework that significantly empowered regional officials in the field of regional development policy. This was done in the name of the "subsidiarity" principle, according to which EU decisions must be taken not at the most centralized but at the most efficient level. On the one hand, the reform provided for a greater coordination of Structural Fund actions on the model of the Integrated Mediterranean Programmes. This both pleased the member states and reinforced the Commission's control over the funds. On the other hand, the Commission was not merely claiming more power for itself. It also introduced new principles such as "partnership" and strengthened previously established rules, especially the rule of "additionality." While partnership was meant to associate regional and state actors in the decision-making process, additionality was designed to ensure that EC funds would not simply replace preexisting national regional development spending.

These new principles were politically savvy. The indigenous nature of partnership programs enabled the Commission as well as local actors to claim a greater influence over their implementation than with the large infrastructure projects typically run by national officials.[39] The Commission promoted a concept of decentralized political power and transparent fiscal management that

36. Ross, *Jacques Delors and European Integration*, 243–44.

37. See Hooghe and Keating, "Politics of EU Regional Policy," 378.

38. Interview, European Commission, Brussels, May 20, 1997.

39. On this political dynamic, see Liesbet Hooghe's introduction to Hooghe, ed., *Cohesion Policy and Regional Integration*, 11.

was consistent with broad expectations about public policymaking in the mid-1980s. It was bound to rally a number of local actors, including some that were initially reticent at the prospect of increasingly centralized decision making in Brussels. For example, Commission and regional officials were increasingly able, as "partners," to form an alliance against state actors to ensure that Structural Fund aid was "additional" to regional development funds that came from the national budget, that is, they prevented state officials from using EC funds as a substitute for national funds.[40] Unlike some politicians in regions such as Catalonia, the Commission never intended to create a "Europe of regions" that would squeeze power away from the member states and toward the regions and Brussels.[41] This prospect was just as unrealistic as the prospect of a full-fledged social policy financed out of a federal budget. The upgrade of "social and economic cohesion" into a full-fledged Community objective served a clear political purpose—to enlist the support of regions behind the single market without alienating the member states. The 1988 reform of the Structural Funds supplied money and autonomy to the regions—this made them happy, but these new European bounties came with strings attached, which kept the member states happy. In this important but limited sense, the adoption of partnership and the participation of subnational as well as supranational authorities was a crucial political linchpin of the 1988 Structural Funds reform.

THE INSTITUTIONALIZATION OF STRUCTURAL POLICY

By the late 1980s, the precondition, the spirit, and the constituency of the reform were all in place—financial discipline, complementarity with the single market, and limited regional empowerment. The 1990s saw the institutionalization of the Structural Funds as an essential plank of what the European Union was about. The new policy was consolidated as its main actors engaged in codifying and implementing structural actions. Although the policy was increasingly under fire in the context of Europe-wide budgetary retrenchment in the 1990s, its three basic elements remain valid and the policy has been remarkably resilient in the face of difficulties.

Economic and Social Cohesion as Acquis Communautaire

At the Edinburgh summit in 1993, the member governments agreed on a budgetary package for the 1993–99 period.[42] The main provision of the Delors

40. See Christopher K. Ansell, Keith Darden, and Craig Parsons, "Dual Networks on European Regional Development Policy," *Journal of Common Market Studies* 36, no. 3 (September 1997): 347–75.

41. In his memoirs, Delors is crystal clear on this count: "We had no intention whatsoever to use the funds as a means to control the regions, or to become the unwilling auxiliaries of the regions' promotion at the expense of national interests." See Delors, *Mémoires*, 254.

42. On the details of the 1993 reform, see esp. Council of Ministers, "1993 Amendments to the 1989 Regulations," July 1993. On the 1999 reform, see Presidency Conclusions, Berlin European Council, March 24–25, 1999.

II package was another major increase in the Structural Funds budget, from 19.3 billion ecus in 1993 to a projected 27.4 billion ecus in 1999 (measured in 1993 prices). This budgetary increase was essentially meant to accommodate the entry of East German *Länder* into the European Union. For this reason, Germany once again agreed to act as paymaster of Europe. As a result, the 1999 Structural Funds budget was four times bigger than in the 1987 budget. This brought Structural Funds expenditures to over one-third of the Community's budget. The 1993 reform also created a new fund called the Cohesion Fund, in order to support environmental programs and transportation network development in countries in which GDP was less than 90 percent of the Community average (Ireland, Spain, Portugal, and Greece). A final objective of the reform was to further rationalize the Structural Fund decision-making process along the lines of the 1988 reform. And while the 1999 ("Agenda 2000") financial package for 2000–2006 did not fundamentally change the parameters of EU structural policy, it was very significant. First, the Agenda 2000 chapter on regional policy ensured that Structural Fund expenditures would be maintained above 30 billion euros, subject to the existing ceiling of 0.46 percent of the European Union's GDP. Second, it was decided to further concentrate these resources by reducing the number of objectives to three.[43]

In comparison with the 1988 overhaul of Structural Funds, the reforms of the 1990s appear relatively modest. Much of the content of the 1993 Delors II budgetary package goes back to the Maastricht treaty as it was negotiated in 1991. In particular, the treaty created the Cohesion Fund in addition to the three existing funds, thus satisfying a Spanish demand in exchange for its consent to the European Economic and Monetary Union.[44] Although this deal has been widely interpreted as a side payment to Spain, Delors and the Commission also supported it for more fundamental reasons. The Maastricht treaty confirmed the Single Act's elevation of "economic and social cohesion" to the status of an official Community objective. It contained a full title (Title XIV) and a special protocol (no. 28) on this subject. The primary rationale for this objective was to compensate for the unequal capacity of EU subnational regions to perform in the marketplace and in the context of an economic and monetary union. The Maastricht treaty also buttressed the regional dimension of the European Union through the creation of the Committee of Regions, a new consultative body.

Not only the 1993 package but even the 1999 budget package followed the track of the 1988 reform—their precondition, spirit, and constituency were exactly the same. The 1993 package and, especially, the 1999 package did not de-

---

43. The three new objectives are promotion of lagging regions with a GDP per capita of less than 75% of Community average (Objective 1, identical to the previous Objective 1); the economic conversion of regions in structural difficulties (Objective 2, combining the previous objectives 2 and 5b); and human resource development (Objective 3, which carries over the previous Objectives 3 and 4).

44. Moravcsik, *Choice for Europe*, 446–48.

part from the financial discipline requirement. The Structural Funds were increased in 1993, but this was presented as nothing more than the necessary counterpart of German reunification. A much-publicized 1993 Commission-sponsored report—with the telling title of *Stable Money, Sound Finances*—was squarely in line with the 1987 Padoa-Schioppa Report.[45] The budgetary framework of cohesion policy was presented as nothing more than the microeconomic counterpart to the macroeconomic stability goal of future EU monetary policy. The report also stated that the budget ceiling of 1.27 percent and the level of interregional transfers were sufficient.[46] Structural policy was not meant to address short-term financial crisis situations but long-term unequal economic development within EMU. In an integrated European market endowed with its own currency, the subnational regions are (relatively) sheltered from monetary fluctuations, but they are not sheltered from economic stagnation. According to the report, financial resources should be mobilized at the Community level to deal with this problem, and they should be allocated according to a set of predefined priorities. The report thus advocated an incentive-based developmental strategy, not a system of fiscal federalism geared for countercyclical macroeconomic management.

The report was fully in step with Delors' rejection of the Keynesian rationale of the 1970s as expressed in the 1977 McDougall Report. The report's rejection of a federalization of fiscal policy was predicated on the notion that the European Union's foremost priority was fiscal discipline rather than a unified fiscal policy. While the McDougall Report had advocated the creation of a countercyclical federal redistribution scheme, the background for *Stable Money, Sound Finances* was a "different economic theory" and "more political realism."[47] The emphasis in the 1990s on "stability" and "sound" financial management further reassured the member states that there was no danger of moving toward a federal budget, even after monetary unification. By keeping the budget focused on limited structural actions, the advocates of structural policy were able to say that they were doing something both coherent and different than "old-fashioned Keynesianism."[48] As in the late 1980s, the architects of structural policy in the 1990s were careful to distinguish it from other European programs that over time had become identified as purely distributive mechanisms, such as the common agricultural policy.[49] In sum, the Commis-

---

45. This report was published as a special issue of *European Economy*, no. 53 (1993).

46. The budget ceiling was later adjusted to 1.24% as part of a technical overhaul of European public finances.

47. Interview with a member of the drafting teams for both reports, Brussels, October 7, 1997.

48. Interviews with Commission officials at DG XVI (Regional Policy) and DG II (Economic and Financial Affairs), Brussels, September 16, 1997, and October 17, 1997.

49. According to an interview with a Commission official in charge of structural policy, achieving efficiency is a primary concern in implementing structural policy: "There is no common measure with the common agricultural policy. The CAP is inherently inefficient, bureaucratic, and messy." Brussels, October 17, 1997.

sion incorporated the member states' concern with budgetary orthodoxy into its own presentation of the EU budget.

It is difficult to disentangle economic beliefs from political calculations in the development of the Commission's concern with budgetary discipline. With the prospect of the future economic and monetary union, many actors were increasingly concerned about the lack of fiscal policy coordination. A form of fiscal federalism could have made economic sense from the standpoint of member states that were about to forego their national monetary autonomy. At the same time, Commission officials understood that, in a context of national budgetary restraint, it was difficult to argue in favor of this option. Therefore, they never seriously proposed turning structural policy into an active macroeconomic (fiscal) policy. Likewise, the early 1990s debate on the eurozone's future capacity to absorb "asymmetric shocks" did not lead to any decisive outcome. Although the Commission went so far as to propose a formal treaty procedure to deal with such problems, only a watered-down version of this provision was included in the Maastricht treaty.[50] One reason the Structural Funds were so liberally increased between 1987 and 1993 is that the Commission did not push for fiscal federalism and generally preferred to go along with the member states' preference for budgetary orthodoxy. Thus, in 1993 as in 1988 massive increases in structural expenditures did not foster any real controversy precisely because the prospect of fiscal federalism was explicitly downplayed.

The 1980s definition of structural actions as a flanking policy was also further codified and thus consolidated. The basic idea was to foster regional development on the supply side at the microeconomic level rather than to support demand through macroeconomic or nationwide infrastructure development. The label of "cohesion policy"—which explicitly referred to the treaty-sanctified objective of "economic and social cohesion" after 1986—was also used. Alternatively, the actors also spoke of an EU structural policy, in reference to the Structural Funds. The Commission was keen on preserving the ambiguous definition of its policy because it could win the support of different constituencies while avoiding the impression that the Commission was claiming power for itself. The label of "structural" is especially interesting because it reflects the reorientation of Community policies toward a supply-side approach that focused on economic "structures." The Commission was essentially marking its distance vis-à-vis more traditional social and demand-side policies that focused on distributional transfers or state-sponsored national infrastructure projects.

Throughout the 1990s, the European Commission also continued the rationalization undertaken by Delors, albeit unevenly. Greater coordination

50. Article 103a makes the granting of Community financial assistance to a member state in "severe difficulties caused by exceptional circumstances" subject to a unanimous decision of the Council of Ministers (except in the case of a natural disaster).

was introduced, especially with the creation of a new directorate-general within the Commission in charge of structural policy coordination.[51] This DG unsuccessfully competed with the more established Directorate General for Regional Policy (DG XVI). It was dismantled in 1992, but DG XVI was upgraded to the status of leading department (*chef de file*) in charge of coordinating Structural Funds programming within the Commission. The idea remained to have three Structural Funds but only one structural policy. Policy was formulated within a comprehensive, multiyear blueprint. The European Commission followed a trend in international development policies here, since the International Monetary Fund and the World Bank were adopting multiyear blueprints at about the same time. And the successive reforms of the Structural Funds each reasserted the need for a rational, priority-based approach that concentrated the most resources on the most needy areas and on core tasks of cohesion. According to the philosophy of structural policy, structural aid would be phased out as lagging regions caught up; it would then be reallocated to other regions facing economic difficulties. The 1999 reform continued to reflect this concern for a coherent framework, by reducing the number of objectives.

The rationalization of structural policy also began to affect areas that originally had little to do with regional policy. The effort to generalize and conceptualize the principles underlying structural policy has had an impact on EU actions in areas as diverse as agriculture and employment. Under agriculture commissioner Ray McSharry, the Directorate General for Agriculture was rechristened Directorate General for Agriculture and Rural Development. The Community was increasingly appropriating funds from the European Social Fund and the Agricultural Guarantee and Guidance Fund for policies that had a regional development focus.[52] Some even spoke of the birth of a "developmental ideology" within the Commission.[53] The common agricultural policy, the best-endowed but also the most criticized Community policy, began a slow conversion into a "rural development" policy. Likewise, structural policy's new emphasis on boosting employment levels is critical, since unemployment is a primary political concern of the European public. While the European Social Fund was always designed to address unemployment, the first attempt to systematically link EU structural policy to the problem of unemployment dates back to the Commission's 1993 white paper.[54] With the Amsterdam Treaty in

51. For a brief history of DG XXII, see Hooghe, "Building a Europe with the Regions: The Changing Role of the European Commission," in Hooghe, ed., *EU Cohesion Policy and Regional Integration.*

52. On this tendency of the European Social Fund, see Anderson, "Structural Funds and the Social Dimension of EC Policy."

53. See esp. Andy Smith, *L'Europe politique au miroir du local* (Paris: L'Harmattan, 1995), 65–68.

54. Commission, *Growth, Competitiveness, and Employment: The Challenges and Ways Forward into the 21st Century* (Luxembourg: Office for Official Publications of the European Communities, 1993).

1997, the EU member states called for an "employment strategy" and designated structural policy as an important element of this strategy. The upgrading of the fight against unemployment as one of the three new objectives ("human resource development" is now Objective 3) of the funds reflects this priority.

Yet perhaps the most concrete manifestation of the member states' long-term commitment to structural policy was the creation of the Instrument for Structural Policies for Pre-Accession (ISPA). This new EU instrument, which covered environment and transportation, was part of the 2000–2006 budgetary package. It was intended to assist in preparing for Europe's enlargement to include central and eastern Europe. Its resources served to cover some adjustment costs, especially in "aligning applicant countries on Community infrastructure standards."[55] It was an addition to existing EU development assistance programs to central and eastern European countries and was appropriated a budget of 7.28 billion euros per year—exactly twice the budget of the preaccession instrument for agriculture (3.64 billion).[56] This represents a change of budgetary priorities compared with the fifteen member states of the EU, since by the late 1990s the common agricultural policy still absorbed more EU funds than did structural policy. The change indicated a trend in spending priorities in an enlarged European Union. The ISPA clearly signaled to the new member states that structural funding, not agricultural assistance, was going to be the primary way the European Union would channel funds to them in the future.

EU-level developments in the 1990s confirmed the moderate regional political orientation of European integration. On the one hand, regions were empowered as they became partners of European officials in the integration process. Many of them established representation offices in Brussels, some of them quite lavish. Besides the Committee of Regions created by the Maastricht treaty as part of the institutional framework of the European Union, some member states also began to send regional elected officials as their representatives to the Council of Ministers. This was the case especially for Germany, where the *Länder* had greater powers than the federal government in some policy areas under EU jurisdiction. Europe's regions acquired more visibility and a higher political profile in Brussels throughout the 1990s. On the other hand, the role of the regions was mostly consultative. The Committee of Regions as such did not acquire any real say in EU decision making—even at the Convention on the Future of Europe that produced the draft of a European constitution. The statute of the Committee of Regions does not even require that regional representatives be locally elected politicians, which means that some of

---

55. Article 4 in Council Regulations No. 1267/1999 of June 21, 1999, establishing an Instrument for Structural Policies for Pre-Accession.

56. See Presidency Conclusions, Berlin European Council, March 24–25, 1999.

them could be regional representatives of the state. Regional empowerment thus remained modest and certainly did not signal any radical changeover from a Europe of states to a Europe of regions.

The 1990s and Beyond: Consolidation or Retrenchment?

After the upsurge of 1988 and 1993, the budget devoted to structural expenditures entered into a period of relative stagnation. Although the 1990s did not see a significant cutback of EU structural expenditures, some of the ambitious plans of the early 1990s were quietly shelved. For example, the white paper of 1993—Delors' final legacy—had envisioned the development of "trans-European networks" in such sectors as transportation, telecommunications, and energy. These ideas were not implemented to this day because the member states never appropriated sufficient funds. On the contrary, the overall impression was one of declining relevance of the EU budget. Capped at the level of 1.24 percent of the European Union's GDP, the EU budget remained small in comparison with even the most modest national or federal state budgets. This only seems to confirm the developmental nature of structural policy, but the open question is whether the EU budget can be sustained over the long term at its small yet not insignificant level.

Undoubtedly, the 2000–2006 budget marked a pause in the fiscal expansion of the European Union. It is very difficult to interpret the underlying trend without sufficient historical hindsight. The widely feared reversal of the 1980s and 1990s increases of structural policy expenses did not materialize. In an EU-wide context of fiscal discipline and amid widespread criticism of Community budgetary practices, the commitment of the member states to the operation of the Structural Funds was far from given at the outset.[57] This tends to refute the thesis that Structural Funds are merely one-shot side payments for market integration. The regions, the Commission, and net recipient member states have a built-in interest in continuing the policy. In a budget negotiation, not everything is up for grabs—contrary to a purely intergovernmental bargaining situation. If we consider national interests as the ultimate driver of structural policy, the surprise is not that structural expenditures have stagnated but that they are so resilient. Given the challenge of deteriorated national budgetary situations and EU enlargement, one could have expected a much more massive retrenchment.

The mood of EU budgetary politics has certainly become less congenial to preserving EU expenditures, even at relatively modest levels. Actual budgetary expenditures continue to hover around 1.1 percent of EU GDP, which is well below the ceiling of 1.24 percent. In 2004, the European Commission came up

---

57. In the run-up to the budget negotiations of 1999, many observers predicted a retrenchment of the Structural Funds. See, for example, Liesbet Hooghe, "EU Cohesion Policy and Competing Models of European Capitalism," and David Allen, "Cohesion and the Structural Funds," in Wallace and Wallace, eds., *Policy-Making in the European Union* (Oxford: Oxford University Press, 2000).

with a budget proposal for 2006–2013 that is only 1.14 percent of EU GDP—once again well below the cap. Still, the governments of the six biggest contributors to the EU (Germany, France, Britain, the Netherlands, Sweden, and Austria) expressed their discontent with the Commission's proposal and in December 2003 issued a letter in favor of a budget at 1 percent of EU GDP. The budget negotiations for 2006–13 were particularly bitter in the spring and again in the fall of 2005. The French and British governments were at loggerheads over French benefits from the CAP to the budget and Thatcher's hard-won "rebate" on Britain's contribution to the EU budget. In a context where member states were increasingly obsessed with the bottom line of net contributions, the EU capacity to preserve the coherence of its structural policy has been threatened by the intergovernmental tug-of-war over different budgetary lines.

Two main factors help explain the new mood of retrenchment. First, and most obviously, the economic climate changed in the 1990s. Economic slowdown and national-level fiscal consolidation throughout Europe under the Maastricht treaty made it more difficult to expand the EU budget. Confronted with diminishing tax returns and increasing budgetary expenditures, the member states had a very difficult time meeting the criteria for adopting the euro as their currency. Some analysts have cast the EU budgetary debate as an ideological battle between neoliberalism and regulated capitalism. Although this may have been part of the story, there were other arguably more critical factors at play. If they wanted their public deficits to be under 3 percent and public debt under 60 percent of national GDP, the member states had to save money. The national contribution to the EU budget was as good a place as any to save. In addition, it became difficult for the Commission to insist on a steady inflow of national funds while advocating lower public expenditures as part of the Stability and Growth Pact around the euro. Ironically, the EU budget was one of the first victims of the Commission's advocacy of fiscal discipline.

Second, the European Union's addition of ten new member states in central and eastern Europe raised new and potentially serious questions for the future of structural policy. Because GDP per capita was significantly lower in these new member states than in the rest of the European Union, all observers predicted a major reallocation of Structural Funds toward these countries. Thus, the very eligibility criteria that provided a rational basis for need-based action threatened to deprive the poor regions of rich countries of any EU funding. There was some wiggle room around this problem, since some of the criteria were specifically designed to favor certain member states or sectors. For example, the criteria of 90 percent of the average EU GDP established for national eligibility under the Cohesion Fund was created to accommodate the demand of some fast-growing member states (especially Spain) that could claim only a diminishing portion of the Structural Funds under the more demanding Objective 1 criterion (75% of EU GDP). Likewise, the "industrial decline" and "rural development" objective responded to requests from individual countries (especially France and Britain) that were confronted with these problems. But the main objective was to develop the poorest regions of Europe that had a GDP of less than 75 percent of the EU average. Thus, enlargement of the union meant that even the poorest regions within the existing fifteen member states would mechanically jump above that 75 percent average.

Related to the prospect of EU enlargement, there was a change of mood among the existing member states regarding the EU budget. In the 1990s, some of the largest contributors to the EU budget—especially Germany—became increasingly reluctant to act as paymasters of Europe. Once Germany was reunified, the political rationale of paying for European membership became more elusive. In the mid-1990s, there was a powerful movement against "excessive" German contributions to the EU. This movement was also fueled by widespread resentment in western Germany against the staggering cost of absorbing eastern Germany. Influential politicians in Germany—most notably Edmund Stoiber in Bavaria—ran on platforms that advocated the end of subsidies to poorer regions, both within Germany and at the EU level more generally. Meanwhile, the political economy of contributions to and receipts from the EU budget was changing. With decreasing agricultural expenditures and the shifting geographical focus of structural expenditures, some of the traditional supporters of the EU budget, like France, became net contributors to the EU budget. The CAP share of the EU budget has gone down from about 60 percent in 1985 to 45 percent in the 2000–2006 budget, and in 2007 France was set to no longer benefit from the Cohesion Fund. All other things being equal, this affected states' willingness to support the European Union's budgetary claims.[58] In sum, the looming enlargement drove some of the main national forces that accepted the 1980s push for Structural Funds to reconsider their tolerance for an increasing EU budget.

Whether these new factors will thwart the further institutionalization of structural policy remains an open question. If we consider EU structural policy as a developmental policy and not as an embryonic social policy, there are good reasons to think the policy has a future. In hard economic times, the EU budget has stagnated, but that is not surprising—and hard times do not last forever. When the EU experienced an upturn in its economic cycle in the late 1990s, actors started to unearth projects from the early 1990s such as the transEuropean networks. Of course, the enlargement to include eastern European countries is a more permanent phenomenon, and the 1980s political balance in favor of cohesion policy is no longer operating. But the new member states also form a substitute coalition backing cohesion policy. The EU made promises that existing policies such as the common agricultural policy and the Structural Funds would be progressively extended to the new member states. This was important because the candidate countries were required to make

58. Interview, French Ministry of Finance, July 5, 2004.

considerable efforts in adopting the *acquis communautaire*, that is, the enormous body of Community law that has been inserted in the national laws of all the member states. It will therefore be hard to renege on these promises.

More fundamentally, the developmental rationale behind structural policy remained valid and difficult to question. The European Union has a problem of unequal development that is not about to go away. This continues to threaten the integrity of the single market and the political cohesiveness of the European Union. It is difficult for the wealthiest member states to claim market access to their less developed neighbors and to ask them to follow European rules, while denying them any form of economic assistance. So the problem remains the same, and the remedies at hand are not plentiful. At the turn of the century, the common agricultural policy and the Structural Funds were the only instruments of financial action at the EU level. But Structural Funds are not a target of criticism by the European Union's trading partners—unlike the CAP system of export subsidies. Given the pressure of global trade negotiations and the diminishing political power of agricultural interests, the common agricultural policy is under siege. The French government fought hard against agriculture commissioner Franz Fischer's proposal to reform the CAP, which mandated a partial decoupling of agricultural production and agricultural subsidies. In October 2003, France reached a deal with Germany and then with other member states to preserve CAP spending until 2013 but to cap it at its current expenditure level, despite the arrival of new member states. The reform of the CAP has therefore considerably slowed down, but it has not stopped, and the European Parliament is further pushing in the direction of reform. The desire of the majority is still to reform the common agricultural policy and to shift a greater share of the Community budget away from straightforward agricultural subsidies and toward structural policy.

In contrast to the common agricultural policy, the idea that some form of regional policy is desirable is not fundamentally in doubt, even though many acknowledge the policy must be reformed.[59] As one observer put it, "EC regional policy has exhibited a remarkable capacity to innovate and evolve."[60] In the 1990s, the policy was subjected to periodic evaluations and audits, by both internal and external experts.[61] Some audits were very critical of Commission

59. Interviews with Commission officials, Brussels, September 27, 2005, and December 6, 2005.
60. Armstrong, "Role and Evolution of European Community Regional Policy," in Jones and Keating, eds., *European Union and the Regions*, 53.
61. Internal audits were mandated by the 1988 reform and were conducted in a thorough and self-critical way. See, for example, Commission, *Community Structural Policies: Assessment and Outlook*, COM (92) 84 final, March 18, 1992; Commission, *Competitiveness and Cohesion: Trends in the Regions* (Luxembourg: Office for Official Publications of the European Communities, 1994); Commission, *First Report on Economic and Social Cohesion* (Luxembourg: Office for Official Publications of the European Communities, 1996); Commission, *The Impact of Structural Policies on Economic and Social Cohesion in the Union, 1989–99* (Luxembourg: Office for Official Publications of the European Communities, 1997). External evaluations were entrusted to academic researchers, including the yearly publication *European Regional Incentives*, which carefully inventories the achievements and shortcomings of EU regional policy.

"mismanagement," but Commission officials bounced back with reform initiatives. Periodic frictions surfaced between Commission officials in charge of structural aid and those in charge of monitoring state aid to industry in the Directorate General for Competition.[62] But the disputes were resolved and did not fundamentally affect the Community's ability to intervene in regional development policies. As a result, the combination of competition and structural policy represents "a significant intervention by the EC in member state regional development policies."[63] In fact, the Commission's work toward the "cohesion" objective strengthened the legitimacy of its efforts to establish a competitive "level playing field."

Yet the Commission's handling of structural policy has always been the subject of intense criticism from the member states. The rather complex application and decision-making process was simplified in 1993 and 1999 in order to reduce the lag between project selection and implementation and to give a greater say to national and local actors.[64] Some analysts argue that this amounted to a partial renationalization of the Structural Funds, while others argue that the renationalization effort failed.[65] What these debates show is that the Commission has always had to fight hard to impose an "integrated" approach to structural policy, whereas member states are always tempted to focus on their individual bottom lines and to claim national budgetary control.[66] The Commission's desire to coordinate structural actions is inherently difficult to reconcile with the horse-trading among the member states eager to create and then secure particular budget lines and also to maximize their control over EU spending.

The most revealing debate came in 2003, when the Sapir Report spurred a controversy within the Commission on the effectiveness of the EU budget.[67] The report criticized structural policy for being weakly effective and insufficiently targeted toward poor regions. The question, as always, was to find the right balance between a meaningful policy and political considerations. Everyone in the Commission agreed that EU policies must be effective, but they must also garner sufficient political support to ensure the budgetary sustain-

62. See, for example, Douglas Yuill, Kevin Allen, John Bachtler, Keith Clement, and Fiona Wishlade, *European Regional Incentives, 1992–93* (London: Bowker-Saur, 1992), 93–96, and *European Regional Incentives, 1993–94* (London: Bowker-Saur, 1993), 80–104.

63. Armstrong, "Role and Evolution of European Community Regional Policy," 49.

64. The 1988 reform required a three-step submission and policy formulation process. The procedure was simplified in 1993 and the remaining two steps gave greater influence to state and local actors on funding decisions.

65. On "re-nationalization," see Pollack, "Regional Actors in Intergovernmental Play," and Ian Bache, *The Politics of European Union Regional Policy: Multilevel Governance or Flexible Gatekeeping?* (Sheffield: Sheffield Academic Press, 1998), 127–33. On the failure of renationalization, see Gary Marks, "Exploring and Explaining Variations in EU Cohesion Policy," 397, and Liesbet Hooghe, "Building Europe with the Regions," 99, in Hooghe, ed., *Cohesion Policy and European Integration.*

66. Interview, European Commission, September 27, 2005.

67. *An Agenda for a Growing Europe: Making the EU Economic System Deliver* (July 2003), report of the Independent High-Level Study Group (André Sapir, chairman) established by the president of the European Commission.

ability of EU policies over time. In the turn-of-the-century mood of budget retrenchment, it had become more difficult to square that circle. The report highlighted the risk that the EU budget and its effectiveness were continuing to erode. It recommended that the EU budget be overhauled to reestablish its effectiveness. But many feared that this would lead to a downsizing of European policy ambitions. In the end, the Commission chose to shelve it away to preserve the political constituency for the policy in the richer member states. Michel Barnier, the French commissioner for regional policy, fought hard to preserve a policy that would sprinkle money all over Europe. Barnier's logic was aimed at preserving a wide constituency for the Structural Funds in the member states. At the same time, the choice to spread limited EU resources over a vast number of regions did not coincide with the immediate needs of the poorest European regions, especially among the new member states. It also entailed a risk that structural policy as well as the entire EU budget would become even more vulnerable to criticisms framed in terms of policy effectiveness.

In this chapter I have argued that the success of cohesion policy was due to a near-universal acknowledgement that something must be done to alleviate regional disparities within an integrated market. The new policy thus took up the idea that the internal market should be a space for economic development. Its political foundation was always a two-way street. The developmental rationale worked because all parties—especially the beneficiaries and the contributors—agreed that the new policy would be neither too costly nor market distorting. Even for the most die-hard opponents of redistribution at the EU level, it was difficult to argue against such a minimalist "social dimension" of the European Union. Procedural and budgetary centralization was introduced in order to implement the new policy as evenly as possible over the entire space of the internal market. At the turn of the century, there was a visible backlash against EU financial handouts and controversial practices in structural policy. But even in the unfavorable context of enlargement and deficit reduction, the necessity of preserving adequate albeit modest levels of interregional transfers was rarely questioned by those who still agreed with the goal of an "ever closer union."

This argument challenges the scholarly insistence on the redistributive aspects of structural policy—under both its utilitarian and its institutionalist or constructivist versions. First, the increasing budgetary importance and the reform of the Structural Funds in the 1980s were not mere side payments in exchange for the single market and the euro. In hindsight, the policy was upgraded because the member states were *not* obsessed by narrow calculations of national economic interest. Although Spain and other prospective recipients of EU funds insistently pressed for new funds, actors that were initially most reluctant could have played hardball and ignored calls for new EU funding. Instead, the actors that favored fiscal conservatism and free-market economics came to terms with the upgrading of flanking policies. They increasingly saw these policies as useful in rebuffing calls for more wide-ranging social policies at the European level. Spain and other recipient countries were able to push the envelope, but only within reasonable bounds and with the Commission's support. Only when political integration started to lose steam in the late 1990s did the member states tend to return to narrow self-interested reasoning, thus fueling a backlash against existing policy.

Second, EU structural policy did not clearly embody an unambiguous choice in favor of "multilevel governance" and "regulated capitalism." Although the reforms of structural policy empowered Europe's regional actors, both the Commission and member states were jealous of their control over procedures and expenditures. Above all, the new policy can hardly be described as inherently antineoliberal, even though it does entail some redistribution. Structural policy was born when neoliberal ideas were particularly salient in Western Europe. The paradox is that the justifications for the new policy were designed in that prima facie unfavorable ideational context. The 1980s is widely remembered as a "lost decade for economic development." At the level of international institutions like the International Monetary Fund and the World Bank, the thinking and practice of development economics traversed a particularly severe intellectual crisis and diminishing resources. Meanwhile, at the European level, structural policy was successfully grafted onto the panoply of single market measures that the member states adopted after the white paper and the Single Act. Thus, the key to its success is not that European political leaders truly believed in "regulated capitalism"—although some probably did. More important, the advocates of the policy were careful never to identify it as an instrument of pure social redistribution.

What this case proves, then, is that the relationship between ideas and policy outcomes is not a simple causal relationship. Certain ideas have particular currency at certain times and they have effects because actors find them useful. Under constant pressure to explain their actions, political actors tend to adjust their justifications to whichever ideas are most dominant. On the face of it, the rise of market ideas in the 1980s and 1990s did not bode well for the growth of EU regional development policies. It could have resulted in the demise of Community development policies, as occurred on a global scale. But in Europe, the 1980s rejuvenation of market ideas spurred policymakers in the European Commission to modify the rationales for what they were doing. Whether the relevant actors believed in the new ideational framework is, strangely, almost irrelevant. The more important fact is that new ideas became part of the panoply of European developmental thinking. In the context of Europe's quiet revolution, the advocates of EU structural policy in the European Commission increasingly resorted to market ideas and recipes. In the end, the policy was considerably upgraded not despite but because its advocates quickly moved to incorporate new and potentially threatening ideas.

EIGHT

The Market as a Talisman

On January 1, 2002, a new currency, the euro, began to circulate within and across twelve member countries. As euro coins and bills entered the daily lives of millions of people, the European Union suddenly became a much more tangible reality than ever before. What the future holds for the euro and for the European Union remains to be seen, but the advent of the European Economic and Monetary Union can already be described as an enormous institutional transformation. Europe's new currency is run by the newly created European Central Bank. Like the Commission or the Court of Justice, the ECB is an independent supranational body. Monetary policy powers are now fully transferred to the European Union level, with the ECB in charge of implementing the same interest rates for all countries in the euro-zone. In addition, European member governments are subject to a legally binding framework of economic policy coordination and surveillance. Although they retain their national prerogatives over fiscal policy, they now exercise the power of taxing and spending within the framework of the Stability and Growth Pact.

This momentous institutional transformation presents a deep puzzle. The power to issue money is often described as an essential attribute of the state, so a central question is why the EU member governments decided to shed this attribute. The objective of forming a monetary union had been around since the 1950s, but attempts to achieve that goal had repeatedly failed up until the late 1980s. In recent scholarship, EMU is often interpreted as a logical response to global economic forces, as the apotheosis of a neoliberal ideational consensus, or as the outcome of Europe's historical acceleration toward unity with the fall of the Berlin wall. However, all three of these views miss the mark. European Economic and Monetary Union is the child of the single market agenda of the 1980s, but in a very specific and deeply political sense. Contrary to standard arguments, my strategic constructivist argument concerning the process and outcome of EMU is that progress toward monetary unification did not stem from economic necessity or from ideas. Rather, it resulted from the actions of pro-European actors that pursued EMU in the name of consolidating the single market. Starting with Jacques Delors in the late 1980s, a small group of European Commission officials began to develop a powerful political strategy that paved the way for EMU. Over time, the promoters of Europe successfully advocated economic and monetary union as a coherent solution to the problems created by financial globalization and the end of the cold war. In turn, the significance of that strategy derives precisely from the fact that monetary union was neither the uncontested solution to economic problems nor an easily obtainable response to German reunification.

More specifically, the EMU advocates' political strategy consistently took advantage of the talisman-like nature of the market. The market is not a single set of beliefs but a particularly versatile notion. The spectrum of attitudes about what the market entails is very broad. In the context of EMU, "the market" provided a convenient, albeit artificial, common ground between those with two very different sets of motivations. The promoters of Europe encouraged governments to envision the market as a new environment for the exercise of sovereignty. In view of the national reluctance to abdicate monetary powers, they worked to reframe actors' understandings of sovereignty in a global economy. At the same time, they hailed the market as a healthy source of discipline. By paying tribute to German-style orthodoxy, they gained the support of a core coalition of financial and monetary officials. Altogether, the EMU advocates' relentless invocation of market integration served both as a rationale and as a coalition-building device for monetary union.

Victory always has many fathers, and I will not try to decide between "supranational" as against "intergovernmental" actors. Of course, EMU would have never got off the ground without rallying the support of a sufficiently broad coalition. National governments made the decision and national central bankers accepted the logic of EMU. Commission officials nonetheless performed a pivotal role as recruiting agents for the cause of EMU. The coalition behind EMU was not a homogenous constituency with clearly articulated economic interests or ideas in common. Despite its remarkable heterogeneity, the pro-EMU coalition sustained the dynamic of EMU even at the most ominous moments. In this sense, the Commission's discovery and strategic utilization of "the market" as a talisman paved the way for EMU. Building on timely perceptions of the single market's desirable nature and shape, the promoters of Europe induced key actors to reframe their preferences in terms of EMU. Although they managed to engineer major institutional change, the method they chose to achieve this goal also illuminates the unresolved issues and debates about EMU.

EMU AS A LEAP OF FAITH

European Economic and Monetary Union, the main raison d'être of the Maastricht treaty, is obviously central to the European Union's quiet revolution. Because EMU went against the grain of deeply institutionalized interests and practices in the political economy of EU nation-states, it also represents a genuine puzzle. In a context of high uncertainty regarding the costs, benefits, and even the viability of EMU, the twelve initial members of the euro club took important and often painful measures to make that leap. Although the broad political and economic consequences of this formal institutional change remain elusive, its symbolic significance is obvious. Today, EMU is a key feature of the European Union's emerging model of political economy. In turn, the nature of that model cannot be understood without an examination of the process that led to EMU.

Most of the recent literature on EMU focuses on economic, ideational, and historical determinants of EMU. A first group of analysts focuses on the role of economic interests in driving EMU.[1] They note that rapid innovation in finance and telecommunications made governments' traditional ways of restraining cross-border capital movements increasingly obsolete. Because European currencies were also part of the European Monetary System that had quasi-fixed exchange rates, these movements increased the potential for currency crises. Thus, economic interests converged in favor of a transition to a full-fledged economic and monetary union. As one scholar put it, "the creation of the euro was the natural last step to be taken by European countries on the historical path toward powerful international financial markets, the decline of capital controls, and the demise of one-country Keynesian policies."[2] A second group of analysts stress instead the power of neoliberal ideas in the transition toward EMU.[3] Within the European Monetary System, most European monetary officials had progressively adopted the German central bank's anti-inflationary doctrine of monetary stability. The creation of the euro and of the European Central Bank further institutionalized those neoliberal ideas. Finally, a third group of observers stresses the importance of historically contingent developments, especially the fall of the Berlin wall.[4] They establish a

1. Jeffry Frieden, "Invested Interests: The Politics of National Economic Policies in a World of Global Finance," *International Organization* (Autumn 1991); Daniel Gros and Niels Thygesen, *European Monetary Integration* (London: Longman, 1992), chap. 10; John B. Goodman, *Monetary Sovereignty: The Politics of Central Banking in Western Europe* (Ithaca: Cornell University Press, 1992), chap. 6; Barry J. Eichengreen and Jeffry A. Frieden, *Forging an Integrated Europe* (Ann Arbor: University of Michigan Press, 1998); Andrew Moravcsik, *Choice for Europe*, chap. 6; Carles Boix, "Partisan Governments, the International Economy, and Macroeconomic Policies in Advanced Nations, 1960–1993," *World Politics* 53, no. 1 (October 2000).

2. See Boix, "Partisan Governments, the International Economy, and Macroeconomic Policies," 73.

3. Wayne Sandholtz, "Choosing Union: Monetary Politics and Maastricht," *International Organization* 47 (Winter 1993); McNamara, *The Currency of Ideas*; Kenneth Dyson and Kevin Featherstone, *The Road to Maastricht* (Oxford: Oxford University Press, 1999); Amy Verdun, "The Role of the Delors Committee in the Creation of EMU," *Journal of European Public Policy* 6, no. 2 (June 1999); Martin Marcussen, "The Dynamics of EMU Ideas," *Cooperation and Conflict* 34, no. 4 (December 1999): 383–411.

4. Geoffrey Garrett, "The Politics of Maastricht," *Economics and Politics* 5 (July 1993); David M. Andrews, "The Global Origins of the Maastricht Treaty on EMU," in *The State of the European Community*, vol. 2, ed. Alan W. Cafruny and Glenda G. Rosenthal (Boulder: Lynne Rienner, 1993); Michael J. Baun, "The Maastricht Treaty as High Politics: Germany, France, and European Integration," *Political Science Quarterly* 110, no. 4 (Winter 1995–96); McNamara, *Currency of Ideas*.

link between EMU and the process of German reunification. The sudden acceleration of German history boosted the prospects of EMU, then, because it raised the specter of German hegemony and induced the German government to reassert a national commitment to the integration of Europe.

These three dominant themes—the economic, ideational, and historical-institutional—traverse many accounts of the sudden reemergence of EMU on the European political agenda. To be sure, various elements of each dynamic were undeniably present, and they are not necessarily incompatible. Yet they each beg further questions concerning what counts as valid explanations of EMU. To be sure, there were economic incentives for moving toward the euro, but the huge costs and uncertainties of EMU make it difficult to say that EMU was fundamentally the result of a rigorous cost-benefit analysis.[5] It is also true that a certain degree of consensus emerged among European financial and monetary officials on the German model of central bank independence and "sound money" policy. Yet the resilience of that apparent consensus in the face of huge adversity was not a pure matter of beliefs. Finally, the choice of EMU was certainly one solution but a priori not the most obvious solution to the reemergence of the "German problem." The difficulties of monetary union between the two German states easily could have deterred German and European political leaders from entering the logic of Europe-wide monetary union. In sum, if the goal is to explain the birth of the euro, we must pay attention to how pro-EMU actors marshaled and articulated various material, cognitive, and historical rationales.

My central claim is that European Commission officials performed exactly that role. They self-consciously mobilized a political rationale and consolidated a political coalition to support EMU. At various points in the EMU process, key officials exercised political leadership and contributed to the emergence, within the Commission, of a political strategy for converting the tide of market interest and ideas and the sudden advent of German unification into political momentum for EMU. Thus, the European Commission can be seen as the pivotal actor that integrated the various and loosely related demand-side factors of monetary integration under the banner of market rationality, making it the "logical" next step after the 1992 initiative. That strategy was political not only because it conferred cohesiveness to the Commission's action on the issue of EMU but because it continuously attempted to reorganize the ways in which domestic-level actors conceived of their interests in terms of EMU, in order to appeal to the greatest number of constituents.

---

5. Academic economists are often more skeptical of the economic logic of EMU than many political scientists. As Benjamin J. Cohen puts it, narrow cost-benefit analysis "pays little attention to the value of political symbolism or insulation from foreign influence." And according to Paul De Grauwe, "Not a single monetary union in the past came about because of a recognition of the economic benefits of the union. In all cases the integration was driven by political objectives." See Benjamin J. Cohen, *The Geography of Money* (Ithaca: Cornell University Press, 1998), 63; Paul De Grauwe, "The Political Economy of Monetary Union in Europe," *World Economy* 16, no. 6 (November 1993): 656.

Political strategy played an important part in the drive toward EMU precisely because monetary union was neither the uncontested solution to economic problems nor an obvious or easily obtainable response to German reunification. Although both trends clearly called for something to be done, the choice of EMU was not a foregone conclusion. The process of monetary unification was beset by successive waves of Euro-optimism and Euro-pessimism, German reunification, national referenda, electoral campaigns, currency crises, and the ups and downs of the economic cycle. Economic and monetary union almost died around 1993, but it reemerged in 1995–96 riding a propitious economic recovery that eased the pain of the "convergence criteria." Neither interests nor ideas nor even history really explains the resilience of the EMU process during the decade of the 1990s. It took a very skillful political strategy to galvanize energies and to build the missing political momentum behind originally lukewarm demands for EMU. The political coalition in support of EMU gathered together a strange clique of national politicians, government officials in national central banks and finance ministries, and members of the business community. Because these actors did not share common interests and ideas, the EMU advocates' political strategy was crucial to keeping the coalition together.

The logic of the political strategy behind EMU emerged over time, partly though a process of trial and error. Retrospectively, two facets can be distinguished that illustrate the talisman-like nature of the market. For one thing, the advocates of EMU within and outside the Commission played what I call the politics of sovereignty. They contributed to and relied on the member governments' perception that the single market, and market globalization more generally, altered the meaning of sovereignty and that national interests would be best served through the pursuit of EMU. They praised the merits of EMU at a time when many state actors believed that their autonomy was threatened by the increasing internationalization of financial markets. To raise the stakes, Delors' Commission took steps to ensure the complete liberalization of capital movements across borders. Worries about a "loss of sovereignty" were especially widespread in the face of currency crises and rising fears of German dominance. In that context, the advocates of EMU worked behind the scenes to channel, rather than to buck, the trends of financial market integration and German unification, with the consistent intention of promoting EMU.

In addition, the promoters of Europe knew that, in order to achieve EMU, they needed to co-opt certain crucial constituents whose consent and support was indispensable for progress toward EMU. The other side of the coin, therefore, was the politics of orthodoxy. EMU advocates increasingly played up the theme of "sound money policies," promoting EMU as part of an orthodox economic policy agenda centered on the fight against inflation. Because it was important to have Germany on board at the outset, Commission officials adopted a very orthodox economic policy discourse. As the EMU process came increasingly under fire, the political necessities of sticking to the terms of the Maastricht treaty and of consolidating a core political constituency pushed the advocates of EMU even further in that direction. Presenting EMU in technical terms as complementary to the single market was part of a strategy to mobilize and consolidate the same proliberalization coalition that had most openly supported the single market and to help member governments overcome domestic obstacles to EMU.

All this is not to suggest that European Commission officials single-handedly did everything. Their activism on the monetary front was all the more surprising in that the Commission had very few prerogatives in this area. The Commission's role cannot be understood in isolation from intergovernmental monetary cooperation within the EMS and from the actions of key governments, especially France and Germany.[6] Heavyweight political actors that had much more say than the Commission over the precise development and nature of EMU became actively involved in favor of monetary union.[7] Without the support of these actors, EMU would have never gotten off the ground. But the actions of Commission officials were essential in continuously steering the relevant actors and especially the French-German couple—the "motor" of European integration—in a direction consistent with progress on the EMU front. From the mid-1980s through the completion of EMU, the Commission was the only institutional actor that consistently devised and pushed strategies specifically designed to achieve that outcome. If we want to explain the momentum behind EMU, as well as its timing and content, we need to examine the Commission's political strategy and its peculiar utilization of market rationality in the service of the EMU cause.

In stressing the Commission's political strategy in the advent of EMU, my goal in this chapter is twofold. The first goal is critical. The argument that it develops casts doubt on some of the assumptions that are widespread or at least implicit in much of the literature on EMU. Economic and monetary union was neither a pure product of high-political contingencies nor a result of incremental institutional evolution. It is not particularly useful to interpret EMU as the thoroughly unpredictable and contingent choice made by "pro-Europe" statesmen at the critical historical conjuncture of German reunification. The grand political choice of regional integration by heads of state in the pursuit of a common peace and prosperity has formed the basis of the European idea since the very beginning. Although this continues to be an important rationale for European integration in the eyes of many of its statesmen and citizens—particularly in Germany—the grand politics of European integration is insufficient

---

6. For an attempt to understand the Commission from a purely internal perspective, however, see Ross, *Delors and European Integration*, chaps. 3, 5, and 6.

7. For an argument that a transnational community of European central bankers had a preponderant influence in shaping the EMU initiative, see David R. Cameron, "Transnational Relations and the Development of European Economic and Monetary Union," in *Bringing Transnational Relations Back In*, by Thomas Risse-Kappen (Princeton: Princeton University Press, 1994). For an argument stressing the role of governmental actors, see Moravcsik, *Choice for Europe*, chap. 6.

to explain its concrete dynamic and shape.[8] At the same time, an analysis in terms of a purely continuous evolution can be equally misleading. It is tempting, retrospectively, to take that outcome for granted and to analyze it as the logical and rational consequence of existing structural or institutional trends. To be sure, the idea of EMU has always been around as a diffuse objective of the European Community. Furthermore, in the process of getting there, pro-EMU actors understandably tried to minimize the political importance of that change in order to achieve it more safely. Altogether, the assumption that EMU was simply a natural or optimal next step on the path toward European economic and political integration is quite common.[9] It is important to remember, however, that EMU represented at the outset an enormous political challenge and that the long march toward the euro was fraught with uncertainties. The failure of the first initiative in the 1970s is a testimony to the political difficulties involved in moving toward a common currency and monetary policy in an era of floating exchange rates and growing capital mobility. In fact, there was remarkably little continuity, substantive learning, or functional incrementalism involved in moving toward EMU. Thus, there are many good reasons to doubt whether the most recent EMU initiative can be explained entirely as the result of economic necessity and/or the expression of a spontaneous consensus or convergence on the "German model" since the 1980s.

My second goal in this chapter is constructive. The case of monetary union is particularly instructive because it shows that "the market" served as a talisman that actors used to advance objectives that were loosely connected with it and partly contradictory. These objectives went far beyond the strict outcome of what one would expect (ex ante) either from hard-nosed diplomatic bargaining between states or from the member states' adherence to a lofty community ethos. In the name of "the market" the Commission fanned a diffuse demand for a solution to the perceived problems of globalization and gave shape to this demand in such a way that EMU came to be perceived as necessary. The two main facets of the Commission's political strategy—the politics of sovereignty and the politics of orthodoxy—were two opposite sides of the same coin. Commission officials derived tremendous transformational power from the timely possibility of invoking an overarching market rationality that had recently acquired a remarkable salience in the worldviews of both national economic decision makers and central bankers. Many actors, especially those who identified with the political Left, viewed the market with resignation; typ-

8. The search for concrete causes of the success of European integration, beyond the generic geopolitical justification for political unity, was pioneered by Ernst B. Haas, *The Uniting of Europe: Political, Social, and Economic Forces* (Stanford: Stanford University Press, 1958).

9. This assumption is much more controversial among professional economists, however. While economists recognize that the combination of trade integration and flexible exchange rates increases the temptation of competitive devaluations and thus the risk of a protectionist backlash, a majority also think that, in principle, trade integration is quite compatible with flexible exchange rates. See esp. Barry Eichengreen, "A More Perfect Union? The Logic of Economic Integration," *Essays in International Finance*, no. 198 (1996).

ically, these actors continued to search for new ways of asserting a measure of political control. Meanwhile, others, especially those who for various reasons were on the side of fiscal conservatism, considered the market as a salutary source of financial discipline for governments; they were therefore not at all unhappy with a situation in which market actors increasingly possessed the power to impose their preferred policy outcomes. Since the market was perceived in such radically different ways by the concerned actors, it can hardly be considered as an object of ideational consensus. Yet it was crucially important as a talisman to justify monetary union, and, in the end, monetary union was sold to both constituencies in the name of "the market." Thus, the various market-based arguments waged by the proponents of EMU in Brussels allowed them to seduce the French, to co-opt the Germans, and to begin a process of redefinition of economic policymaking within a European-level framework.

In the remainder of this chapter I will examine the two facets of the Commission's political strategy and the ways in which they fed into what I call the politics of sovereignty and the politics of orthodoxy. Although both political dynamics have been apparent since the mid-1980s, each has been relatively more prominent than the other during certain key acts of the most recent EMU saga. Simply put, Commission officials played up the politics of sovereignty when their priority was to generate a demand for EMU among state actors; they increasingly relied on the politics of orthodoxy when the problem was to find a politically palatable recipe to achieve EMU in the face of political and economic adversity. Therefore, the development of the Commission's political strategy can be followed in a relatively linear chronological fashion. Consistent with the argument, however, I want to emphasize causal and strategic linkages rather than the well-known chronological development of EMU punctuated by European summits and the release of numerous reports and statistics.

THE POLITICS OF SOVEREIGNTY

Commission officials praised the merits of EMU at a time when many state actors were worried by the increasing fluidity of financial markets. While taking steps to further liberalize financial markets, they channeled these concerns into the paradoxical idea that national sovereignty could best be preserved by transferring it to the European level. They presented EMU as an improvement over a de facto situation in which most member states no longer controlled their own monetary policies. The underlying logic of the Commission's strategic reliance on the politics of sovereignty becomes apparent in the form of three basic figures: seducing the French; promoting EMU in parallel with the liberation of capital movements; and co-opting the Germans.

The Seduction of the French: Nurturing a Growing Political Demand for EMU

The EMU campaign of the 1980s was officially launched by a series of memorandums circulated among French, Italian, and German government ministers. In December 1987, French finance minister Edouard Balladur issued the first proposal to move toward a "common currency." This move was immediately followed by a memorandum from Italian finance minister Giuliano Amato and a response from German foreign minister Hans-Dietrich Genscher in January 1988. Yet the sudden proliferation of governmental initiatives in this area was not merely a result of political leaders' good will.[10] Delors, already a fervent supporter of the European Monetary System as French finance minister from 1981 to 1984, was perhaps the first Frenchman to be seduced by the idea of monetary union. He tried to sell the idea of economic and monetary union as soon as he became president of the European Commission in 1984.[11] Despite his persistent lobbying of European governments before and during the Single Act negotiations, Delors did not win the member states' clear consent to move toward monetary union. He did get agreement, however, that EMU should be reasserted as a "long-term" objective of the European Community and as a natural counterpart to the single market. As it turned out, the political linkage established between the idea of EMU and the single market agenda encountered increasing success in the following years.

The Commission's support of EMU intersected with a powerful surge of political interest in monetary integration by most members of the EMS exchange rate mechanism. Strangely, many accounts of the recent EMU process imply that the only real puzzle is why Germany would willingly give up its deutsche mark—perhaps because German officials, for political and bargaining purposes, often portrayed EMU as a pure act of Europeanist generosity. Germany's attachment to its national currency was particularly strong for historical identity reasons, but the same could be said of Germany's attachment to European integration—and in the past Germany's Europeanist commitments had always come first. When the first blueprint for EMU (the Werner Report) came out in the 1970s, the German government of Chancellor Willy Brandt was ready to sacrifice its national monetary autonomy on the European altar.[12] Despite serious misgivings by Bundesbank officials and the German public, Brandt chose to commit to the Community and to the enduring primacy of *Westpolitik* over the then nascent *Ostpolitik*. The continuity of German governmental support of EMU as a foreign policy objective is perhaps best represented in the actions and thinking of the long-time foreign minister, Hans-Dietrich Genscher.[13] Thus, by extending his benediction to EMU after much

10. A former close adviser to Jacques Delors said, "We knew we had to be ready, because this was going to happen sooner or later—and we were ready when it happened!" Interview with Commission official, Brussels, June 17, 1997.

11. See, for example, Delors' speech to the European Parliament on January 14, 1985.

12. See Loukas Tsoukalis, *The Politics and Economics of European Monetary Integration* (London: George Allen and Unwin, 1977), 106; Donald C. Kruse, *Monetary Integration in Western Europe* (London: Butterworth, 1980).

13. In his memoirs, Genscher traces the process of EMU back to the Genscher-Columbo initiative of 1981 and even to the prospects of European Union as outlined by European governments in the early 1970s. See Genscher, *Rebuilding a House Divided*, 140. (Translated from Genscher, *Erinnerungen* [1995]).

hesitation, Helmut Kohl was simply reiterating a long-held tenet of postwar German foreign policy, which was that any move toward greater European unity was desirable in principle.

A simple methodological point is necessary here. If variation in outcomes—that is, the success of EMU in the 1980s and 1990s as opposed to failure in the 1970s—is to be explained by variation in causes, then Kohl's magnanimity is not a particularly enlightening explanation of EMU. Although the German chancellor's steadfast personal commitment to the process certainly played an important role in the advent of EMU, his conceptualization of German national interest was not particularly new. Yet until the 1980s Germany's interest in European integration, including monetary integration, had never been sufficient to bring about EMU. Therefore, it is at least as useful to ponder France's strong push for EMU as it is to look at Germany's continued commitment to it. In contrast to Germany, the reasons for a growing French demand for EMU were new. And these reasons are not at all self-evident. It is often forgotten that, in the 1970s, the biggest hurdle to monetary unification was domestic political opposition and lack of governmental commitment in France. The national malaise vis-à-vis what many French citizens considered an unacceptable dilution of sovereignty was much more salient than the Germans' angst about the possible loss of the deutsche mark.[14] By the 1980s, this state of affairs had changed so radically that most analysts tend to take for granted the existence of a French national interest in moving toward EMU.

French interest in EMU must be understood in light of the early 1980s currency crises and the important political decision, made by Mitterrand in March 1983, to remain in the EMS.[15] Until that decision, French government officials typically envisioned the EMS as a convenient instrument for conducting anti-inflationary policies in the name of "Europe."[16] After March 1983, however, the EMS could no longer be seen as a mere tool in the service of broader government objectives. It was de facto institutionalized as a permanent feature of and constraint on French economic policymaking. The return to floating exchange rates was politically ruled out, because it was equated with macroeconomic mismanagement and the "illusion" that France could durably pursue a different course from its main trade partners in the EC. This evolution is perhaps best epitomized by the personal trajectory of Pierre Bérégovoy, a prominent member of the French government who originally favored the idea of opting out of the EMS and later became, as finance minister and

---

14. Stanley Hoffmann, in his 1974 article "Obstinate or Obsolete?" (reprinted in Hoffmann, *European Sisyphus*), identified the French concern for sovereignty as a permanent obstacle to monetary union.

15. On this well-known episode, see Philippe Bauchard, *La guerre des deux roses* (Paris: Grasset, 1986); Hall, *Governing the Economy*, esp. chap. 8; Pierre Favier and Michel Martin-Rolland, *La décennie Mitterrand*, vol. 1, *Les ruptures, 1981–1984* (Paris: Seuil, 1990), 438–64; Attali, *Verbatim I*, 252–409.

16. On the French motivations for creating the EMS, see Peter Ludlow, *The Making of the European Monetary System* (London: Butterworth, 1982), 199.

then prime minister, the staunchest advocate of a *franc fort* policy in the EMS.[17] Following the 1983 decision, France was therefore caught in the EMS predicament.

From a strictly economic standpoint, the EMS carried both costs and benefits for a country like France. In the context of the EMS and in an era of growing capital mobility, foregoing national monetary autonomy was one possible solution to a dilemma that is well-known to economists under the name of the Mundell-Fleming "inconsistent trinity" or the incompatibility between fixed exchange rates, freedom of capital movements, and national monetary policy autonomy. In other words, there was a coherent economic case in favor of "tying one's hands" to the German currency "anchor."[18] For example, Belgium, the Netherlands, and other small member states saw the supremacy of the deutsche mark as the inevitable ransom they would have to pay to gain monetary stability and economic interdependence. The Belgian-Dutch choice of preference ordering was both logically coherent and economically sustainable. Of course, "tying one's hands" to the deutsche mark within the EMS was a costly option, since the alignment of national monetary policy with Germany's policy could be inadequate when economic cycles were not synchronized. But it also presented some benefits, because it lowered inflationary pressures and the threat of currency speculation. Thus, Belgium and the Netherlands managed, over time, to credibly commit to a policy framework in which the "peg" to the German mark was a foremost macroeconomic priority. These two countries' currencies were able to graduate to the status of strong currencies, which, in combination with low inflation, made their economies more competitive.[19] France could have conceivably done the same thing by forcefully committing to a particular exchange rate vis-à-vis the German mark. After nearly a decade of relatively successful "competitive disinflation" in France, many French policymakers became convinced of the virtues of fixed exchange rates within the EMS.[20] Clearly, some French officials, especially in the French Ministry of Finance and the Bank of France, converted to the economic rationale that justified the operation of the EMS around its anchor, the deutsche mark.

17. For an insiders' account of Bérégovoy's evolution as guardian angel of Mitterrand's March 1983 choice, see Favier and Martin-Rolland, *La décennie Mitterrand*, 1:489; Favier and Martin-Rolland, *La décennie Mitterrand*, vol. 3, *Les défis, 1988–1991* (Paris: Seuil, 1996), 67. See also Jean-Claude Trichet, "Dix ans de désinflation compétitive en France," *Notes Bleues du Ministère des Finances* (October 16, 1992).

18. For the economic argument in favor of "tying one's hands," see Francesco Giavazzi and Marco Pagano, "The Advantage of Tying One's Hands: EMS Discipline and Central Bank Credibility," *European Economic Review* 32 (1988).

19. Interviews with Belgian and Dutch monetary officials, Brussels, July 1, 1997; Amsterdam, February 10, 1998.

20. Interviews with French, Belgian, and Dutch monetary officials, Brussels, July 1, 1997, and September 17, 1997; Amsterdam February 10, 1998. For an official retrospective justification of the French policy of "competitive disinflation," see Trichet, "Dix ans de désinflation compétitive en France." For the argument that France was converted to Germany's monetarist ideas, see McNamara, *Currency of Ideas.*

Yet from a *political* standpoint, the renunciation of monetary autonomy was difficult to sustain for the government of a country like France. For clear historical and electoral reasons, the preservation of national policy autonomy remained a potent symbol as well as a policy objective, especially in relation to Germany. The Bundesbank had become "the bank that ruled Europe." Ever since the creation of the EMS, successive French governments consistently tried to prevent France's transformation into a de facto deutsche mark zone.[21] The "asymmetry" of the EMS was not primarily an economic problem, however. As long at Germany's partners accepted the German dominance of the system, the EMS did not require institutional symmetry in order to function well. While small countries like Belgium and even the Netherlands could accept living in a deutsche mark zone, and even turn it to their advantage, the bigger states like France and Italy increasingly perceived it as an unacceptable subordination to German power. There was a contradiction at the heart of the French embrace of EMS discipline, because French officials never came to terms with the consequences of that choice, which was accepting Germany's superior position within the monetary system.[22]

In that context, key Commission officials became ardent advocates of EMU vis-à-vis elite actors, both in France and in other member states that were in a similar position in the EMS. By taking up the growing French and Italian criticism of the EMS and officially supporting EMU as a way to "rebalance" the EMS, Delors and his advisers regained the initiative on monetary reform.[23] Monetary union was increasingly presented as the "logical" counterpart to the single market and the logical next step toward European integration. While this message was buttressed by some economic cost-benefit analyses, it was far from universally accepted by economists.[24] Economists were divided as to

21. On the German opposition to the French idea of a European Monetary Fund, which was led by the Bundesbank, see Ludlow, *Making of the European Monetary System*, 196–205. On the evolution of the EMS and its "asymmetry," see Francesco Giavazzi, Stefano Micossi, and Marcus Miller, eds. *The European Monetary System* (Cambridge: Cambridge University Press, 1988); Francesco Giavazzi and Alberto Giovannini, *Limiting Exchange Rate Flexibility: The European Monetary System* (Cambridge: MIT Press, 1989), esp. chaps. 4–5; Gros and Thygesen, *European Monetary System*, chaps. 7–9.

22. Against McNamara's thesis of a Europe-wide conversion to monetarism, Moravcsik argues that France pursued EMU because the burden of adjustment within the EMS was too costly. But he does not acknowledge the benefits of "tying one's hand," which could counterbalance these costs, nor the contradiction between the French choice of *franc fort* and the resentment against German dominance. For these two reasons, the argument is extremely weak. See Moravcsik, *Choice for Europe*.

23. Delors started working on EMU with a very small team of advisers directly around himself and in the Directorate General for Economic Affairs (DG II) who de facto would increasingly define the Commission's official line on EMU. See Ross, *Delors and European Integration*, 81–84; Delors, *Mémoires*, 197, 339.

24. The Commission published a positive report on the costs and benefits of EMU: "One Market, One Money," *European Economy* 44 (October 1990). The broader community of professional and academic economists, however, remained divided on the desirability of EMU from a strictly economic standpoint. See Barry Eichengreen, "Should the Maastricht Treaty Be Saved?" *Princeton Studies in International Finance* 74 (December 1992).

whether the balance between the costs and benefits of EMU was positive or negative. This does not mean that EMU was (or is) "irrational," but it does make it difficult to argue, in a causal sense, that the primary motivations behind EMU were economic. The Commission's primary goal was to surmount the political contradictions of EMS membership. The franc and the lira remained periodically the object of market tensions, because the depth of French and Italian commitment to the EMS was in doubt. After the currency crisis of January 1987, in which France was forced to devalue the franc and raise interest rates, despite its unflinching commitment to the *franc fort* policy, the demand for a reform of the EMS became more pressing.[25] At that point, of course, French political support of EMU partly expressed a generic and somewhat idealistic choice in favor of "European union" as a remedy to the failures of policy coordination.[26] Yet, there also existed clear reasons for favoring monetary integration as the best way to achieve regional integration. Many in the French political elite were seduced by the notion that EMU would reinvigorate, rather than dilute, French "sovereignty."[27] As national monetary policies were de facto aligned with Germany's, Prime Minister Thatcher's fierce critique of EMU in the name of "sovereignty" was quite atypical.[28] The anti-EMU position never took hold in the political establishments of those member states that were strongly committed to the EMS, except, of course, Germany.

The Strategy of "Parallelism": Jointly Promoting the EMS and Capital Liberalization

Although Commission officials capitalized on French and Italian desires to recover some of their lost sovereignty, this very prospect could easily alienate traditional German sympathies to the cause of European economic integration. Thus, something had to be done to reassure the Germans that "strengthening the EMS" was not a thinly veiled way of shifting the burden of adjustment onto strong-currency countries. Commission officials effectively dodged this problem by advocating a transition to EMU in parallel with capital liberalization. On the one hand, they became ever more vocal public advocates of EMU in

25. French finance minister Edouard Balladur authored an article titled "EMS: Advance or Face Retreat" in the *Financial Times*, June 17, 1987. By 1987–88, mainstream French policy circles were actively discussing the EMS, and monetary reform was one of the issues at stake in the 1988 electoral campaign. See "Barre, Balladur, Bérégovoy: Les projets des '3 B'," *La Tribune de l'Expansion*, April 22, 1988.

26. EMU was then modestly envisioned as a movement toward permanently fixed exchange rates, some degree of pooling of national monetary reserves, and increased reliance on the ecu. See Eric Aeschimann and Pascal Riché, *La guerre de sept ans* (Paris: Fayard, 1997), 86–93.

27. Note that this was not a prominent motivation in the 1970s, according to Tsoukalis: "From the French point of view, monetary integration used to be desirable only as a means of promoting EEC unity in external relations. In this respect, French politicians were torn between the objective of having a common external monetary policy and their fear of loss of national sovereignty" (*Politics of Economic and Monetary Integration*, 80).

28. For a critical assessment of Thatcher's position on EMU, see Ian Harden, "Sovereignty and the Eurofed," *Political Quarterly* 61, no. 4 (1990).

European policy circles, even though there was no legal basis for Commission initiatives on the monetary front. On the other hand, Commission officials used their formal prerogatives in financial market integration to set capital liberalization firmly on the EC agenda as early as 1986. The strategy of "parallelism" is an old European Community recipe for engineering integrative spillovers.[29] With their campaign in favor of EMU, however, Delors and his team carried this art to a wholly unprecedented high-political dimension. It soon became clear that the EMU objective raised the ante far beyond the neofunctionalist problem of "upgrading common interests." This time, the game of European integration entailed enormous political controversy, as prominent national actors stood to lose some of their power and prerogatives.

By simultaneously promoting the idea of strengthening the EMS and the agenda of financial liberalization, Commission officials were engaging in a risky enterprise. Because the liberalization of capital movements opened the way for unfettered currency speculation, the EMS system of quasi-fixed exchange rates could easily become its victim. Commission officials, especially within the Directorate General for Economic Affairs (DG II), were acutely aware of the economic incompatibility between fixed exchange rates, freedom of capital movements, and national policy autonomy.[30] In 1987, a Commission-sponsored group of experts under the chairmanship of former director-general Padoa-Schioppa published a report on the EMS, recommending a move toward monetary union as a way to solve the economic problem by transferring monetary policy to the Community level.[31] Although the report spelled out a coherent economic rationale to move forward on EMU, the political problem remained that there were few tangible economic pressures or interests that unambiguously pushed in the direction of EMU. Even though there were good reasons to believe that the single market's survival depended politically on a regime of exchange rate stability, such reasons were not sufficiently compelling to spur enthusiasm for EMU.[32] The political decision to move to monetary union still required a genuine leap of faith.

However risky and potentially contradictory the strategy of parallelism may have appeared in economic terms, it made a lot of sense from a political per-

---

29. See Haas, *The Uniting of Europe*; Coombes, *Politics and Bureaucracy in the European Community*.

30. This was one of their central arguments for strengthening the EMS. According to one Commission official, DG II chose to rechristen Mundell's "unholy trinity" as the "inconsistent quartet" to emphasize the condition of free trade—which was implicit in the traditional formulation—and thus the link with the single market. Interview, Brussels, July 2, 1997. See also Tommaso Padoa-Schioppa, "European Capital Markets between Liberalization and Restrictions" (1982), reprinted in Padoa-Schioppa, *Money, Economic Policy and Europe*, and "The EMS Is Not Enough: The Need for Monetary Union" (1987), reprinted in Padoa-Schioppa, *Road to Monetary Union in Europe*.

31. A useful summary of that report, "After the Single European Act: Efficiency, Stability, and Equity" (1987), can be found in Padoa-Schioppa, *Road to Monetary Union in Europe*.

32. The spillover dynamic of market integration in the 1970s "did not succeed in preventing internal crises, nor did it really take place when it was most needed [i.e., in currency crises]" (Tsoukalis, *Politics of Economic and Monetary Integration*, 79).

spective. Delors apparently calculated that the odds of a breakdown of the EMS were sufficiently small at that time to justify a bold initiative in favor of liberalizing capital movements.[33] Meanwhile, the Commission's push for European directives in the area of capital liberalization removed some of the most important political obstacles to EMU. A durable bone of contention between the French and the Germans about EMU was the French reluctance to forego the dirigiste financial policies, traditionally used in industrial policy and for rewarding various interest groups. German monetary officials saw these policies as deeply flawed because of their inflationary potential. Since the early 1980s, German (and Dutch) central bank and financial officials had made it clear that they would be prepared to consider any further strengthening of the EMS only if other countries liberalized capital movements and submitted their economic policies to the test of "market discipline."[34] Even after the French financial system was dramatically liberalized in 1984–86, Germany continued to suspect that France's interest in strengthening the EMS was motivated by a desire to shun the cost of expansionary macroeconomic policies by "exporting" French inflation to Germany. Thus, by standing behind the German-Dutch demand to liberalize capital movements, Commission officials were not only balancing their support of France's demand for a more "symmetric" EMS, they were effectively countering both the dirigiste nostalgia of French politicians and the German apprehensions regarding their partners' "inflationary" temptations.

On the one hand, the removal of capital controls meant that France's monetary policy autonomy appeared more illusory than ever. It massively reinforced an already strong desire to somehow compensate for a perceived loss of sovereignty vis-à-vis market actors and the German central bank. Of course, it was always possible for politicians to argue against EMU in the name of preserving French sovereignty, but this argument rang increasingly hollow. In this respect, the objective situation of French subordination to German monetary policy was an important difference from the 1970s. On the other hand, the removal of controls made it increasingly hard for Germany to resist the pressure of its neighbors and the Commission in favor of EMS reform. German government officials saw the EMS as a haven of relative stability in a highly volatile international monetary environment and in the context of recurring conflicts between German and U.S. priorities.[35] Although German

33. According to Age Bakker, Delors gave two reasons for full capital liberalization at a May 1986 meeting of the EC Monetary Committee: the existence of the 1992 objective and that greater freedom of capital would be necessary to make monetary cooperation more effective (see chap. 6 in Bakker, *Liberalization of Capital Movements*). Thus, Delors apparently gambled that nobody would dare to question the value of these two sacred cows.

34. Bakker, *Liberalization of Capital Movements*.

35. On the international economic context, see chap. 4 in I. M. Destler and C. Randall Henning, *Dollar Politics: Exchange Rate Policymaking in the United States* (Washington, D.C.: Institute for International Economics, 1989); Henning, *Currencies and Politics in the United States, Germany, and Japan* (Washington, D.C.: Institute for International Economics, 1994), 203–9; Henning, "Systemic Conflict and Regional Monetary Integration: The Case of Europe," *International Organization* 52, no. 3 (1998).

government officials did not have an obvious interest in revamping the EMS, they continued to express a very clear preference for preserving it as an instrument of external stability for the German mark in relation to the currencies of its most important trade partners.[36] Whether this preference corresponded to the "true" economic interests of Germany is debatable, but that view was very consistently and strongly held by the German elite, especially in the run-up to EC 1992.[37] That outside Germany the EMS was increasingly seen as the embodiment of German monetary hegemony was a genuine cause for concern, since it carried the threat that other member states would eventually defect from the EMS.[38] If the EMS collapsed, the German mark might have become, as in the 1970s, the object of massive speculation, with potentially negative consequences for the growth of the German economy. Thus, German government officials believed they had a lot at stake in the preservation of the EMS in some form. Only later was this point obscured by the portrayal of EMU as an act of pure Europeanism and a concession by Germany— a convenient way to both package EMU to the German people and to maximize bargaining power.

Delors' promotion of the liberalization of capital movements as part of the single market agenda precipitated a reassessment of the institutional framework of monetary policy and initiated a sequence of events that eventually led to EMU.[39] The EMU drive of the late 1980s can be traced directly back to the Commission's strategy of seducing the French into accepting EMU while systematically removing the only remaining trapping of national sovereignty, discretionary capital controls. In this sense, EMU did not stem from a French process of substantive learning and paradigmatic conversion to the antiinflationary benefits of the "German model" of monetary policy.[40] Nor, in fact,

36. This was an important motivation behind Genscher's support for relaunching the EMU project, as he explained it in a speech to the European Parliament in January 1988. And even Finance Minister Gerhard Stoltenberg, despite his outspoken skepticism about the short-term prospects of EMU, considered that the EMS was valuable for Germany (see Stoltenberg, *Wendepunkte*, 327–29). On the German discussions of EMU in early 1988, see Wilhelm Schönfelder and Elke Thiel, *Ein Markt—Ein Währung* (Baden-Baden: Nomos Verlagsgesellschaft, 1994), 27–38.

37. In *Currencies and Politics*, Henning argues that the German preference for exchange rate stability reflects private preferences that stem from particularly strong ties between bank and industry (see esp. chaps. 2 and 5). See also Carsten Hefeker, "Germany and Monetary Union," a paper prepared for the conference on "The Political Economy of European Integration," Bremen, August 4–16, 1996.

38. For example, French prime minister Jacques Chirac declared that unless the EMS were strengthened, "it would be better to abolish it." See "M. Chirac annonce qu'il prendra des initiatives dans le domaine monétaire," *Le Monde*, January 9, 1988.

39. Delors apparently did not fully realize the success of parallelism until the spring of 1988. He recalls that, at the time, he was reluctant to push too strongly for EMU, because he thought it was dangerous to overload an already crowded EC agenda (Delors, *L'unité d'un homme*, 229). According to Charles Grant, Padoa-Schioppa convinced Delors that the time had come to again champion the idea of EMU (*Delors*, 118–19).

40. On the emergence of a certain "neo-liberal policy consensus" on monetary policy, see esp. McNamara, *Currency of Ideas*, chap. 6. For a related interpretation of EMU based on the concept of "epistemic community," see Verdun, "Role of the Delors Committee in the Creation of EMU."

did it reflect an unquestioned and unanimous consensus even among German politicians.[41]

After all, the French government never positively wanted to conduct inflationary policies. The periodic emergence of inflation in France was an unintended consequence of the government's reliance on loose economic policies in order to defuse political conflicts about the public allocation of economic resources.[42] The main difference between France and Germany was not simply a difference of policy paradigms, between a growth-oriented and a stability-oriented national economic culture. At least as important was the fact that, until capital liberalization, the only limit to the autonomy of the French government's economic policy was the EMS, whereas the German government had to put up with an independent and politically powerful central bank. Of course, many French policymakers, including Delors, clearly saw the EMS as a valuable way to avoid the inflationary spiral of an easy-money policy. Yet there is little evidence that the traditional French political preference for growth and social order over monetary stability has been fundamentally changed.[43] In Germany, by contrast, there was less room for the government to single-handedly pursue growth-oriented policies, because the independent Bundesbank would slam on the monetary brakes at the first worrying signs of inflation.

Whatever bridging occurred between French and German macroeconomic conceptions was the result, rather than the cause, of a progressive transition from a politically controlled monetary policy apparatus toward a regime of free capital movements and, later, central bank independence in combination with EMS membership.

Delors' Gamble: Co-opting the Bundesbank

In June 1988, a few days after the stumbling block of capital liberalization was finally eliminated by the EC Capital Movements Directive, Chancellor Kohl decided to move on the EMU front. The European Council at Hanover decided to commission a feasibility study of EMU from a committee of central bankers and experts chaired by Delors. After Hanover—and thus well before German

41. According to Peter Katzenstein, "The Bundesbank's pursuit of monetary stability has been the most constant element in West Germany's economic policy to the chagrin of the Christian Democrats and the Social Democrats alike" (*Politics and Policy in West Germany* [Philadelphia: Temple University Press, 1987], 97). See also Fritz W. Scharpf's account of the conflict between Chancellor Helmut Schmidt and the Bundesbank in the early 1980s: *Crisis and Choice in European Social Democracy* (Ithaca: Cornell University Press, 1991 [1987]), 150–57.

42. This is very well explained in Shonfield, *Modern Capitalism*, 133.

43. An assessment by two French economists of France's deflationary policy during the 1980s and 1990s suggests that the "implicit framework [of policymakers] was a neo-Keynesian model under fixed exchange rates, in which disinflation automatically translates into real exchange rate depreciation, gains in market shares, and growth." See Christian de Boissieu and Jean Pisani-Ferry, "The Political Economy of French Economic Policy in the Perspective of EMU," in *Forging an Integrated Europe*, ed. Barry Eichengreen and Jeffry Frieden (Ann Arbor: University of Michigan Press, 1998), 66–67.

reunification—Delors was increasingly able to count on Kohl's support.[44] Even at that point, however, EMU was not yet a done deal. Delors reasoned that enhancing the political credibility of his pet project would require a seal of approval from national central bankers.[45] Such formal endorsement was all the more necessary because EMU was bound to stir controversy in central banking circles, as it threatened to deprive the national central banks of their most important prerogatives.

After nine months of deliberations, the Delors Committee came up with a sweeping report, unanimously approved by its members, which concluded not only that EMU was possible but that the right way to proceed toward this goal was to move decisively toward a single currency for Europe. In retrospect, the most remarkable achievement of the Delors Committee was to extract the consent of the most serious potential opponent to EMU among national central bankers, namely German Bundesbank president Karl Otto Pöhl. There was no a priori guarantee that this would happen, yet the political momentum behind European integration in 1988–89 was such that no single member of the committee openly questioned the objective of EMU.[46] The Bundesbank had initially agreed to participate in the committee for fear of being presented with a political fait accompli, like the introduction of the EMS in the not-so-distant past.[47] This time, German central bank officials clearly hoped to influence the terms of whatever compromise was achieved on EMU. The other members of the Delors Committee, including Delors himself, quickly understood that EMU would have to proceed on terms that were roughly agreeable to the German central bank.[48] This political reality later became clear after the French government issued a proposal to promote the role of the ecu as a "common currency" before moving toward the single currency, attempting to bridge the gap between the idea of a single currency and a (half-hearted) British proposal to develop a "parallel" currency.[49] The German central bank then bluntly rejected the British proposal, so that the schema put forward by the Delors Report remained the only option on the table.

Although Pöhl's signature was probably a sine qua non for EMU to pro-

44. At the time of the Hanover summit, the *Financial Times* reported Kohl's belief that "some form of monetary union is 90 percent certain by the end of the century": "Beaming Kohl Glories in Summit Euphoria," *Financial Times*, June 29, 1988. Kohl did not openly champion EMU until late 1989, however, and it is difficult to know exactly what he was thinking on this subject in 1988–89. He apparently adopted the role of referee in the German cabinet's internal debate between his pro-EMU foreign minister Hans-Dietrich Genscher and his more skeptical finance minister Gerhard Stoltenberg.

45. Delors, *L'unité d'un homme*, 238.

46. Interview with member of the Delors Committee, Paris, October 10, 1997.

47. On the well-publicized opposition of the German central bank to the creation of the EMS, see Ludlow, *Making of the European Monetary System.*

48. The press echoed the strong German flavor of the Report: "One committee member said the document contained 'a lot of German thinking.' Another said Mr Pöhl 'had good reason to look happy.' " ("Bankers Agree on EC Route to Unity," *Financial Times*, April 13, 1989). One committee member was reported as saying that "Karl Otto got everything he wanted" (*Institutional Investor*, May 1989).

49. On the ill-fated British proposal, see Colchester and Buchan, *Europe Relaunched*, 174.

ceed, it also triggered a political process that largely escaped the control of the Bundesbank. The publication of the report was a breakthrough that opened the road for the Maastricht treaty. In substance, the Delors Report went far beyond the more incrementalist approach envisioned by most EMU advocates. The Delors Report jumped well ahead of the game by definitively shifting the object of the debate from a "common currency" to a "single currency." It stated that, once the political decision to move toward EMU was made, the transition process should be irreversible and proceed in three successive phases. It recommended that the management of the newly created currency be entrusted to an independent central bank at the European level—a principle that understandably was palatable to a committee primarily made up of central bankers.[50] Finally, by specifying that "the decision to enter upon the first stage should be a decision to embark on the entire process," the report implied that EMU was indeed possible in the near future, since by definition the first phase of EMU could start as soon as the Capital Movements Directive became effective. On the whole, the Delors Report built a high degree of automaticity into the EMU process. German central bank officials apparently underestimated the powerful logic of France's or Italy's desire for sovereignty and their unwillingness to live under the current conditions.[51] When the European Council decided to move forward on the basis of the Delors Report, they could hardly conduct a frontal attack on a plan they had essentially preapproved.

Of course, EMU was not sealed as a political deal until the Maastricht treaty was signed; and, even after Maastricht, the future of EMU remained uncertain. The fluctuating fortunes of EMU were influenced by the geopolitical and economic context. The sudden advent of German reunification provided a useful public rationale for Kohl's very strong personal investment in favor of EMU.[52] Concurrently, French and Italian pressures on Germany to allow the steady progress of EMU became extremely pressing only after November 1989.[53] Yet

---

50. David Cameron argues that many provisions of the Delors Report closely reflect the collective preferences of the central bankers who made up the majority of the Delors Committee (Cameron, "Transnational Relations").

51. Following the publication of the report, Pöhl tried to minimize its impact by saying that "we can live very well with the status quo." In a later interview with Charles Grant, Pöhl expressed regrets about his decision to participate in a committee where he "couldn't defend German interests" (*Delors*, 121). David Marsh gives the following overall appraisal of the Bundesbank's attitude toward EMU: "Up until the last moment, the Bundesbank did not realize that, to release themselves from the grip of the D-mark, the French and the Italians were ready to promise almost anything" (*The Bundesbank: The Bank That Rules Europe* [London: William Heinemann, 1992], 215).

52. Delors' unmitigated support of German reunification—in contrast to Mitterrand's and especially Thatcher's colder reception of the event—apparently contributed to reinvigorating Kohl's support of EMU. A senior adviser to Kohl reports that Delors was the first foreign political leader to be informed of the chancellor's decision to push for immediate German reunification; Kohl also assured Delors that German reunification would occur within the framework of the European Community (Horst Teltschik, *329 Tage: Innenansichten der Einigung* [Berlin: Goldmann Verlag, 1991], 144). On the relationship between Kohl and Delors, see also Grant, *Delors*, 139–42.

53. Increasingly, Mitterrand viewed EMU as a critical way to "anchor" Germany to the European Community (Pierre Favier and Michel Martin-Rolland, *La décennie Mitterrand*, vol. 3, *Les défis, 1988–1991* [Paris: Seuil, 1996], 201–5, 243–46).

it is worth stressing that the Delors Report was formally approved by the European Council in Madrid as early as June 1989, that is, well before German unity was remotely in sight.[54] In addition, the "German problem" and the French fear of Germany's drifting eastward were not particularly new and do not in themselves explain the choice of monetary integration as a focus of French pressure. Finally, it is often forgotten that German reunification almost derailed the EMU process. To offset the inflationary risks of East Germany's consumer boom, the German Bundesbank began a policy of high interest rates, with a base rate that went as high as 13 percent, but with little regard for the consequences to Germany's EMS partners. In this sense, Germany's reunification made EMU more difficult by driving a wedge between the economic policy cycles of Germany and the rest of Europe.

It would be risky to make the counterfactual claim that EMU would have come about even in the absence of German reunification. But the political pressure in favor of EMU clearly predated and outlived the advent of German reunification. The true political root of EMU in the 1980s was the demand for more "symmetry" in the EMS, in the context of the 1992 program and capital liberalization. The Delors Committee was established to deal with that problem. And while the Delors Report was followed by many more reports and high-level meetings up until December 1991, it was the blueprint for the EMU provisions in the Maastricht treaty. Fundamentally, the Maastricht treaty only added three elements to the prior political endorsement of the Delors Report—the formal decision to move forward, the start dates of EMU's second and third phases, and the convergence criteria. The Delors Report triggered a dynamic of institutional reform that propelled EMU through to its completion.

THE POLITICS OF ORTHODOXY

Although the pursuit of sovereignty was an important motivation for state actors in the 1980s, another set of considerations emerged in the run-up to the Maastricht treaty and during the transition process to EMU throughout the 1990s. During that period, the Commission's EMU strategy increasingly rested on the politics of orthodoxy, that is, the political promotion of an orthodox economic policy agenda centered on the fight against monetary inflation. From the Commission's perspective, that campaign served two main political purposes: the advocacy of "stability-oriented" monetary policies secured German commitment to EMU, and the orthodox technical presentation was a way

---

54. Thatcher (who cannot be suspected of being overoptimistic about the prospects of the EMU) summarized the results of the Madrid process: "The heart of the matter is that the European Community has just passed a watershed in its political history . . . The Madrid summit is likely to prove the most important decision point since the signing of the Rome Treaty" (interview with the *Financial Times,* June 29, 1989).

to consolidate a core political constituency and to defuse potential political opposition to EMU at the domestic level.

The Origins of Orthodoxy: A German Solution to a Common Problem

The Delors Report's argument in favor of making the fight against inflation the cardinal priority of macroeconomic policy appeared as an unavoidable political step toward EMU. As one Commission official summarized the situation, "With the Delors Report, things became very clear: either the German model became the model for EMU, or the independence of the European Central Bank was rejected—but there was no third option."[55] The progressive turn toward strict orthodoxy largely reflected German preferences in a particular strategic context. Basically, the bargaining situation over EMU was stacked in favor of Germany. Because the German mark was the de facto anchor currency of the EMS, at any point in the EMU process Germany could easily decide it was better off with the status quo—however fragile. Although the formal decision to engage in a transition process toward EMU was a sovereign prerogative of the federal government, the Bundesbank informally possessed an important say on the official German position regarding the modalities of that transition process.[56] This helps explain the rather draconian provisions of the Maastricht treaty. In turn, that EU governments stood tightly by their commitments to implement the treaty underscores not only the resilience of the politics of sovereignty but also the growing power of orthodoxy as a political logic for pursuing EMU.

The political logic of orthodoxy did not emerge all at once. The Commission consistently spread the message that EMU was a logical extension of the single market, but its nature was left relatively open until very late, in part because it was politically risky to venture into specific details. As early as the mid-1980s, however, the highly asymmetric bargaining situation was clear to Delors and monetary policy experts within the European Commission. Their response was to co-opt Germany not only formally, by taking the German central bank on board within the Delors Committee, but also informally, by praising the "German model." The Commission's official support of the German model reflected a set of beliefs that were widespread in the late 1980s among European officials. Yet during those times of robust economic growth, the prospect of renewed inflation was everybody's bogeyman, not just a monetarist fear. Many saw the German model not so much in terms of giving up the possibility of conducting expansionary policies in times of recession but in terms of accepting the single, albeit significant, institutional change of central bank independence.

55. Interview with Commission official, Brussels, September 16, 1997.
56. For analyses of the politics of central banking in Germany as compared to other countries, see Goodman, *Monetary Sovereignty,* and Henning, *Currencies and Politics.*

The sudden tendency of state and EC officials to heap praise on the German model owes more to the attraction of shared sovereignty than to a wholesale convergence of elite opinion on the alleged superiority of monetarist policies and central bank independence. For precisely this reason, the French government supported an "economic government" as a counterpart to the independent European Central Bank.[57] The fact that many countries had anti-inflationary policies resulted in large part from prior political choices to stick with the EMS and to accept the logic of capital liberalization, rather than from a complete cognitive alignment with Germany's economic priorities. The Commission did nothing to dissipate this potential source of conflict. In fact, any potentially controversial implications for fiscal policy were studiously avoided.[58] While Delors and other Commission staff had no reason to be particularly enamored of the idea of central bank independence, they considered that the price to pay for EMU was to transfer many features of the German model to the EU level.

In the run-up to the Maastricht treaty, however, it became clear that central bank independence would be only one element of orthodoxy among others.[59] The idea of establishing quantitative "convergence criteria" to ensure steady progress toward the ultimate goal of EMU quickly gained support among national monetary officials and central bankers. At that point, the Commission was internally divided on these criteria and more generally on the method of EMU.[60] Delors himself was against adopting excessively strict criteria, whereas some of his advisers thought the criteria were a necessary price to pay for a treaty on EMU. In any case, since the Commission had no formal prerogative in the intergovernmental conference, Delors' team could only hope to influence the modalities of EMU by circulating treaty drafts on an informal basis.[61] Thus, in the end, the quantitative approach prevailed, albeit with qualifying

57. Bérégovoy was very clear about this in a French parliamentary debate on the constitutional revision required by the Maastricht treaty (May 9, 1992): "If I came over to the idea of central bank independence, which Germany considered a sine qua non [for EMU], it is because it appeared to me that the central bank would be counterbalanced by a strong and democratic economic authority that would determine the most important things: the general orientation of economic policy and exchange rate policy" (my translation).

58. Already in the Delors Report, it is stated that "subsidiarity" would be the rule, except insofar as "uncoordinated and divergent national budgetary policies would undermine monetary stability and generate imbalances in the real and financial sectors of the community."

59. For a discussion of the makeup of the German negotiating position at Maastricht, see Henning, *Currencies and Politics*, 228–37; Dyson and Featherstone, *Road to Maastricht*, 370–451.

60. The most scathing critique of Delors' EMU strategy came from a former senior monetary official within the European Commission. His narrative is too polemical to be treated as fact, but it indicates a certain diversity of opinion on EMU within the Commission (see Bernard Connolly, *The Rotten Heart of Europe: The Dirty War for Europe's Money* [London: Faber and Faber, 1995]).

61. The Commission's drafts, as well as the main provisions of the Maastricht treaty regarding EMU, are discussed in detail by Alexander Italianer, "Mastering Maastricht: EMU Issues and How They Were Settled," in *Economic and Monetary Union: Implications for National Policy-Makers*, edited by K. Gretschmann (Maastricht: European Institute of Public Administration, 1993). See also Sandholtz, "Choosing Union"; Kenneth Dyson, *Elusive Union: The Process of Economic and Monetary Union in Europe* (London: Longman, 1994); Dyson and Featherstone, *Road to Maastricht*.

clauses that left some room to assess the degree of fulfillment of the convergence criteria.[62] These criteria embodied a definite turn toward orthodoxy, since they mandated tight control of national economic policies in order to fight inflationary pressures.

In view of subsequent events, it is hard to understand why the governments of Europe agreed to bind themselves to the strict "convergence criteria" contained in the Maastricht treaty. As Germany's EMS partners were forced to adjust to the Bundesbank's postreunification interest rate hike by adopting restrictive monetary policies, the convergence criteria increasingly appeared as quantitative straitjackets on economic growth.[63] The 1980s convergence around fighting inflation began to crumble in the face of a serious economic recession and in the absence of inflationary tensions. The controversies over EMU that erupted across Europe after the Danish failure to ratify the Maastricht treaty manifested a certain decay of pro-Europe enthusiasm. To fulfill the criteria, many governments had to cut public expenditures and possibly forego some economic growth. In Germany, the dilemma was not so stark, but Kohl's government was weakened domestically by the problems of German reunification.[64] The credibility of governmental commitments to respect the convergence criteria and to achieve EMU was increasingly in doubt, which repeatedly triggered monetary crises in the EMS in 1992–93. When Delors left the Commission in 1994, his political capital was considerably lower, especially vis-à-vis the French government.[65] His successor Jacques Santer and the new EMU commissioner Yves-Thibaut de Silguy inherited the task of introducing EMU in a very unfavorable context. From then on, the advocates of EMU chose to adopt a very orthodox discourse as a way to effectively insulate the EMU process from outside interference.

Keeping Focused on EMU: Orthodoxy as Political Technology for EMU

After it was enshrined in a treaty, the recipe of orthodoxy acquired legal force. Consequently, the promoters of EMU in the European Commission and in the member states increasingly chose to adopt an orthodox and legalistic discourse as a way to insulate the EMU process from political attacks. This orientation no longer embodied a policy consensus so much as it formed the cement of a bizarre coalition between a variety of political and institutional

62. The criteria (setting numerical targets for inflation, budget deficits, public debts, exchange rate fluctuation margins, and long-term interest rates) are detailed in Protocol 21 of the Maastricht treaty, and their utilization is defined in Articles 104c and 109j.

63. Professional economists were often among the most vocal critics of the criteria. For an example of a neo-Keynesian critique of the convergence criteria, see Paul De Grauwe, *The Economics of Monetary Integration* (Oxford: Oxford University Press, 1992), and De Grauwe, "The Political Economy of Monetary Union in Europe," *World Economy* 16, no. 6 (November 1993). For a U.S. and monetarist version of the critique, see Martin Feldstein, "Europe's Monetary Union," *Economist*, June 13.

64. On Kohl's domestic political problems in Germany, see Schönfelder and Thiel, *Ein Markt— Ein Währung*, 157.

65. On Delors' misfortunes in 1992–94, see chap. 10 in Grant, *Delors*.

actors with divergent preferences and motivations. Paradoxically, the enterprise of EMU, which originally stemmed from the desire of sovereignty-seeking politicians to shed German orthodoxy, began to appear as the ultimate triumph of the Bundesbank.

The incorporation of orthodoxy into the Commission's EMU strategy was neither immediate nor exclusive of other political tactics. Most visibly, Commission officials conducted several public relations campaigns to convert elite opinion to EMU. As early as 1990, they attempted to capitalize on the success of the 1992 program by presenting EMU as the "logical" next step after the single market.[66] Europe's internationally oriented firms, wary of a potential spiral of competitive devaluation that could undermine the integrity of the single market, began to mobilize around that message in forums such as the Committee for the Monetary Union of Europe. After 1994, the Commission was no longer alone in lobbying for EMU, since the newly created European Monetary Institute (precursor to the European Central Bank) immediately joined the EMU camp. Commission officials took the initiative in January 1995 of preparing a green paper on the practical implications of the introduction of the euro. Put together after extensive hearings of professional associations, the Commission's green paper was intended to demonstrate to the member governments that its scenario for EMU was realistic and had the support of the private sector.[67] It was discussed at the Madrid summit of December 1995 and the governments reiterated their commitments to EMU by formally approving the Commission's practical agenda.

In retrospect, the Madrid Council marked the moment when the financial markets started to take EMU seriously and to prepare for its advent.[68] Yet there is little evidence that EMU was intrinsically in the economic interest of particular social groups.[69] To muster the support of a broad and stable political coalition, therefore, EMU also had to be sold in more concrete terms than the abstract logic of economic necessity. Commission officials progressively realized that while the political constituency that was likely to support EMU per se remained elusive, there existed a clear constituency for orthodoxy. It was made

66. Following the Cecchini Report's successful formula on the "costs of non-Europe" in the 1992 campaign, in the fall of 1990 the Commission published a study on the costs and benefits of EMU: Commission of the European Communities, "One Market, One Money: An Evaluation of the Potential Benefits and Costs of Forming an Economic and Monetary Union," *European Economy* no. 44 (1990). Although the report was largely favorable to the idea of EMU, professional and academic economists remained divided on the feasibility and desirability of EMU from a strictly economic standpoint. For a critical assessment, see Eichengreen, *Globalizing Capital.*

67. When Commissioner de Silguy launched this initiative, even Commission insiders were skeptical. According to one interview: "The idea was to go ahead as if nothing bad had happened and to outline the concrete steps that had to be taken to get there. And it worked!" Interview, Brussels, October 1, 1997.

68. "Traders Are Warming to EMU," *Financial Times*, April 9, 1996.

69. This view is advanced in Frieden, "Invested Interests." For a useful critique, see McNamara, *Currency of Ideas*, 32–40.

up of national politicians who favored a leaner state and/or leaner public budgets, national central banks and finance ministry officials, members of the business community, especially in the financial sector, and, more generally, all actors or social groups that conceived a political, bureaucratic, or economic interest in the provision of fiscally conservative policies. As unemployment rates reached all-time highs and the recession increased pressure on public budgets, these actors and groups were searching for ways to secure their policy preferences.

To obtain the support of these actors, the Commission increasingly framed EMU in terms of consolidating the free-market economic policy orientation present in the EMS and the single market. Despite certain misgivings about the Maastricht criteria within its ranks, the stakes of EMU were extremely high for the Commission. In the long march toward EMU, Commission officials needed to mobilize all the political supporters they could find. And for fear of jeopardizing the prospect of EMU, they could not afford to condone member states' behavior that deviated from the terms of the treaty.[70] Thus, the Commission increasingly took up the defense of the criteria as a way to smooth out the political transition to EMU. As early as 1994–95, Commission officials emphasized the "necessity" of stabilizing public deficits and that the "Keynesian model" of countercyclical economic policy was "dead."[71] At a time when the recession was barely coming to an end and growth prospects remained fragile, the desirability of a swift transition to fiscal austerity was arguable, to say the least. By then, however, what was originally a set of concessions to co-opt the advocates of strict orthodoxy had become a political technology to achieve EMU.

Commission officials also realized that orthodoxy, while useful as the cement for a liberal pro-EMU coalition, could also be used as a front to conceal divergent purposes. That front served an economic function, since market pressures on the EMS mandated a certain show of determination to proceed with the EMU project. Just as important, however, the façade of orthodoxy served the political function of fudging potentially divisive issues until the EMU process was completed. For some actors, especially in France, the painful economic prescription of respecting the Maastricht treaty was a necessary evil in order for EMU to happen.[72] There clearly were some moments of uneasiness in the French government, especially on the part of President Mitterrand, which created serious frictions with the Bundesbank and the German govern-

70. Interview with Commission official, November 20, 1996.
71. See, for example, "Brussels Points Finger at Fiscal Policy Laggards," *Financial Times*, May 26, 1994; interview of Commissioner de Silguy by *Le Monde*, December 12, 1995; "Santer Makes Plea on Public Spending Cuts," *Financial Times*, June 27, 1995; Yves-Thibault de Silguy, "Vers la monnaie unique," *Commentaire*, no. 74 (Summer 1996).
72. In an interview, this choice was presented to me by a French high-level government official: "Assuming that we sacrificed one percentage point of growth [in the early 1990s] and in the end we obtain EMU, then the balance sheet will be positive." Interview, Brussels, May 2, 1997.

ment.[73] Meanwhile, the official Bundesbank position in favor of strictly respecting the criteria was probably not motivated only by the objective of preserving and diffusing the German model of monetary policy.[74] Commission officials consistently tried to prevent or defuse potential conflicts about the political meanings and purposes of EMU. For example, when prominent French politicians started to demand a "weak" euro at a time when the German government was trying to convince the German public that the euro would be "as strong as the mark," Commission officials tried to deflate this controversy by saying that it was "completely beside the point" since the value of the euro would be decided primarily by the market actors.[75]

The Commission's support of the orthodox terms of the Maastricht treaty was motivated not only by its commitment to the goal of EMU but also by incentives to carefully jockey its political capital in the course of ongoing EMU-related negotiations. After the Maastricht treaty was signed, it became ipso facto a negotiating baseline as well as an instruction manual for the member states that aspired to EMU. Any deviation from its specific terms weakened not only a country's chances of reaching the promised Euroland but also its bargaining position for deciding the details of EMU.[76] The many aspects of EMU left relatively open for negotiation—including the possibility of anticipating certain deadlines, the identity of the final participants, the degree of monetary policy coordination during the long first and second stages of EMU, the character of economic policy coordination in the third stage, the location of the European Central Bank, and the external representation of the euro—constituted a strong set of incentives for the member states to adhere to orthodoxy. Because they too hoped to exert some influence on the specific terms of EMU, Commission officials had bargaining incentives to appear as tough defenders of orthodoxy.

73. On September 3, 1992, Mitterrand appeared to renege on central bank independence by saying that monetary policy was part of economic policy, which was primarily in the hands of the Council of Ministers. This immediately provoked a series of articles, "Paris Calls ECB Independence into Question," in *Auszüge aus Presseartikeln*, the Bundesbank's weekly publication. As late as November 1996, Prime Minister Alain Juppé blundered by saying that the "economic government" favored by the French government would "control interest rates."

74. Thus, when the Bundesbank raised interest rates in 1992, many speculated that this move was aimed at forcing a realignment within the EMS or even an indefinite postponement of EMU (see Henning, *Currencies and Politics*, 236–37). Paul De Grauwe argues that, from the standpoint of German policymakers, the convergence criteria conveniently served the political purpose of excluding weak-currency countries and thus of preserving Germany's "dominating position in the monetary policy making process" (De Grauwe, "Political Economy of Monetary Union," 660).

75. "Bonn et Paris se mobilisent pour dégripper le moteur européen," *Le Monde*, December 10, 1996.

76. According to a French official, the government's decision to levy a special contribution from France Telecom to round off the 1996 budget was detrimental to that country's bargaining position. Conversely, when the German government indicated that it intended to reevaluate the Bundesbank's gold reserves in the spring of 1997, the German advocacy of strict orthodoxy was considerably weakened. That immediately boosted the chances for "Club Med" countries, especially Italy, to enter the euro club. Interview, Brussels, May 2, 1997.

More generally, the political pressures in favor of orthodoxy increased as the member states encountered difficulties in abiding by the convergence criteria. In many member states, opposition or challenger politicians often seized on these difficulties. Kohl's government was under heavy pressure from the central bank and the parliament to remain a staunch advocate of the convergence criteria. In the course of the German parliamentary ratification debate, the government had to commit to pledge allegiance to the convergence criteria as a prerequisite for German consent to EMU.[77] By the mid-1990s the *dreikommanull* coalition (named after the 3 percent convergence criterion on public deficits) led by Bavarian premier Edmund Stoiber also pushed the German government in the direction of greater orthodoxy. Domestic criticism reached a peak in 1996, when the German finance ministry was trying to tamper with the rigor of the convergence criteria. The German government's response to criticism was to demand a "stability pact" that would extend the convergence criteria beyond completion of EMU. In the end, the member states adopted the pact alongside the Amsterdam Treaty in the spring of 1997.[78] Despite the objections of the newly elected socialist government in France, the French government did not go to war against it, for fear of alienating the German government. The only real substantive change that the French obtained was changing the name of the pact to the "Stability *and Growth* Pact." The French government, like the Commission, remained willing to accept a certain dose of orthodoxy rather than to jeopardize EMU.

Finally, at a time when European integration and the Commission's role in particular were subject to controversy, there was inevitably a dimension of defense of its turf in the Commission's retrenchment behind the Maastricht treaty. In the late 1990s, the commission president, Jacques Santer, repeatedly said that his idea was to try to do "less" but "better."[79] The most promising way to do this was to reassert the Commission's role as "guardian of the treaties," while shielding EMU from potential political bickering. That, in applying the Maastricht treaty, the Commission was responsible for the "multilateral surveillance" of member states' macroeconomic performance certainly contributed to its acceptance of the convergence criteria, and then of the sanction-based approach of the German-sponsored stability pact.[80] The Com-

77. Schönfelder and Thiel, *Ein Markt—Ein Währung*, 157.

78. The pact, which consists of a resolution and two binding regulations, obligates member states to aim for public budgets "close to balance or in surplus" and provides for financial sanctions if a member state's deficit exceeds 3 percent of national GDP.

79. On Santer's attitude toward challenges to the Commission's prerogatives in the context of the 1996 intergovernmental conference, see also "On Guard: Santer and the European Union," *Economist*, January 21, 1995; "The Big Countries' Poodle? The Timid European Commission," *Economist*, July 15, 1995.

80. For example, before the Council of Ministers defined "exceptional circumstances" (under which a member state would be allowed to have a deficit-to-GDP ratio higher than 3%) as a negative growth rate of -0.75%, the Commission was considering the more restrictive figure of -1.5%. See "Ministers to Seek Pact on EMU Budget Deficit Rules," *Financial Times*, November 11, 1996.

mission stayed officially neutral in the debate between the member states—mostly France and Germany—on fiscal policy coordination or the exchange rate policy of the euro, but it was often very "German" in its watchdog insistence on macroeconomic convergence and stability-oriented policies. In the face of member state pressures and a logic of competition with the European Monetary Institute, the Commission's institutional prerogatives were at stake and therefore Commission officials could not afford to appear "soft" on the Commission's interpretation of macroeconomic convergence.[81] At the same time, Commission officials in charge of EMU were also under strong internal pressure to prove their neutral benevolence vis-à-vis all prospective EMU members.[82] In the end, this dilemma was attenuated by a welcome Europe-wide upturn in the economic cycle, which definitively secured the prospect of a broad-based EMU.

THE GOVERNANCE OF EUROPE'S ECONOMIC AND MONETARY UNION

The politics of sovereignty created and sustained a strong demand for EMU, while the politics of orthodoxy increasingly gave it a sense of direction. Both emerged over time and by design, as they were incorporated into the Commission's strategy to obtain EMU. France was especially interested in EMU for sovereignty-related reasons in a context of rising capital mobility and German reunification, while Germany's strong bargaining position in the context of the EMS largely explains the turn toward orthodoxy. Yet the strange combination of these two orientations was not the object of straightforward quid pro quo bargaining. The direct economic benefits of Maastricht-style EMU were not sufficiently clear to warrant a strict utilitarian decision. Likewise, the convergence of macroeconomic policies after 1983 was not sufficiently deep to construct an ideational basis for EMU. And, finally, there is little evidence that German reunification really enhanced the prospects of EMU or that the two processes naturally went hand in hand—even though Chancellor Kohl and President Mitterrand (for perfectly self-interested reasons) spoke as if it were so. If we bracket Delors' and other actors' pro-EMU initiatives, it is perfectly possible to imagine a counterfactual scenario that combines a protracted unraveling of the EMS, under the pressure of increasing capital mobility, with a retention of the deutsche mark by a reunited Germany.

But this was not the course that history took. And the two kinds of politics that led to EMU also left very characteristic and different legacies. On the one

81. During the stability pact negotiations, Germany stepped up its demands for more intergovernmentalism and more automaticity of sanctions, and the official EMI line was quite restrictive. See "Stark Home Truths of a Stability Pact," *Financial Times*, December 4, 1996; "EMI Chief Takes Hard Maastricht Line," *Financial Times*, November 20, 1996.

82. Italian commissioner Emma Bonino publicly clashed with Commissioner de Silguy on the treatment of Italy's deficits in Commission forecasts of economic convergence: "EU Battle against Deficit Forecast," *Financial Times*, April 22, 1997.

hand, the politics of orthodoxy has led to a distinctive orientation toward market-friendly policies. The orthodox dimension of EMU is perhaps the most obvious legacy of the EMU process. First, the European Central Bank is an inflation fighter. Under the terms of the treaty, it can pursue other economic objectives, but only "without prejudice" to its primary objective of price stability. Many observers think this creates a bias toward excessively cautious monetary policy. Second, the ECB's independence is very extensive. It sets its own targets and determines its policies without entering any kind of negotiation with the member states. Third, the member states of Europe's Economic and Monetary Union have shed the Maastricht convergence criteria only to find themselves caught in the strictures of the Stability and Growth Pact. Unless they keep their public deficits under 3 percent of GDP, they are subject to the rather stiff sanction mechanism under the pact. Although the 1997 pact was reformed in March 2005 in order to make it less rigid, its disciplinary spirit has remained unchanged.

On the other hand, the politics of sovereignty led to a considerable empowerment of the European Union writ large. This is a legacy that observers often overlook or take for granted, but it is no less real and tangible than the legacy of orthodoxy. First, a supranational ECB means that a Dutch or a French citizen can aspire to become the most powerful central banker in Europe. The Bundesbank is no longer the "bank that rules Europe" and the ECB takes into consideration the eurozone as a whole when it makes its monetary policy decisions. Second, the euro is both a vivid symbol of European unity and a shield against currency crises. Member states are no longer at the mercy of global currency speculation, and they no longer have to pay a currency risk premium for conducting policies that do not meet the expectations of international financiers. Third, fiscal policy has been successfully reasserted as a national prerogative. Of course, individual member states are subject to peer pressures and accountability for the way in which they manage their budgets. But this peer pressure is likely to remain gentle, given that governments generally are reluctant to pillory each other. Compared with the scrutiny that governments had to endure in the EMS under the threat of currency crises, this is a much more comfortable situation.

This remarkable duality of EMU raises an important question: Can these two legacies of the politics of EMU persist in the long run? The irony is that, once the euro is in place, the politics of sovereignty and the politics of orthodoxy both lose some of their urgency. In Europe's Economic and Monetary Union, sovereignty over money is effectively relocated at the EU level—primarily within the ECB. The search for sovereignty takes on new forms in a much more institutionalized European context. By the same token, orthodoxy ceases to be an absolute political imperative. It was largely a function of Germany's dominance over the EMS and of its power to hold up progress toward EMU. Despite all the hype about variations of the euro against the dollar, governments are under much less serious pressure to behave in an orthodox way than during past episodes of currency speculation. And, of course, the very existence of the euro deprives the political advocates of orthodoxy of their most precious bargaining chip. Thus, the political resources available to the advocates of orthodox policies have also radically changed.

The balance of forces between the two tendencies could go in either direction. Governments' desire for maneuvering room is deep, especially in hard times. The Stability and Growth Pact was not enforced against Germany and France, despite their egregious failure to comply with the 3 percent limit. After Germany breached the pact that it had fought so hard to impose in 1997, the orthodox orientation of the European Union's economic policies was seriously in question. At the same time, the advocates of orthodoxy can find reasons for hope in the treaty and in the emerging balance of power. In the absence of a coherent fiscal policy authority at the EU level, central bankers are able to frame much of the European Union's economic policy debate. The October 2003 episode gave a preview of future debates about fiscal policies, with some member states suddenly in a position to castigate the lax policies of deficit spenders and to build political capital out of their more virtuous policies. In the Economic and Monetary Union, new cleavages are emerging between the "hawks," who are especially numerous among central bankers, and "doves," who are to be found in deficit-spending member states.

A critical question is whether economic coordination will go beyond the Stability and Growth Pact and a punishment procedure against fiscally deviant member states. Economic coordination under EMU does not necessarily have to always lean in the direction of strict orthodoxy. Although treaty articles about the "coordination of economic policies" (Articles 102 and 103, now Articles 98 and 99) are extremely vague in comparison with monetary policy provisions, Maastricht does contain a few guideposts for the future. Delors was keen on the economic dimension of Europe's Economic and Monetary Union and, in his eyes, Articles 102 and 103 were vital.[83] So far, however, the economic dimension of EMU exists only in embryonic form, at two levels. First, a modest form of economic coordination takes place at the level of the "eurogroup," a German concession to the French desire for an "economic government" at the EU level. With no recognized existence in the treaty, the "eurogroup" is an informal subdivision of the Council of Economics and Finance Ministers and works on the basis of consensus among its members. Formal voting rules and decision-making power are still in the hands of the Economic and Financial Affairs Council (EcoFin), which is made up of the Economics and Finance Ministers of the member states. Second, the European Parliament is in charge of ensuring the democratic accountability of the European Central Bank (Article 109b). The potential exists for the European Parliament to assert itself as an arena for public EU-wide economic policy debates, involving central bankers and governments.

83. Interview with Commission official, Brussels, July 2, 1997.

Of course, the development of this embryo is not a foregone conclusion. Because of the disconnect between the economic and the monetary dimensions of EMU, Delors called the Maastricht treaty "schizophrenic."[84] The treaty was designed to provide both maximum autonomy to the member states and maximum orthodoxy in the centralized conduct of monetary policy. Since they no longer control monetary policy, member governments may become increasingly jealous of their *national* sovereignty in the area of fiscal policy. Thus, the contradictory logic of EMU not only has deep political roots but could persist for a long time, even if it is economically costly. Whether sovereignty and orthodoxy are compatible and sustainable aspirations in the long run is debatable. The evolution of economic policy institutions and orientations will hinge on domestic situations as well as on the interactions between a variety of actors at the level of the European Union. Thus, the configuration of EMU remains wide open. The Maastricht treaty, precisely because it combines two contradictory visions of the market, leaves a lot of room for political maneuvering. The only certainty is that all concerned actors will fight to defend their prerogatives.

In this chapter I have focused on the actions of EMU advocates that played a pivotal role in engineering EMU. These actors deployed a powerful political strategy that made use of the talisman-like nature of the market. They used sovereignty as a bait to lure government officials to the idea of EMU, and, increasingly, they adopted orthodoxy as a political insulation technology. In both cases, the central linchpin of their action was the market. Depending on the targeted constituency, they presented the market either as a new context for the exercise of sovereignty or as a healthy source of policy discipline. Seen in this light, EMU is not the product of raw economic interests, grand economic or geopolitical ideas, or patient institution building. Rather, the euro embodies a political compromise between two broad and largely contradictory conceptions of the market. Only a detailed investigation and theorization of actors' strategies can show how contradictory ideas can be put to the service of a broader goal—in this case, the creation of the world's only major regional currency, and a powerful symbol of European unity.

This case shows that relative institutional and political weakness can sometimes be a blessing in disguise. I have focused on the role of the Commission because it held a central position in the EMU process. Despite their lack of power resources and monetary prerogatives, Commission officials successfully promoted and engineered a seemingly unrealistic institutional outcome. Perhaps because they were forced to be inventive and could not rely on formal prerogatives and "raw" power, Commission officials developed a remarkably robust political strategy. The strategy of luring sovereignty-conscious state officials to support EMU while adopting orthodoxy as a technology was political

---

84. Delors, *L'unité d'un homme.*

in the sense that it was manipulative—since by definition sovereignty is the opposite of orthodoxy. The advocates of EMU within and outside the European Commission utilized different market ideas to defuse political conflicts and to accelerate an otherwise slow historical and economic evolution. In the end, the views propagated by the Commission and the national governments prevailed with large segments of the elite and the general public across the European Union. At that point, the task of paving the road toward EMU was practically achieved.

All this suggests that interests, institutions, and ideas matter but that so does political strategy. A well-crafted political strategy can bring about a powerful redefinition of the very context within which interests are defined and economic policy is made. In this case, Delors and other promoters of Europe exercised critical leadership at various points in the process. By selectively relying on the talisman-like appeal of the market, they discovered and developed a particularly powerful political strategy that enabled them to jump-start the EMU process. That the politics of sovereignty and the politics of orthodoxy suddenly became so central to the political as well as the monetary evolution of the European Union shows that ideas can be a precious asset for conducting institutional change. And given that institutional change has already occurred on the magnitude of EMU, there is little reason to believe that the present institutional configuration for EU-level economic and monetary policymaking is forever settled.

The irony is that the advent of EMU dramatically changed the very terms of the debate over sovereignty and orthodoxy. Not only does it become more difficult to use the market as a talisman once the single market and the euro exist but the new institutional context changes the nature of the dilemma. EMU means that sovereignty is effectively relocated at the EU level, but it is primarily under the stewardship of the inflation-averse European Central Bank. At the same time, the member governments of Euroland, once released from the Bundesbank's singular veto power over the progress of monetary union, will be able to considerably influence the practical orientation of EMU—if they can manage to establish a coherent collective voice in economic policies. Whatever the future may hold for Europe's Economic and Monetary Union, it is safe to say that its promoters in the European Commission and elsewhere have powerfully reshaped the institutional context within which interests are defined and policies are made.

NINE

The Janus-Faced European Union

The political strategy exposed in this book has run its course. By the late 1990s, the European Union's internal market and its Economic and Monetary Union were realized or already well on track. An EU model of political economy was born, so to speak. This model is not so easy to categorize, however, since it is the legacy of an inherently complex political strategy. Although the promoters of Europe consistently appealed to "the market," many of their motivations were "economic" in only a loose sense. The resulting EU model of political economy cannot be described simply as an international regime designed to facilitate market transactions on a European scale—it certainly serves that purpose, but it cannot be reduced to it. Thus, the characterization of the EU as a straightforward market-friendly regime is a truncated cartoon of reality—equally naïve as the opposite vision of the EU as a supranational state.

Like the ancient god Janus, the EU model of political economy has two faces. The principle of market competition and the emphasis on arms-length regulation rather than direct government intervention were central to the European Union's quiet revolution of the 1980s and 1990s. As a consequence, European economic governance today is much more market friendly, fueling the widespread perception of the European Union as an agent of the free market. Alongside market-oriented governance, however, power has been built at the EU level. Europe's national economies today are no longer governed exclusively at the national level, leading some observers to consider the EU as a powerful reassertion of politics at the supranational level. Today's EU model of political economy, then, is an essentially dual reality—the outcome of both marketization and federalization. Complex patterns of relations have developed between the European Union, the market, and the state.

THE EUROPEAN UNION AND THE MARKET

In the 1980s and 1990s, European economies underwent marketization at a remarkable pace. The institutional frameworks of economic governance that had been established across Western Europe after World War II rested on a mix of free-market liberalism and public intervention—what Andrew Shonfield suggestively called a "balance of public and private power."[1] Toward the end of the twentieth century, this balance was significantly altered. As rapid technological progress affected sectors like finance and information and telecommunications, and as the Soviet bloc crumbled to its collapse, Europeans joined the global rush for "market reforms." The privatization trend is especially interesting because of the historical weight of the public sector in Western Europe. According to the OECD, Britain holds the world record for number of industries privatized between 1990 and 1998, with privatization receipts totaling $64 billion; Italy and France occupy the second and third positions in this ranking; seven of the top ten in the OECD's list are EU countries. All across Europe, many public or semipublic industries and services were opened to market competition and to private capital, not only in technologically fast-moving sectors but also in transportation (trucking, airlines, and railroads), energy (gas and electricity), and postal services.

The European Union was not solely responsible for marketization, but it supported and sometimes even engineered the process. First, the EU acted as *market supporter*. This supporting role is well exemplified by internationally competitive economic sectors like finance, in which the market was considered as a constraint. The European Union quickly established capital liberalization and a number of "single licenses" in European banking, securities, and even insurance. As discussed earlier, national government officials initiated market reforms in the financial sector, believing that global technological and economic changes required the adoption of new and more market-based regulatory frameworks. European Commission officials generally played a secondary role, but they acted in a responsive manner. Business actors welcomed Europe's internal market as a way to alleviate the burden of national regulations, while state actors saw it as the promise of modernized regulatory frameworks to oversee increasingly internationalized and rapidly evolving economic sectors. Because the European Union responded to the demands of both business and member states, European-level marketization usually combined deregulation and substantial re-regulation at the EU level.

The main legacy of this first type of marketization was the establishment of the European Union as a new level of regulatory coordination between European regulatory authorities. The European Union today aims for "one-stop regulatory shopping" and a "level playing field" among firms based in different national markets. The pace of EU-level reforms has been impressive, and marketization took place increasingly under EU auspices. Yet the implementation of market reforms left considerable room for national actors in relevant sectors. On the whole, national authorities have welcomed the intervention of the European Union because it enabled them to consolidate national reform

1. Shonfield, *Modern Capitalism.*

processes without really threatening their regulatory turfs. Far from supplant-
ing national levels of regulation, the European Union serves as a forum for the
continuous coordination of market reforms. Networks of national regulators
took advantage of the internal market to tighten their coordination at the EU
level, as well as in other technical forums such as the Basel Committee of banking regulators or the International Organization of Securities Commissions.
Some firms acquired a European or even a global scale, but this was already
happening before the internal market. When the dust settled, it became clear
that EU-level marketization stirred up only the relatively few industry segments that were truly open to international competition. Even in sectors like
finance or telecommunications, the high costs of market entry and the differences in tax structures enabled many actors to defend their niches.

Second, the EU acted in some cases as *market builder*. This engineering role
was most evident in the more intrusive forms of marketization that affected
sectors not previously subject to powerful market forces, such as major collective service providers. The transition to a liberalized internal energy market illuminates this pattern of EU-instigated marketization. The promoters of Europe pushed through a process that would never have gone so far if it had
been animated solely by economic forces. They used the norm of the market
to reform sectors that had previously been considered natural monopolies.
Many state officials as well as industry representatives in Europe thought that
market reform was not the most rational response to Europe's energy problems. Yet they proved unwilling to question the fundamental objective of an internal energy market. Although liberalization was not a foregone conclusion,
it progressively imposed itself for lack of a viable alternative for creating the internal energy market. As national politicians and interest groups became resigned or even favorable to liberalization, European officials managed to pry
open the economically insulated and politically entrenched model of public
utility regulation.

This second type of marketization enabled a remarkable buildup of EU
oversight capacities, which has become a key feature of economic governance
in Europe. Above and beyond the single market initiative, far-reaching European reforms occurred in slow-moving sectors where the odds were stacked
against marketization at the outset. Networks of national regulators tightened,
for example with the creation of the "Florence forum" of regulators in the
electricity sector. But this time the main novelty was the introduction of EU
oversight over the market. Competition powers, provided by the Treaty of
Rome yet little used before the 1990s, initially served as a legal basis for European officials to assert their oversight role. Then, new EU pro-market legislation was passed, which member governments were obligated to implement.
Paradoxically, the absence of self-enforcing marketization favored rather than
impeded the European Union's oversight capacity. The European Commission
increasingly stepped in as the watchdog of domestic implementation of EU-
mandated liberalization.

In a variety of ways, then, marketization was central to the European integration process of the 1980s and the 1990s. Market competition was strengthened, and a minimalist framework of rule-based economic governance was established at the expense of more direct government intervention in the economy—what Majone has called a "regulatory state."[2] Given the degree of marketization that it has introduced in economic governance structures, the European Union's push for market and monetary integration is often perceived as part of a broader trend of market globalization. Those who think that market globalization was inevitable see the European Union as a valuable instrument of economic modernization, whereas those who are critical of globalization see it as the Trojan horse of neoliberal ideology. Either way, the European Union is depicted as an agent of market globalization. If we consider that marketization led to a remarkable concentration of power at the EU level, however, then the quiet revolution of the 1980s and 1990s has a somewhat different flavor.

THE EUROPEAN UNION AND THE STATE

Alongside marketization, the quiet revolution of the 1980s and 1990s involved a significant federalization of economic governance. The increase in public powers at the EU level is especially obvious in the legislative arena. Although the European Union today lacks the unified governmental apparatus of modern states, it is a prolific maker of legal rules. According to widely cited estimates, 50 to 70 percent of all legislation produced in Europe is of EU origin. Even though these figures are probably inflated, they underscore the fact that almost every aspect of economic governance in Europe now has an EU dimension—not only micro- and macroeconomic policymaking within the framework of the internal market and the Economic and Monetary Union but also welfare and employment policies that remain primarily national yet are increasingly discussed in an EU framework.

The growth of EU powers in economic governance consisted of limited new EU trusteeship and, in exceptional cases, outright EU empowerment. First, the European Union became a *federal trust* of some new aspects of economic policymaking. The birth of EU structural policy is a good example of this limited expansion. European Commission officials were able to establish a geographic transfer mechanism at the European level between rich and poor regions. The new policy was sold to the member states as a way to build the market as a space—less than a federal state but more than simply a free market. Two rationales—economic and social—therefore coexisted to justify structural policy. Unlike other purely distributive programs of European side payments, such as the common agricultural policy, this policy had a strong developmental dimension, as it was designed to facilitate the adjustment of

---

2. Majone, "Rise of the Regulatory State in Europe."

economically lagging regions to Europe's single market. To the extent that the member states were willing to delegate their responsibilities, the European Union established its authority in this area.

This EU structural policy initiative laid the groundwork for the now widely accepted, albeit circumscribed, developmental vocation of the European Union. With the upgrading of Structural Funds into a full-fledged EU policy, the European Union has been able to pursue "economic and social cohesion" beyond the free market and autonomous from the member states. The members have thus entrusted the European Union to perform the state-like function of facilitating adjustment to market competition on a European scale. EU trusteeship remains limited in this area, however. Member state officials do not want to hand over their economic powers to the Commission any more than to the invisible hand of the market. The budget of the European Union remains only slightly above 1 percent of the continent's GDP. In addition, the European Union generally has few direct instruments of implementation in the area of structural policy. All this tends to discourage policy innovation at the EU level beyond the narrow definition of cohesion as an interregional transfer mechanism. At the Lisbon EU summit of 2000, for example, EU governments made a commitment to foster a "knowledge-based economy," but they did not appropriate the funds or delegate powers to the EU level to implement this agenda. As the member states were dragging their feet, the Lisbon agenda did not go far in the following years.

In addition to its role as federal trust, the European Union has become a real *federal power* in some areas of economic governance. The example of economic and monetary union is the most illuminating example, of course, with a new institutional framework for monetary policy and economic policy coordination among the twelve member states that adopted the euro in 2002. Along with the new restraints on the ability of member states to run budget deficits and accumulate debt, the creation of an independent European Central Bank with a primary objective of fighting inflation is generally cited as evidence of the European Union's "neoliberal" proclivities. Yet EMU can just as easily be described as an example of outright EU empowerment. The creation of the euro sheltered the member states from the constraining pressure of currency fluctuations. Although they have transferred their monetary prerogatives to the European Central Bank, governments have regained some maneuvering room vis-à-vis market actors in the conduct of economic policies. Their fiscal policies are now subject to a process of peer evaluation, which enables them to defuse the often much harsher verdict of financial actors. Finally, the treaty provides an embryonic framework for central bank accountability and international economic coordination, potentially empowering the European Union to assert broader collective priorities than merely low inflation. In a nutshell, EU empowerment is just as real as market-friendly policies.

This increase in EU powers has left a profound yet unbalanced legacy. The European Union today has a much greater potential than before the advent of

EMU to assert collective priorities, however, it remains less than a federal state with a unified government. EU empowerment was anything but a negative-sum game at the expense of state powers. Although the member states agreed to fully delegate monetary policy to the European Central Bank, they held on to their other prerogatives. As a result, each member state is naturally tempted to free ride on the new EU powers so as to secure its own priorities, rather than those of the Union. The EU focus on rules actually works as an incentive for national actors to maximize discretion over the policies that remain in the hands of member governments, especially in the area of fiscal policy. Once again, this directly stems from the context of the 1980s and 1990s and from the sensitivity of many national actors to the question of sovereignty. It remains to be seen whether the new EU powerhouse will be able to live up to its potential and to assert collective priorities beyond the nominal adherence to common rules.

In sum, the European Union has become a significant center of power and federal-style decision making but not a full-fledged federal state. On the face of it, the European Union today has a much greater potential to assert collective priorities than in the early 1980s. Its admirers describe it as a benevolent gatekeeper and an emerging federal state; its detractors see it as a bureaucratic Leviathan and worry about its infringement on national sovereignty and democracy. In both cases, the European Union is perceived as a state-like counterweight to the free operation of global market forces. Although this perception of the EU as a state runs counter to the opposite view of it as an agent of globalization, it is equally misguided. The quiet revolution superimposed new EU institutions of economic governance on existing ones at the national level, but the limits of this process are clear: the European Union today remains much less than a "normal" federal state with a unified government.

THE POWER AND LIMITS OF POLITICAL STRATEGY

The two faces of the EU model of political economy result from the fact that marketization and federalization went hand in hand. Adding an unprecedented political dimension to Jean Monnet's "Community method" of upgrading common European interests, the promoters of Europe rallied behind a political strategy of playing the market. That political strategy turned the European Union into a market supporter and a market builder, but also into a federal trust and even a federal power. It did not do away with a deeper contradiction, however. The market can appear as a powerful tool to integrate economies and polities. Adam Smith's "invisible hand" holds the promise of peaceful trade and prosperity for society as a whole. At the same time, the market can uproot communities and undermine democracy. This is the dark side of the market, famously described by Karl Polanyi as a "satanic mill." Since the promoters of Europe did not agree on the same long-term visions, they deliberately left these contradictions unresolved and built an inherently dualistic economic governance model.

Whether this Janus-faced model of political economy is sustainable over time and whether European integration can continue without the European Union clarifying its stance on the balance between the state and the market are quite another set of questions. A political strategy of playing the market is unlikely to sustain the European Union's integrationist momentum much further in the face of growing popular dissatisfaction, as evidenced most recently by the French *non* to the referendum on the EU constitution in May 2005. As both European elite actors and citizens change their expectations vis-à-vis the European Union, the integrationist political strategies of the past cannot be replicated indefinitely. If it is to produce further European unity, the strategy that worked in the 1980s and 1990s must be recalibrated—just like the strategy of the 1950s was retooled for a new context in the 1980s.

Was it a mistake in the first place to pursue an integrationist strategy that relied on the market's compelling appeal? There is an element of gamble in any ambitious political strategy. Actors advance certain ideas, but often they have little control over how these ideas will be implemented. The risk that intermediate goals subvert long-term purposes is thus always present.[3] Once the promoters of Europe jumped on the bandwagon of market reforms, they were caught in a process that was beyond the control of any single actor. Yet it would be a mistake to assume that goal subversion is inevitable. The extent to which different actors in a collective endeavor are successful in reaching their goals is ultimately a matter for empirical analysis and interpretation.

By necessity, Delors was obliged to develop a political strategy that would rally the "powers that be" in Europe. His choice of market rationality as the banner for reform was not innocent. He himself believed that a laissez-faire Europe was politically unsustainable in the long run. Yet he had to adopt a strategy that actors who believed in such a free-market vision could also accept. The federalist dream of a United States of Europe was quietly shelved; the more immediate task was to build the long-awaited regional market. Delors counted on corporate actors to exert pressure on the member governments of the European Union. He gambled that the market rationality underpinning the single market program would lose its Thatcherite flavor when it came in contact with reality. Given the circumstances, this political strategy of playing the market to spur European integration was savvy. To some extent, his vision was vindicated with the continued progress of European unity through the advent of the euro.

Yet Delors' critics have accused him of playing with fire, and this accusation cannot be entirely dismissed. There was always a risk that the harshness of marketization would provoke a backlash against "Europe." Through its implementation of the internal market agenda, the Commission triggered the transformation of Europe from an elite agreement to a large-scale institutional re-

---

3. For a classic story of goal subversion at the Tennessee Valley Authority, see Selznick, *TVA and the Grass Roots.*

ality. This kind of sweeping change could not occur without political conflict. A sure index of controversy was the increasing uneasiness of public opinion over both the means and the ends of the European integration process, which first burst out in the referenda on the Maastricht treaty. Critics of the European integration process have become very vocal in expressing their rejection of a "free-market" or a "technocratic" Europe. The irony is that, for strategic reasons, Delors contributed to these much-criticized aspects of European integration, whereas his ideal vision of Europe was neither economically liberal nor technocratic.

Paradoxically, then, the remarkable success of the integrationist strategy of the 1980s and 1990s could become a liability for future political integration. In the long run, a scenario of progressive decomposition of the European Union is not unthinkable. Although some advocates of the free market genuinely believe in the European Union's added value, others might be easily resigned to, or even pleased with, a backlash against European unity—as long as it does not really jeopardize the internal market. If this decomposition scenario becomes a reality, the title of this book—*Playing the Market: A Political Strategy for Uniting Europe*—may turn out to be misleading after all. Over time, we may come to recognize instead that "Playing Unity: A Political Strategy for Marketizing Europe" would have been a more accurate depiction of what was happening. The late twentieth-century heyday of "Europe" would then be reinterpreted, in hindsight, as a mere transition phase in the advent of a hegemonic global market order. This is not necessarily the most realistic scenario for the future, but it cannot be ruled out either.

This indeterminacy underscores the unwieldy nature of any political strategy and the importance of unintended consequences over long periods of time. My point in this book is certainly not to suggest that political strategies are omnipotent recipes for institutional change. Clearly, the success of the political strategy I document in the preceding chapters is an exception. Many political strategies never achieve sufficient visibility to warrant detailed examination. In such cases, conventional political science models of analysis are quite useful. A bird's-eye perspective on interests, institutions, and ideas is then perfectly sufficient to understand the main driving forces of institutional change. And the fact that most political strategies fail, or achieve minimal results, probably explains why we tend not to pay much attention to them in hindsight when we try to get a big picture understanding of institutional change.

Political strategies are present everywhere around us, however. Actors routinely embark on collective action in the name of ideas whose very terms may remain relatively ill defined. For a variety of reasons, market ideas came to the forefront of political debate in late twentieth-century Europe. In that historical context, the institutional forms of Europe's political economy, as inherited from the post–World War II period, seemed strangely incongruent. That new and unusual situation created room for strategic action. In the absence of deeply shared objectives and values, many actors realized that their actions were subject to great uncertainty, yet they hoped their preferences would prevail in the end. This peculiar type of highly strategic but open-ended behavior is essentially political, and it sometimes appears retrospectively as a critical factor in the politics of change.

The fact that "the market" became the linchpin of such an open-ended political strategy is perhaps especially surprising. Political economy scholars have often called attention to the inexorable logic of market rationality in the modern world—what Max Weber called the "cage of reason." Yet it must also be recognized that imaginative strategic actors can harness the power of this modern rationality into an instrument of open-ended change. Ideas about what is or is not "rational" frame the political debate and constitute crucial points of departure for reform processes. Any investigation of institutional change processes should therefore start by mapping out the different uses of ideas, and their politics. As the European politics of market ideas demonstrates, actors who exploit ideas as strategic resources can partly evade the strictures of even the most cage-like rationality. Under favorable conditions, then, a well-crafted political strategy can impose its own order over the sometime-chaotic dynamics of interests, ideas, and institutions.

References

Aeschimann, Eric, and Pascal Riché. *La guerre de sept ans.* Paris: Fayard, 1997.

Allen, David. "Competition Policy: Policing the Single Market." In *Decision-Making in the European Union,* edited by Helen Wallace and William Wallace. Oxford: Oxford University Press, 1996.

———. "Cohesion and the Structural Funds: Transfers and Trade-offs." In *Decision-Making in the European Union,* edited by Helen Wallace and William Wallace. Oxford: Oxford University Press, 2000.

Alter, Karen J. *Establishing the Supremacy of European Law: The Making of an International Rule of Law in Europe.* Oxford: Oxford University Press, 2001.

Andrews, David M. "The Global Origins of the Maastricht Treaty on EMU." In *The State of the European Community,* vol. 2, edited by Alan W. Cafruny and Glenda G. Rosenthal. Boulder: Lynne Rienner, 1993.

———. "Capital Mobility and State Autonomy: Toward a Structural Theory of International Monetary Relations." *International Studies Quarterly* 38 (June 1994).

Ansell, Christopher K., Keith Darden, and Craig Parsons. "Dual Networks on European Regional Development Policy." *Journal of Common Market Studies* 36, no. 3 (September 1997): 347–75.

Attali, Jacques. *Verbatim I, 1981–1986.* Paris: Fayard, 1993.

———. *Verbatim III, 1988–1991.* Paris: Fayard, 1995.

Bakker, Age. *The Liberalization of Capital Movements in Europe.* Dordrecht: Kluwer Academic, 1996.

Bauchard, Philippe. *La guerre des deux roses.* Paris: Grasset, 1986.

Baun, Michael J. "The Maastricht Treaty as High Politics: Germany, France, and European Integration." *Political Science Quarterly* 110, no. 4 (1996): 605–24.

Behrens, Petra, and Marc Smyrl. "A Conflict of Rationalities: EU Regional Policy and the Single Market." *Journal of European Public Policy* 6, no. 3 (September 1999).

Blyth, Mark. *Great Transformations: Economic Ideas and Institutional Change in the Twentieth Century.* Cambridge: Cambridge University Press, 2002.

Boissieu, Christian de, and Jean Pisani-Ferry. "The Political Economy of French Economic Policy in the Perspective of EMU." In *Forging an Integrated Europe,* edited by Barry Eichengreen and Jeffry Frieden. Ann Arbor: University of Michigan Press, 1998.

Boix, Carles. "Partisan Governments, the International Economy, and Macroeconomic Policies in Advanced Nations, 1960–1993." *World Politics* 53, no. 1 (October 2000).

Brenac, Edith. "L'exemple des télécommunications." In *Le tournant néo-libéral en Europe,* edited by Bruno Jobert. Paris: L'Harmattan, 1994.

Brittan, Leon. Interview in the *New York Times,* May 8, 1991.

———. *Globalization vs. Sovereignty? The European Response.* Cambridge: Cambridge University Press, 1998.

———. *A Diet of Brussels: The Changing Face of Europe.* London: Little, Brown, 2000.

Bryant, Ralph C. *International Financial Intermediation.* Washington, D.C.: Brookings Institution, 1987.

Burley, Anne-Marie Slaughter, and Walter Mattli. "Europe before the Court: A Political Theory of Legal Integration." *International Organization* 47, no. 1 (Winter 1993): 41–76.

Cameron, David R. "The 1992 Initiative: Causes and Consequences." In *Euro-Politics: Institutions and Policymaking in the "New" European Community*, edited by Alberta Sbragia, 23–74. Washington, D.C.: Brookings Institution, 1991.

———. "Transnational Relations and the Development of European Economic and Monetary Union." In *Bringing Transnational Relations Back In*, edited by Thomas Risse-Kappen. Princeton: Princeton University Press, 1994.

Carmoy, Guy de, and Gerard Brondel. *L'Europe de l'énergie: Objectif 1992 et perspective 2010*. Luxembourg: Office for Official Publications of the European Communities, 1991.

Cerny, Philip. "The Little Big Bang in Paris: Financial Market Deregulation in a Dirigiste System." *European Journal of Policy Research* 17 (1989): 169–92.

Christiansen, Thomas. "Tensions of European Governance: Politicized Bureaucracy and Multiple Accountability in the European Commission." *Journal of European Public Policy* 4, no. 1 (March 1997): 73–90.

Christiansen, Thomas, Knud Erik Jørgensen, Antje Wiener, eds. "The Social Construction of Europe," special issue of *Journal of European Public Policy* 6, no. 4 (1999).

Cini, Michelle. *The European Commission: Leadership, Organisation, and Culture in the EU Administration*. Manchester: Manchester University Press, 1996.

Clarotti, Paolo. "Le rôle du processus d'intégration communautaire dans la dérégulation en matière bancaire." *Revue de Droit des Affaires Internationales*, no. 7 (1986).

———. "Le rôle des organes supranationaux en matière de réglementation bancaire." *Revue de Droit Bancaire et de la Bourse*, no. 9 (September–October 1988): 153–57.

———. "La coopération administrative entre organes de contrôle bancaire dans la CE." *Revue de la Banque* (October 1993): 583–88.

Clemens, Elizabeth S. "Organizational Repertoires and Institutional Change: Women's Groups and the Transformation of U.S. Politics, 1890–1920." *American Journal of Sociology* 98, no. 4 (January 1993): 755–98.

Cockfield, Arthur. *The European Union: Creating the Single Market*. London: Wiley Chancery Law Publishing, 1994.

Cohen, Benjamin J. *The Geography of Money*. Ithaca: Cornell University Press, 1998.

Colchester, Nicholas, and David Buchan. *Europe Relaunched: Truth and Illusions on the Way to 1992*. London: Hutchinson Business Books, 1990.

Commission. *The Role of Public Finances in the Process of European Integration* (McDougall Report). Brussels, 1977.

Commission of the European Communities. *Completing the Internal Market*. COM (85) 310 final, published in *Official Journal of the European Communities*, June 14, 1985.

———. "Agenda for a Liberation of Capital Movements." May 23, 1986, COM (86) 292 final.

———. "Creation of a European Financial Space." COM (87) 550 final.

———. *Creation of a European Financial Space: Liberation of Capital Movements and Financial Integration in the Community*. Luxembourg: Office for Official Publications of the European Communities, 1988.

———. *The Internal Energy Market*. Reprinted in *Energy in Europe*, special issue. Luxembourg: Office for Official Publications of the European Communities, 1988.

———. "One Market, One Money: An Evaluation of the Potential Benefits and Costs of Forming an Economic and Monetary Union." *European Economy* no. 44 (1990).

———. *Energy in the European Community*. Luxembourg: Office for Official Publications of the European Communities, 1991.

———. *Energy: A Challenge for Europe and the World*. Brussels: Commission of the European Communities, 1992.

———. *Energy in Europe* 19, July 1992. Luxembourg: Office for Official Publications of the European Communities, 1992.

———. *Eurobarometer: Public Opinion in the European Union*. May 1994.

———. Communication, "Services of General Interest in Europe." Luxembourg: Office for Official Publications of the European Communities, 1996.

———. Interpretative Communication, "Freedom to Provide Services and the Interest of the General Good in the Second Banking Directive." June 26, 1997.

———. *Eurobarometer: Public Opinion in the European Union* (Autumn 1998).

Conant, Lisa. *Justice Contained: Law and Politics in The European Union.* Ithaca: Cornell University Press, 2002.

Connolly, Bernard. *The Rotten Heart of Europe: The Dirty War for Europe's Money.* London: Faber and Faber, 1995.

Coombes, David. *Politics and Bureaucracy in the European Community: A Portrait of the Commission of the EEC.* London: George Allen and Unwin, 1970.

Cooper, Richard N. "Economic Interdependence and Foreign Policy in the Seventies." *World Politics* 24, no. 2 (January 1972).

Cowles, Maria Green. "Setting the Agenda for a New Europe: The ERT and EC 1992." *Journal of Common Market Studies* 33, no. 4 (December 1995): 501–26.

Cowles, Maria Green, James A. Caporaso, and Thomas Risse, eds. *Transforming Europe: Europeanization and Domestic Change.* Ithaca: Cornell University Press, 2001.

Crouch, Colin, and David Marquand, eds. *The Politics of 1992: Beyond the Single European Market.* Oxford: Basil Blackwell, 1990.

De Grauwe, Paul. *The Economics of Monetary Integration.* Oxford: Oxford University Press, 1992.

———. "The Political Economy of Monetary Union in Europe." *World Economy* 16, no. 6 (November 1993): 653–61.

Delors, Jacques. *L'unité d'un homme: Entretiens avec Dominique Wolton.* Paris: Odile Jacob, 1994; book epigraph from page 220.

———. *Mémoires.* Paris: Plon, 2004.

Delors, Jacques, and Clisthène. *La France par l'Europe.* Paris: Grasset, 1988.

Destler, I. M., and C. Randall Henning. *Dollar Politics: Exchange Rate Policymaking in the United States.* Washington, D.C.: Institute for International Economics, 1989.

Diez Medrano, Juan. *Framing Europe.* Princeton: Princeton University Press, 2003.

Douglas, Mary. *How Institutions Think.* Syracuse: Syracuse University Press, 1986.

Duchêne, François. *Jean Monnet: The First Statesman of Interdependence.* New York: W. W. Norton, 1994.

Dumez, Hervé, and Alain Jeunemaître. "Political Intervention v. L'Etat de Droit Economique." *Essays in Regulation,* no. 5. Oxford: Regulatory Policy Institute, 1994.

Dumont, Louis. *From Mandeville to Marx: The Genesis and Triumph of Economic Ideology.* Chicago: University of Chicago Press, 1977.

Dyson, Kenneth. *Elusive Union: The Process of Economic and Monetary Union in Europe.* London: Longman, 1994.

Dyson, Kenneth, and Kevin Featherstone. *The Road to Maastricht: Negotiating Economic and Monetary Union.* Oxford: Oxford University Press, 1999.

Eichengreen, Barry J. "Should the Maastricht Treaty Be Saved?" *Princeton Studies in International Finance* 74 (December 1992).

———. "A More Perfect Union? The Logic of Economic Integration." *Essays in International Finance,* no. 198 (1996).

———. *Globalizing Capital: A History of the International Monetary System.* Princeton: Princeton University Press, 1996.

Eichengreen, Barry J., and Jeffry A. Frieden. *Forging an Integrated Europe.* Ann Arbor: University of Michigan Press, 1998.

Eising, Rainer, and Nicolas Jabko. "Moving Targets: National Interests and Electricity Liberalization in the European Union." *Comparative Political Studies* 34, no. 7 (September 2001): 742–67.

Ellger, Reinhard. "Telecommunications in Europe: Law and Policy of the European Community in a Key Industrial Sector." In *Singular Europe,* edited by William James Adams. Ann Arbor: University of Michigan Press, 1993.

Fair, Donald, and Christian de Boissieu. *International Monetary and Financial Integration.* Dordrecht: Martinus Nijhoff, 1988.

Fair, Donald, and Christian de Boissieu, eds. *Financial Institutions in Europe under New Competitive Conditions.* Dordrecht: Kluwer Academic, 1990.

Favier, Pierre, and Michel Martin-Rolland. *La décennie Mitterrand,* vol. 1, *Les ruptures, 1981–1984.* Paris: Seuil, 1990.

——. *La décennie Mitterrand,* vol. 2, *Les epreuves, 1984–1998.* Paris: Seuil, 1993.

——. *La décennie Mitterrand,* vol. 3, *Les défis, 1988–1991.* Paris: Seuil, 1996.

Fligstein, Neil. "Social Skill and the Theory of Fields." *Sociological Theory* 19, no. 2 (July 2001): 105–25.

Fligstein, Neil, and I. Maradrita. "How to Make a Market: Reflections on the Attempt to Create a Single Market in the European Union." *European Journal of Sociology* 102, no. 1 (July 1996): 1–33.

Fligstein, Neil, and Alec Stone Sweet. "Constructing Polities and Markets: An Institutionalist Account of European Integration." *American Journal of Sociology* 107, no. 5 (March 2002): 1206–45.

Frieden, Jeffry A. "Invested Interests: The Politics of National Economic Policy in a World of Global Finance." *International Organization* 45 (Autumn 1991).

——. "Actors and Preferences in International Relations." In *Strategic Choice and International Relations,* edited by David A. Lake and Robert Powell. Princeton: Princeton University Press, 1999.

Gabel, Matthew J. *Interests and Integration: Market Liberalization, Public Opinion, and European Union.* Ann Arbor: University of Michigan Press, 1998.

Gardner, Richard. *Sterling-Dollar Diplomacy in Current Perspective: The Origins and the Prospects of Our International Economic Order.* New York: Columbia University Press, 1980.

Garrett, Geoffrey. "International Cooperation and Institutional Choice: The European Community's Internal Market." *International Organization* 46, no. 2 (Spring 1992): 533–60.

——. "The Politics of Maastricht." *Economics and Politics* 5 (July 1993).

Garrett, Geoffrey, and George Tsebelis. "An Institutionalist Critique of Intergovernmentalism." *International Organization* 50 (Summer 1996): 269–99.

Garrett, Geoffrey, and Barry Weingast. "Ideas, Interests, and Institutions: Constructing the European Community's Internal Market." In *Ideas and Foreign Policy,* edited by Judith Goldstein and Robert Keohane. Ithaca: Cornell University Press, 1993.

Geertz, Clifford. *The Interpretation of Cultures.* New York: Basic Books, 1973.

Genscher, Hans-Dietrich. *Rebuilding a House Divided: A Memoir by the Architect of Germany's Reunification.* New York: Broadway Books, 1997.

Giavazzi, Francesco, and Alberto Giovannini. *Limiting Exchange Rate Flexibility: The European Monetary System.* Cambridge: MIT Press, 1989.

Giavazzi, Francesco, Stefano Micossi, and Marcus Miller, eds. *The European Monetary System.* Cambridge: Cambridge University Press, 1988.

Giavazzi, Francesco, and Marco Pagano. "The Advantage of Tying One's Hands: EMS Discipline and Central Bank Credibility." *European Economic Review* 32 (1988): 1055–82.

Golember, Carter H., and David S. Holland. "Banking and Services." In *Europe 1992: An American Perspective,* edited by Gary Clyde Hufbauer. Washington, D.C.: Brookings Institution, 1990.

Goodman, John B. *Monetary Sovereignty: The Politics of Central Banking in Western Europe.* Ithaca: Cornell University Press, 1992.

Goodman, John B., and Louis Pauly. "The Obsolescence of Capital Controls: Economic Management in an Age of Global Markets." *World Politics* 46 (October 1993).

Gourevitch, Peter M. *Politics in Hard Times: Comparative Responses to International Economic Crises.* Ithaca: Cornell University Press, 1986.

Grant, Charles. *Delors: Inside the House That Jacques Built.* London: Nicholas Brealey, 1994.

Gros, Daniel, and Niels Thygesen. *The European Monetary System.* Center for European Policy Studies (CEPS) paper 35, Brussels, 1988.
——. *European Monetary Integration.* London: Longman, 1992.
Haas, Ernst B. *The Uniting of Europe: Political, Social, and Economic Forces, 1950–1957.* Stanford: Stanford University Press, 1958.
——. *The Obsolescence of Regional Integration Theory.* Berkeley: University of California, Institute of International Studies, 1975.
——. "Turbulent Fields and the Theory of Regional Integration." *International Organization* 29, no. 3 (Spring 1976): 173–212.
Hall, Peter A. *Governing the Economy: The Politics of State Intervention in Britain and France.* Cambridge: Polity Press, 1986.
——. "The Movement from Keynesianism to Monetarism: Institutional Analysis and British Economic Policy in the 1970s." In *Structuring Politics: Historical Institutionalism in Comparative Analysis,* edited by Sven Steinmo et al., 91–113. Cambridge: Cambridge University Press, 1992
——. "Policy Paradigms, Social Learning, and the State: The Case of Economic Policymaking in Britain." *Comparative Politics* 25, no. 3 (April 1993).
——. "The Political Economy of Europe in an Era of Interdependence." In *Continuity and Change in Contemporary Capitalism,* edited by Herbert Kitschelt et al. Cambridge: Cambridge University Press, 1999.
Hall, Peter A., ed. *The Political Power of Economic Ideas: Keynesianism across Nations.* Princeton: Princeton University Press, 1989.
Harden, Ian. "Sovereignty and the Eurofed." *Political Quarterly* 61, no. 4 (1990): 402–14.
Hay, Colin, and Ben Rosamond. "Globalization, European integration and the Discursive Construction of Economic Imperatives." *Journal of European Public Policy* (April 2002).
Hefeker, Carsten. "Germany and Monetary Union." Paper prepared for conference on "The Political Economy of European Integration," Bremen, August 4–16, 1996.
Helleiner, Eric. *States and the Resurgence of Global Finance.* Ithaca: Cornell University Press, 1994.
Henning, C. Randall. *Currencies and Politics in the United States, Germany, and Japan.* Washington, D.C.: Institute for International Economics, 1994.
——. "Systemic Conflict and Regional Monetary Integration: The Case of Europe." *International Organization* 52, no. 3 (1998): 537–74.
Herring, Richard, and Robert Litan. *Financial Regulation in the Global Economy.* Washington, D.C.: Brookings Institution, 1995.
Hirschman, Albert O. *The Passions and the Interests: Political Arguments for Capitalism before Its Triumph.* Princeton: Princeton University Press, 1977.
Hirst, Paul Q., and Grahame Thompson. *Globalization in Question: The International Economy and the Possibilities of Governance.* Cambridge: Polity Press, 1996.
Hix, Simon. "The Study of the European Union II: The 'New Governance' Agenda and Its Rival." *Journal of European Public Policy* 5, no. 1 (March 1998): 38–65.
——. *The Political System of the European Union.* New York: St. Martin's, 1999.
Hoffmann, Stanley. *The European Sisyphus: Essays on Europe, 1964–1994.* Boulder: Westview Press, 1995.
Hooghe, Liesbet. *Cohesion Policy and European Integration.* Oxford: Oxford University Press, 1996.
——. "Images of Europe: Orientations to European Integration among Senior Officials of the Commission." *British Journal of Political Science* 29, no. 2 (April 1999): 345–67.
——. "Supranational Activists or Intergovernmental Agents? Explaining the Orientations of Senior Commission Officials." *Comparative Political Studies* 32, no. 4 (June 1999): 435–63.
——. *The European Commission and European Integration.* Cambridge: Cambridge University Press, 2001.

Hooghe, Liesbet, and Michael Keating. "The Politics of European Union Regional Policy." *Journal of European Public Policy* 1, no. 3 (1994).

Hooghe, Liesbet, and Gary Marks. *Multi-level Governance and European Integration.* Lanham, Md.: Rowman and Littlefield, 2001.

Italianer, Alexander. "Mastering Maastricht: EMU Issues and How They Were Settled." In *Economic and Monetary Union: Implications for National Policy-Makers,* edited by K. Gretschmann. Maastricht: European Institute of Public Administration, 1993.

Jabko, Nicolas. "In the Name of the Market: How the European Commission Paved the Way for Monetary Union." *Journal of European Public Policy* 6, no. 3 (September 1999): 475–95.

Jachtenfuchs, Markus, Thomas Diez, and Sabine Jung. "Which Europe? Conflicting Models of a Legitimate European Political Order." *European Journal of International Relations* 4, no. 4 (December 1998): 409–45.

Joannes, Alain. "L'acte unique dans le discours politique français." *Revue Politique et Parlementaire* (January–February 1988): 32–36.

Jobert, Bruno, ed. *Le tournant néo-libéral en Europe.* Paris: L'Harmattan, 1994.

Joscow, Paul. "The Role of Transaction Cost Economics in Antitrust and Public Utility Regulatory Policies." Special issue of the *Journal of Law, Economics and Organization* 7 (1991).

Joscow, Paul, and Richard Schmalensee. *Markets for Power: An Analysis of Electric Utility Deregulation.* Cambridge: MIT Press, 1985.

Kapstein, Ethan B. *Governing the Global Economy.* Cambridge: Harvard University Press, 1994.

Katz, S. "The Second Banking Directive and the General Good Clause: A Major Exception to the Freedom to Provide Services." *CEPS Research Report* no. 9. Brussels: Center for European Policy Studies.

Katzenstein, Peter J. *Politics and Policy in West Germany.* Philadelphia: Temple University Press, 1987.

——. "The Smaller States, Germany, and Europe." In *Tamed Power,* edited by Peter J. Katzenstein. Ithaca: Cornell University Press, 1997.

Katzenstein, Peter J., ed. *Between Power and Plenty: Foreign Economic Policies of Advanced Industrial States.* Madison: University of Wisconsin Press, 1978.

Kelemen, R. Daniel. *The Rules of Federalism: Institutions and Regulatory Politics in the EU and Beyond.* Cambridge: Harvard University Press, 2004.

Key, Sidney. "Mutual Recognition: Integration of the Financial Sector in the European Community." *Federal Reserve Bulletin* (September 1989).

Kitschelt, Herbert, Peter Lange, Gary Marks, and John D. Stephens, eds. *Continuity and Change in Contemporary Capitalism.* Cambridge: Cambridge University Press, 1999.

Kohler-Koch, Beate. "Catching Up with Change." *Journal of European Public Policy* 3, no. 3 (1996): 359–80.

Krasner, Stephen. "Approaches to the State: Alternative Conceptions and Historical Dynamics." *Comparative Politics* 16 (January 1984): 223–46.

Kruse, Donald C. *Monetary Integration in Western Europe.* London: Butterworth, 1980.

Kurzer, Paulette. *Business and Banking: Political Change and Economic Integration in Western Europe.* Ithaca: Cornell University Press, 1993.

Lannoo, Karel. "The Single Market in Banking: A First Assessment." In *The Single Market in Banking: From 1992 to EMU. CEPS Research Report* No. 17. Brussels: Center for European Policy Studies, June 1995.

——. "The Draft Pension Funds Directive and the Financing of Pensions in the EU." *Geneva Papers on Risk and Insurance,* no. 78 (January 1996).

Lawson, Nigel. *The View from No. 11: Memoirs of a Tory Radical.* London: Bantam Press, 1992.

Leblebici, Husayin, Gerald D. Salancik, Anne Copay, and Tom King. "Institutional Change and the Transformation of Interorganizational Fields: An Organizational History of the U.S. Radio Broadcasting Industry." *Administrative Science Quarterly* 36, no. 3 (September 1991): 333–63.

Leibfried, Stephan, and Paul Pierson, eds. *European Social Policy: Between Fragmentation and Integration*. Washington, D.C.: Brookings Institution, 1995.

Lelakis, Vassili. "La libération complète des mouvements de capitaux au sein de la Communauté." *Revue du Marché Commun* 320 (September–October 1988).

Lequesne, Christian et al. "La Commission Européenne." Special issue of *Revue Française de Science Politique* 46, no. 3 (June 1996).

Levi-Faur, David. "On the 'Net Impact' of Europeanization: The EU's Telecoms and Electricity Regimes between the Global and the National." *Comparative Political Studies* 37, no. 1 (February 2004): 3–29.

Levy, Jonah D. *Tocqueville's Revenge: State, Society, and Economy in Contemporary France*. Cambridge: Harvard University Press, 1999.

Lieberman, Robert C. "Ideas, Institutions, and Political Order: Explaining Political Change." *American Political Science Review* 96, no. 4 (December 2002): 697–712.

Lindberg, Leon, and Stuart Scheingold. *Europe's Would-Be Polity*. Englewood Cliffs, N.J.: Prentice-Hall, 1970.

Loriaux, Michael. *France after Hegemony: International Change and Financial Reform*. Ithaca: Cornell University Press, 1991.

Ludlow, Peter. *The Making of the European Monetary System*. London: Butterworth, 1982.

Lütz, Susanne. "The Revival of the Nation-State? Stock Exchange Regulation in an Era of Globalized Financial Markets." *Journal of European Public Policy* 5, no. 1 (March 1998).

Majone, Giandomenico. "The Rise of the Regulatory State in Europe." *West European Politics* 17 (July 1994): 77–101.

———. *Regulating Europe*. London: Routledge, 1996.

Marcussen, Martin. "The Dynamics of EMU Ideas." *Cooperation and Conflict* 34, no. 4 (December 1999): 383–411.

Marks, Gary, Liesbet Hooghe, and Kermit Blank. "European Integration from the 1980s: State-Centric vs. Multi-level Governance." *Journal of Common Market Studies* 34, no. 3 (September 1996): 341–78.

Marsh, David. *The Bundesbank: The Bank That Rules Europe*. London: William Heinemann, 1992.

Matlary, Janne H. *Energy Policy in the European Union*. London: Macmillan, 1997.

Mattli, Walter. *The Logic of Regional Integration: Europe and Beyond*. Cambridge: Cambridge University Press, 1999.

Mazey, Sonia, and Jeremy J. Richardson. *Lobbying in the European Community*. Oxford: Oxford University Press, 1993.

McNamara, Kathleen R. *The Currency of Ideas: Monetary Politics in the European Union*. Ithaca: Cornell University Press, 1998.

Mélitz, Jacques. "Financial Deregulation in France." *European Economic Review* 34, nos. 2–3 (May 1990): 394–402.

Menon, Anand. "Member States and International Institutions: Institutionalizing Intergovernmentalism in the European Union." *Comparative European Politics* 1, no. 2 (July 2003): 171–201.

Mercer, Jonathan. "Rationality and Psychology in International Politics." *International Organization* 59 (Winter 2005): 77–106.

Meunier, Sophie. *Trading Voices: The European in International Commercial Negotiations*. Princeton: Princeton University Press, 2005.

Meyer, John W., and Brian Rowan. "Institutionalized Organizations: Formal Structure as Myth and Ceremony." In *The New Institutionalism in Organizational Analysis*, edited by Walter W. Powell and Paul J. DiMaggio. Chicago: University of Chicago Press, 1991.

Milner, Helen V. *Resisting Protectionism: Global Industries and the Politics of International Trade*. Princeton: Princeton University Press, 1988.

Milward, Alan S. *The European Rescue of the Nation-State*. Berkeley: University of California Press, 1992.

Ministère de l'Economie et des Finances (France). "La réforme des marchés financiers français." *Notes Bleues* 250 (October 21–27, 1985).

Ministère de l'Industrie (France), Rapport du groupe de travail. *La réforme de l'organisation électrique et gazière française.* Paris: Ministère de l'Industrie, 1994.

Moran, Michael. *The Politics of the Financial Services Revolution: The USA, the UK, and Japan.* Basingstoke: Macmillan, 1991.

———. "The State and the Financial Services Revolution: A Comparative Analysis." *West European Politics* 17, no. 3 (July 1994).

Moravcsik, Andrew. "Negotiating the Single European Act." In *The New European Community,* edited by Robert Keohane and Stanley Hoffmann. Boulder: Westview Press, 1991.

———. "Why European Integration Strengthens the Nation-State." CFIA Working Paper. Cambridge: Harvard University, 1993.

———. *The Choice for Europe: Social Purpose and State Power from Messina to Maastricht.* Ithaca: Cornell University Press, 1998.

Mosley, Layna. *Global Capital and National Governments.* Cambridge: Cambridge University Press, 2003.

O'Brien, Richard. *Global Financial Integration: The End of Geography.* New York: Council on Foreign Relations, 1992.

Oliver, Peter, and Jean-Pierre Baché. "Free Movements of Capital Markets between the Member States: Recent Developments." *Common Market Law Review* 26 (1989).

Organization for Economic Cooperation and Development. *Prudential Supervision in Banking.* Paris: OECD, 1987.

———. *Banks under Stress.* Paris: OECD, 1992.

Padgett, John F., and Christopher K. Ansell. "Robust Action and the Rise of the Medici, 1400–1434." *American Journal of Sociology* 98, no. 6 (May 1993): 1259–1320.

Padgett, Stephen. "The Single European Energy Market: The Politics of Realization." *Journal of Common Market Studies* 30, no. 1 (March 1992): 53–75.

Padoa-Schioppa, Tommaso. *Money, Economic Policy and Europe.* Luxembourg: Office for Official Publications of the European Communities, 1985.

———. *The Road to Monetary Union in Europe.* Oxford: Clarendon Press, 1994.

Palier, Bruno, and Philippe Pochet. "Toward a European Social Policy—at Last?" In *With US or Against US? European Trends in American Perspective,* edited by Nicolas Jabko and Craig Parsons, 253–73. Oxford: Oxford University Press, 2005.

Parsons, Craig A. "Domestic Interests, Ideas and Integration: The French Case." *Journal of Common Market Studies* 38, no. 1 (March 2000): 45–70.

———. *A Certain Idea of Europe.* Ithaca: Cornell University Press, 2003.

Pierson, Paul. "The Path to European Integration: A Historical Institutionalist Analysis." *Comparative Political Studies* 29, no. 2 (April 1996).

Pinder, John. *European Community: The Building of a Union.* Oxford: Oxford University Press, 1991.

Polanyi, Karl. *The Great Transformation: The Political and Economic Origins of Our Time.* Boston: Beacon Press, 1957 [1944].

———. "The Economy as an Instituted Process." In *Trade and Market in the Early Empires,* edited by Karl Polanyi, Conrad M. Arensberger, and Harry W. Pearson. Glencoe, Ill.: Gateway, 1957.

Posner, Elliot. "Stock Exchange Competition and the NASDAQ Bargain in Europe." In *With US or Against US? European Trends in American Perspective,* edited by Nicolas Jabko and Craig Parsons. Oxford: Oxford University Press, 2005.

Powell, Walter W., and Paul J. DiMaggio, eds. *The New Institutionalism in Organizational Analysis.* Chicago: University of Chicago Press, 1991.

Radaelli, Claudio, and Vivien A. Schmidt. "Policy Change and Discourse in Europe." *West European Politics* 27, no. 2 (March 2004): 183–379.

Rosamond, Ben. "Discourses of Globalization and the Social Construction of European Identities." *Journal of European Public Policy* 6, no. 4 (1999): 652–68.

Ross, George. *Jacques Delors and European Integration.* New York: Oxford University Press, 1995.

Ruggie, John G. "International Regimes, Transactions, and Change: Embedded Liberalism in the Postwar Economic Order." *International Organization* 36 (Spring 1982): 379–415.

Sandholtz, Wayne. "Institutions and Collective Action: The New Telecommunications in Western Europe." *World Politics,* no. 45 (January 1993).

———. "Choosing Union: Monetary Politics and Maastricht." *International Organization* 47 (Winter 1993).

Sandholtz, Wayne, and John Zysman. "1992: Recasting the European Bargain." *World Politics* 42, no. 1 (October 1989).

Sbragia, Alberta M., ed. *Euro-Politics: Institutions and Policymaking in the "New" European Community.* Washington, D.C.: Brookings Institution, 1991.

Scharpf, Fritz W. *Crisis and Choice in European Social Democracy.* Ithaca: Cornell University Press, 1991 [1987].

Scharpf, Fritz, and Vivien Schmidt. *Welfare and Work in the Open Economy.* Oxford: Oxford University Press, 2000.

Schmidt, Susanne K. "Commission Activism: Subsuming Telecommunications and Electricity Policy under European Competition Law." *Journal of European Public Policy* 5, no. 1 (March 1998).

Schmidt, Vivien A. *The Futures of European Capitalism.* Oxford: Oxford University Press, 2002.

Schneider, Volker, Godefroy Dang-Nguyen, and Raymund Werle. "Corporate Actor Networks in European Policy-Making: Harmonizing Telecommunications Policy." *Journal of Common Market Studies* 32, no. 4 (December 1994): 473–98.

Schönfelder, Wilhelm, and Elke Thiel. *Ein Markt—Ein Währung.* Baden-Baden: Nomos Verlagsgesellschaft, 1994.

Selznick, Philip. *TVA and the Grass Roots: A Study of Politics and Organization.* Berkeley: University of California Press, 1949.

———. *Leadership in Administration: A Sociological Interpretation.* Berkeley: University of California Press, 1984 [1957].

Servais, Dominique. *Un espace financier européen.* Luxembourg: Office for Official Publications of the European Communities, 1995.

Shapiro, Martin, and Alec Stone, eds. "The New Constitutional Politics of Europe." *Comparative Political Studies* 26, no. 4 (January 1994): 297–420.

Shepsle, Kenneth A. "Studying Institutions: Some Lessons from the Rational Choice Approach." *Journal of Theoretical Politics* 1, no. 2 (1989).

Shonfield, Andrew. *Modern Capitalism: The Changing Balance of Public and Private Power.* London: Oxford University Press, 1969.

Slot, Piet Jan. "Energy and Competition." *Common Market Law Review* 31 (1994): 511–47.

Sobel, Andrew C. *Domestic Choices, International Markets: Dismantling National Barriers and Liberalizing Securities Markets.* Ann Arbor: University of Michigan Press, 1994.

Steil, Benn, ed. *The European Equity Markets: The State of the Union and an Agenda for the Millennium.* London: Royal Institute for International Affairs, 1996.

Steinherr, Alfred, ed. *The New European Financial Marketplace.* London: Longman, 1992.

Steinmo, Sven, Kathleen Thelen, and Frank Longstreth. *Structuring Politics: Historical Institutionalism in Comparative Analysis.* Cambridge: Cambridge University Press, 1992.

Stoltenberg, Gerhard. *Wendepunkte: Stationen deutscher Politik, 1947–1990.* Berlin: Siedler Verlag, 1997.

Story, Jonathan, and Ingo Walter. *Political Economy of Financial Integration in Europe: The Battle of the Systems.* Manchester: Manchester University Press, 1997.

Swidler, Ann. "Culture in Action: Symbols and Strategies." *American Sociological Review* 51, no. 2 (1986): 273–86.

Teltschik, Horst. *329 Tage: Innenansichten der Einigung.* Berlin: Goldmann Verlag, 1991.

Thatcher, Margaret. *The Downing Street Years.* London: Harper and Collins, 1993.

Thelen, Kathleen. "How Institutions Evolve: Insights from Comparative-Historical Analysis." In *Comparative Historical Analysis in the Social Sciences*, edited by James Mahoney and Dietrich Rueschemeyer. New York: Cambridge University Press, 2003.

Thelen, Kathleen, and Sven Steinmo. "Historical Institutionalism in Comparative Politics." In *Structuring Politics: Historical Institutionalism in Comparative Analysis*, edited by Steinmo, Thelen, and Frank Longstreth. Cambridge: Cambridge University Press, 1992.

Tilly, Charles. *From Mobilization to Revolution*. Reading, Mass.: Addison-Wesley, 1978.

Trichet, Jean-Claude. "Dix ans de désinflation compétitive en France." *Notes Bleues du Ministère des Finances* (October 16, 1992).

Tsebelis, George. "The Power of the European Parliament as a Conditional Agenda Setter." *American Political Science Review* 88, no. 1 (March 1994): 128–42.

Tsoukalis, Loukas. *The Politics and Economics of European Monetary Integration*. London: George Allen and Unwin, 1977.

———. *The New European Economy: The Politics and Economics of Integration*. New York: Oxford University Press, 1993.

Underhill, Geoffrey R. D. "Markets beyond Politics? The State and the Internationalization of Financial Markets." *European Journal of Political Research* 19 (1991): 197–225.

Van Schendelen, Marinus P. C. M. " 'The Council Decides': Does the Council Decide?" *Journal of Common Market Studies* 34, no. 4 (December 1996): 531–48.

Védrine, Hubert. *Les mondes de François Mitterrand*. Paris: Fayard, 1996.

Verdier, Daniel. *Moving Capital: Banking and Finance in the Industrialized World*. Cambridge: Cambridge University Press, 2002.

Verdun, Amy. "The Role of the Delors Committee in the Creation of EMU: An Epistemic Community?" *Journal of European Public Policy* 6, no. 2 (June 1999): 308–28.

Vigneron, Philippe. "Le concept de réciprocité dans la législation communautaire: L'exemple de la deuxième directive bancaire." *Revue du Marché Commun*, no. 337 (May 1990).

Vogel, Steven K. *Freer Markets, More Rules: Regulatory Reform in Advanced Industrialized Countries*. Ithaca: Cornell University Press, 1996.

Wallace, Helen, and William Wallace. *Policy-Making in the European Union*. Oxford: Oxford University Press, 1996.

———. *Policy-Making in the European Union*. Oxford: Oxford University Press, 2000.

Weber, Max. "Politics as a Vocation." In *From Max Weber: Essays in Sociology*, edited by H. H. Gerth and C. Wright Mills. New York: Oxford University Press, 1946.

Weber, Steven, and Elliot Posner. "Creating a Pan-European Equity Market: The Origins of EASDAQ." *Review of International Political Economy* 7, no. 4 (Winter 2000): 529–73.

Weiler, Joseph H. H. "The Transformation of Europe." *Yale Law Journal* 100 (June 1991).

———. "The Reformation of European Constitutionalism." *Journal of Common Market Studies* 35, no. 1 (March 1997): 97–131.

———. *The Constitution of Europe*. Cambridge: Cambridge University Press, 1999.

Wessels, Wolfgang. "The EC Council: The Community's Decisionmaking Center." In *The New European Community*, edited by Keohane and Hoffmann. Boulder: Westview Press, 1991.

———. "An Ever Closer Fusion? A Dynamic Macropolitical View on Integration Processes." *Journal of Common Market Studies* 35, no. 2 (June 1998): 267–99.

Western, Bruce. *Between Class and Market: Postwar Unionization in the Capitalist Democracies*. Princeton: Princeton University Press, 1997.

Westlake, Martin. *The Council of the European Union*. London: Catermill, 1995.

Williamson, Oliver. *The Economic Institutions of Capitalism*. New York: Free Press, 1985.

Woolcock, Stephen, Michael R. Hodges, and Kristin Schreiber. *Britain, Germany, and 1992: The Limits of Deregulation*. New York: Council on Foreign Relations, 1991.

Zavvos, Georges S. "L'acte bancaire Européen: Objectif et conséquences." *Revue d'Economie Financière* 4 (1989).

Zysman, John. *Governments, Markets, and Growth: Financial Systems and the Politics of Industrial Change*. Ithaca: Cornell University Press, 1983.

Index

CPSIA information can be obtained
at www.ICGtesting.com
Printed in the USA
LVHW031751301018
595365LV00007B/102/P